BALANCING on BLUE

A Dromomaniac Hiking

KEITH FOSKETT

Balancing on Blue

By Keith Foskett

Produced by Createspace.com

www.keithfoskett.com

ISBN: 978-1480176416

Illustrations by Derek Smith

Contents

Praise for Balancing on Blue

A highly anticipated Appalachian Trail memoir, and well worth the wait.

Daniel Neilson (The Great Outdoors Magazine)

Following on from his entertaining account of his Pacific Crest Trail hike, The Last Englishman, Keith Foskett tackles the Appalachian Trail. Written with his usual energy and style the book covers motivation and the story of the trail as well as his personal hike. A good read for anyone interested in long distance journeys.

Chris Townsend (Author and hiker)

Long distance hikes are simultaneously life-affirming and total agony. Walking 2000 miles would be a phenomenal journey wherever in the world you did it. To tackle the legendary Appalachian Trail is a truly special experience, and one I dream of attempting sometime in my life. Amongst the bears, moose and rattlesnakes, climbing to 2000 metres, and countless aches and pains lives the memory of a special journey, the wonderful people who briefly share the experience with you, and the knowledge that lasts long after the final blister has healed. It's a lifetime's worth of adventurous memories crammed into one simple walk.

Alastair Humphreys (Author, adventurer and A National Geographic Adventurer of the Year 2012)

With thru-hiking gaining in popularity, many look to the Appalachian Trail to test out their trail legs, and discover why it holds the reputation it does.

The wilds of this planet are serene, peaceful and offer the chance to break away from a normal existence. Keith's wonderful perspective of the trail reflects this freedom.

Jennifer Pharr Davis (Author and record holder for the fastest ever thru-hike of the Appalachian Trail).

An entertaining and inspiring account of one of the world's longest walks and the people who walk it. Keith is a perfect walking companion for the ups and downs of the trail – his easy and understated style kept me turning the pages.

Essential reading for those contemplating their own big adventure.

David Lintern (Editor - **Outdoor Enthusiast Magazine**)

Long distance backpacking trips can be monotonous, and it's often the same story for most books about them. Balancing on Blue is something completely different and once again, Keith invites you to the world that he calls home.

Be prepared for great story telling, unique and interesting characters, humour and insight.

Andrew Skurka (Long distance hiker, adventurer and National Geographic Adventurer of the Year 2007).

This book is for anyone who's ever dreamed about a big adventure, as Fozzie spins a funny, thought-provoking and inspiring tale of thru-hiking the Appalachian Trail. You'll be handing in your notice and packing up your rucksack as soon as you've finished reading.

Jenny Walters (Country Walking Magazine)

Other books by Keith Foskett

The Journey in Between

(ISBN: 978 - 1480176393)

A 1,000 mile walk along El Camino de Santiago in France and Spain.

The Last Englishman

(ISBN: 978 - 1480169111)

A 2,640 mile hiking adventure on the Pacific Crest Trail.

This book is dedicated to the Appalachian Trail Class of 2012.

And – to those who didn't come home:

Dwight Cope, Dagan Cope, Thomas Andersen,
Carmen Kotula and Paul Bernhardt.

Thru-Hiker

Someone who hikes a long distance trail end to end, usually in one, continuous attempt.

The Appalachian Trail

The Appalachian National Scenic Trail, known simply as the AT, is a 2,180 mile hiking route in the eastern United States. Starting at Springer Mountain in Georgia and passing through fourteen states to finish on Mount Katahdin in Maine.

Dromomania

From the Latin dromas (runner) and mania (excessive or unreasonable desire, even insanity) is an uncontrollable impulse to wander.

Acknowledgements

First and most importantly, thank *you* for buying this book. Following an unconventional dream of hiking and writing is a long road, full of setbacks which require a strength and stubborn determination to follow. It is people like you, who buy my books that allow me to continue to live it.

The proof readers who took time out to help me: Caroline Morse, Chris Partridge, Dan McCormack, Tom Moose, Cliff Martin, Derek Vreeland, Charley Seger, Frank Patriot, Sarah Van Vliet, Nina Smirnoff, Michelle Markel, Patti Kulesz and exceeding the call of duty honourably - Kate Bryant.

Alex Roddie of Pinnacle Editorial for pointing out my dangling participles, and for his top notch editing.

Jeremy 'Obs da Blobs' Rowley and Samantha 'Mumfa' Rowley for the continued dedication to the formatting cause.

For those who provided quotes - Daniel Neilson, Alastair Humphreys, Jennifer Pharr Davis, David Lintern, Andrew Skurka, Rosie Fuller and Chris Townsend.

The Appalachian Trail Conservancy, whose help with trail and history facts was much appreciated.

Those that helped me prior to starting the trail and their hospitality; Gariele Marewski, Keith 'Hiker X' Baitsell, Sarah 'Sami' Van Vliet, Lauren 'Swiss Miss' Moran and Kathryn 'Dinosaur' Herndon.

The group that I hiked most of the trail with comprised of Peter 'PJ' Semo, Sam 'Daffy' Ridge, Chris 'Juggles' Chiappini, John 'Thirsty' Beshara, Dallas 'Bush Goggles' Nustvold and Phillip 'Lazagne' Colelli. My thanks to them for keeping such a great group together and also for their individual work on the first and last chapters.

All the hikers I met on trail, friendships made, and missed; PJ, Lady Forward, Chatterbox, Bowser, Byline, Pork Chop, Lazagne, Daffy, Bill, Kindle Ninja, Juggles, Bush Goggles, Thirsty, Desperado, Ninja, Jack, Shakespeare, Eastwood, Susan, Poco 'n Poco, Beacon, Mousy, Cheryl, Patrick, Cassie, Daniel, Tom and his dog Dakota, Tyler, Dirt Farmer, Central Booking, Jonathan, Grady, Turtle, Funny Bones, Slayer, Wildflower, Ken, Hoot, Lord Horatio Fonsworth Belvidere Bentley Tiberius III Esq, Tree Hugger, Mary Poppins, Honey Badger, Road Runner, Walking Man, Ninja Turtle, Jonah and his dog Dingleberry,

Onespeed, W, Balls, Sunshine, Pops, Earthling, Carrie, Willy, One Speed, Honey Badger, Margaret, Roadrunner, Spam, Mattress Pad, Chez 11, Nito, Bonk, Saint, Cheddar, Hill Walker, Snot Rocket, Anchor, Tripping Yeti, Embassador, Flint, Tyvek, Wiffle Chicken, Apollo, Ken, Yodler, K9, Tarp Water, Tinkerbell, Rainbow Eyes, Plant Man, Socks, White Wolf, Kaleidoscope, Not Worthy, Chef, Turtle, Day-Glo, Sun, Slims, Turbo Toes, Wise Guy, Socks, Atlas, Hotshot, Hippity Hop, Medic, Easy Rider, Dog Whisperer, Easy Mile, Danish, Don Quixote, Two, Bad Dinner, Grok, Metric, Willie, Indiana, Warlie, Johaness, Cat Woman, Meat, Connect 4, Stingray, Resource, Whoop, Danish, Houdini, Pedestrian, Great Dane, Banjo, Skunkape, Roadhouse, Chesty, Stingray and Poncho.

The immense artistic talent of Derek Smith, whose sketches illustrate this book. David Taylor and Faye Fillingham's advice and tweaks to the front cover.

Thanks to David 'Awol' Miller, whose excellent book - The AT Guide, I used both on trail and in writing this book. It was invaluable for both.

The equipment manufacturers, and suppliers who helped me with gear for the trip; Rand Lindsly of Trail designs, Jake Bennett at Numa Sport Optics, Dan Thompson at Rab, Chris McMaster at ULA Equipment, Niels Overgaard Blok of Backpacking Light Denmark, Richard Codgbrook from Smartwool, Ron Bell at Mountain Laurel Designs, Tom Hennessy at Hennessy Hammocks and Joe Valesko at ZPacks.

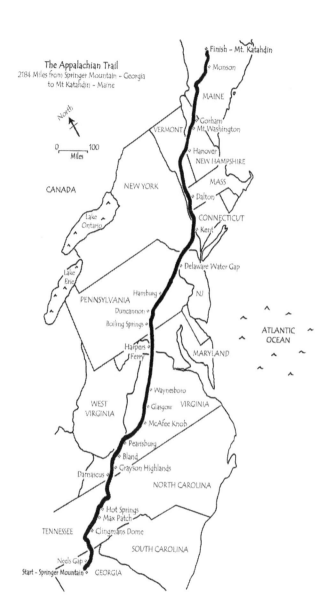

The Appalachian Trail
2184 Miles from Springer Mountain - Georgia
to Mt Katahdin - Maine

North

0   100
    Miles

Finish - Mt. Katahdin
Monson

MAINE

Gorham
Mt. Washington

VERMONT

Hanover
NEW HAMPSHIRE

CANADA

NEW YORK

MASS

Dalton

CONNECTICUT

Lake
Ontario

Kent

Delaware Water Gap

Lake
Erie

Hamburg   NJ

PENNSYLVANIA

Duncannon

Boiling Springs

ATLANTIC
OCEAN

Harpers
Ferry

MARYLAND

Waynesboro

WEST
VIRGINIA

Glasgow   VIRGINIA

McAfee Knob

Pearisburg

Bland
Grayson Highlands

Damascus

NORTH CAROLINA

Hot Springs
Max Patch

TENNESSEE

Clingmans Dome

SOUTH CAROLINA

Neels Gap
Start - Springer Mountain   GEORGIA

Chapter 1
The Converging

Peter 'PJ' Semo

I had to tell her, but every time my mouth opened in anticipation, I fell silent. The plan of confronting her when she returned from work had been delayed. At each attempt to break the news that I was leaving in the morning, I clammed up and put it off for another ten minutes, which in turn never arrived.

Just tell her PJ, get it out of the way.

I can't.

You have to tell her, there's not much time.

I know.

Just do it!

Enough! I'm going to tell her when we go to bed!

I looked over at my wife, who was just falling asleep. I had only minutes left, but still I kept delaying the inevitable.

You have to tell her now.

I know.

This is your last chance; you won't get another one. You have to leave soon.

I know!

Turning my head towards her and fighting back some tears, I finally broke the silence.

"I didn't tell you, but I have to catch a train. I'm leaving to hike the Appalachian Trail in the morning."

Jess shot up in bed.

"What?"

I explained as calmly as possible, foolishly thinking that this would make the situation acceptable.

"And you were going to just, to just, leave me?"

"Yes."

1

"And not say anything? When were you going to tell me?"

I looked sheepishly into her eyes, felt her anger and sensed her sadness. Feeling a slight pang of guilt, I quickly realized it was hollow.

"I'm telling you now."

With that, I went to the closet where my backpack was stored. Most of the packing had been done in preparation for a quick departure.

"So you have a new backpack too?"

"Yeah."

She hovered; I felt her staring and it made me nervous.

If you turn back now, if you wait, you won't do it.

It took just ten minutes to finish getting my stuff together, which was ten minutes too long. I told her I loved her but that this was goodbye. Was it possible to love someone and leave them for good?

"When will you be back?"

Why was she asking me this when I thought she had realized it was permanent? I paused to think of an answer. Not wanting to remind her in case she had misunderstood, I replied simply.

"I don't know. The trail should take six months tops."

Avoiding any further eye contact, I grabbed my trekking poles, opened the door and started to walk to the Amtrak station.

***

I was born Peter John Semo, but my neighbour, Tom, nicknamed me 'PJ' when I was a baby. As my father was also called Peter, the nickname helped avoid confusion. I suppose I'm grateful for it; it has always felt more fitting for me.

I had decided to hike the Appalachian Trail, or the AT for short, when I was sixteen. I had just returned from a camping trip with my family and was experiencing my first real taste of life dissatisfaction. On one side was Jess, my girlfriend back then, trying to persuade me to move to South Dakota once I had finished high school, and she often made phone calls to my family's house to try and persuade them to let me go. My family, in particular my father, were pulling me in the opposite direction and urging me to move to Pennsylvania to attend college, as my sister and brother had done before me. Neither side was shy about expressing their opinions. My father would take the opportunity to lecture me during long drives to go fishing. Being trapped in the car, I had no choice but to listen. It infuriated me.

Jess and my family loved me dearly, which was comforting but also the problem. I had been presented with plan A and plan B but sorely needed a plan of my own, a different plan, a plan that I wanted, not one that everyone else had in mind for me. This was plan C.

I knew what plan C entailed: I just didn't know where it would be. Plan C was to hike, to hike for miles, to hike for such a distance that people would deem it impossible to go that far. For whatever reason, I didn't make the choice then, but instead chose to go and live with Jess in South Dakota.

My family treated my decision with disdain and, on the day before my departure, some hostility. I ended up in a fight with my brother, and my father cried for one of the first times in his life.

"I just don't want you to go," he sobbed.

They drove me to the airport. We were all in tears as I got my luggage from the car. I can't remember my last words to my father, but I do remember him holding me, feeling his bristly chin, his strong, wide chest and the way he patted my back in a silly rhythm. That was the last time I ever saw him.

I was still clueless, not knowing whether to stay with Jess on arrival, go back to Pennsylvania after a couple of weeks or do some more work on plan C. Landing at Detroit to change planes, I pondered fleeing, going somewhere, anywhere.

It's Detroit, for God's sake, you'll get killed.

The closer my plane got to Jess, the more urgent plan C became. Her parents picked me up at the airport, leaving no time for another getaway or a last-ditch attempt at fleeing by going to Wal-Mart, kitting myself out with hiking gear and escaping to the American Discovery Trail.

We got married on July 9th, 2010. My family wasn't invited, as we had stopped speaking by that point, still down to the aftermath of my decision to move. It was so bad that the last words I had said to my father over the phone were "Fuck you." Those proved to be the last words we ever shared.

I started working in retail, which became bearable, my good-spirited co-workers making up for any career disappointments. Having received news that my father was suffering from pancreatic cancer, which could be terminal, I applied for a leave of absence to see him. Owing to misunderstandings between my employer and my father's doctor, I never received the paperwork in time. It arrived on September 2nd, 2011, the day after my father passed away.

***

The train lurched, brakes squealing as I awoke from another sleep. Harpers Ferry in West Virginia is considered the halfway mark of the AT. Nestled at the confluence of the Potomac and Shenandoah Rivers, it is a hugely important target for thru-hikers. I had dozed off several times on the train but smiled as I saw the Harpers Ferry sign. I knew its significance and thought it was a good omen that I had woken there.

Making a final change in Gainsville, I knew I had eventually arrived in the state of Georgia and disembarked. It was late, dark, I was tired and confused as to my next step. Looking around for inspiration, I spotted another guy with a large backpack and we got to talking. His name was Adam. I put my faith in him and we decided to share a taxi to Amicalola Falls State Park, where an approach trail leads nine miles to Springer Mountain and the true start of the AT.

I spent my first night in a hostel and in the morning I trod carefully. I had researched a method of running and walking called POSE, which reduces injuries. I guess I was taking it easy in order to find my feet and break my body in for the mammoth task I was asking of it. People passed me but I didn't care, it wasn't a race. Some guy with a silver umbrella came by me and nodded a greeting, smiling.

"You walk carefully. It's interesting to watch! What's your name?" His accent sounded British.

"PJ," I replied. "And yours?"

"Fozzie, nice to meet you."

"Are you British?"

His stride slowed as though he was going to stop but he didn't.

"Yes, English to be exact. See you up the trail I expect?"

"For sure, it's all good."

I rested a while, drank some water, took stock of the events of the past few days and looked skyward, silently saying, "I don't ask for much from the universe but I'm grateful to be here. Please accept me for my faults and mistakes and let me make something right. Let me do something that makes my father proud of me, wherever he is now. Let me finish this trip, every

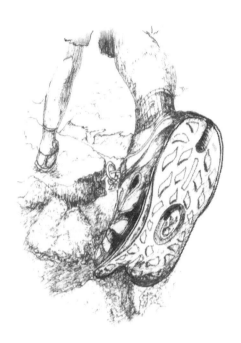

step. Please, world, just give me a shot and lead my footsteps in the right direction."

Phillip 'Lazagne' Colelli

I was well qualified in fort and dam construction. It was hard work digging with shovels, chopping with hatchets, moving fallen trees and amassing a pile of sticks into a fortress, but I enjoyed it. From my present standpoint, my early career as an engineer obviously didn't amount to much. But when you're a kid, surveying the small reservoir, flanked by your impregnable garrison, your achievement seems huge and life feels rich and rewarding.

My father had also taken me camping during those times. Not exactly in the remote wilderness, but to me, a flat area of gravel next to the parked car with a fire ring was just as exciting. We'd unpack a huge tent, coolers packed with ice and drinks, hot dogs, hamburgers, condiments, eggs, bacon and oatmeal. I had the time of my life, all the comforts and luxuries a boy needs, right on his own private camping spot.

I was too young then to know what the AT was, but my father and uncle occasionally used to spend a few days there. It was years before curiosity got the better of me. Dad had guidebooks for the North Carolina and Pennsylvania sections of the trail and I would pull them out and study them. I was especially intrigued by the maps: the trail was a series of red dashes playing with black contour lines, passing by the blue outlines of rivers, lakes and occasionally meeting a road.

I was still a kid when Dad agreed to a short hike on the trail and we parked at Trent's Grocery near where the trail crossed the road, a few miles from Bland, Virginia. The instant we left the road, the beauty of the woods enveloped me, and I felt I was in another world that was peaceful, quiet and leisurely. We just slowed down and walked.

Passing the Kimberling Creek Suspension Bridge and Dismal Falls, we continued up steep hills until we were too tired to carry on. We hastily pitched our tent as a storm threatened, then cooked a simple dinner on the camp stove and read the books we had each brought. I fell asleep quickly, tired from the hiking.

Wonderful though that trip was, it was years before I set foot back on the AT. It was as if I'd read one chapter from a great book and then put it aside. I was working a miserable job at a burger bar and became good friends with a guy called Sam Ridge, who spoke of his plans to thru-hike the entire trail the following year. Before long, Sam and I were planning a trial trip to see if our hopes had any chance of being realised.

We planned on hiking into the Great Smoky Mountains National Park and trying out a forty mile section of the AT from Newfound Gap to Davenport Gap. Again I became immersed in the woods: spotting all the different types of wildlife was mesmerising, even smelling that mountain air validated my being there and reawakened lost memories.

We reached Ice Water Spring shelter and set up our sleeping mats and bags inside. Again, after eating and chatting to some of the other hikers, I fell asleep quickly, but I remember waking in the early hours, astonished at the clarity and brightness of the night sky away from the lights of town. The stars were simply incredible. Reinvigorated in both body and mind, we hit the ridge of the Smoky Mountains the next day, with Tennessee on our left, North Carolina to the right and with epic views in all directions. That book from long ago had been opened again and I loved what I was reading.

It didn't take long for me to decide that I wanted to thru-hike the AT and Sam encouraged me. Soon, all I could focus on was the trip. Work became even more mundane and I ended up quitting a full month before we planned to start because I couldn't deal with it any longer. I stayed in touch with Sam; we had decided to start together but agreed we were each free to make our own plans on the trail. We spoke daily on the phone, making arrangements, discussing gear and took various day hikes around the area. I repeated a five-mile loop on a local trail three times a day to gain some fitness. It was repetitive and tiresome sometimes, especially in the rain, but I persevered to get in shape and also to test my mind and resolve further. I wanted to know that I could push on when the going got tough.

The final week dragged and I feared I would go nuts just waiting. I don't like wishing my life away but I wanted that week gone. I longed for that feeling of being cradled in the woods once more.

We arrived at Amicalola Falls and hiked a few miles before camping, completing the short distance to Springer Mountain the following day.

At last, I was back in the woods.

Sam 'Daffy' Ridge

Many people hike the Appalachian Trail to see some of the world. I wanted to hike to get away from it.

Needing to be different and break out of a conventional life, I wanted to experience and appreciate an adventure that I could call my own. I had just been arrested and kicked out of school for selling weed in my dorm room. Having blacked out, which is how I got caught, I only remembered tiny parts, like being cuffed and led away. I don't remember them taking my mug shot but when I saw it, my face was streaked from crying. I'd been selling weed and getting into trouble, or dodging trouble, since I was fifteen. I'm not proud of it, that's just how things turned out. Every time I got into hot water, I chastised myself and told myself to stop dealing but I never did.

I came to in a prison cell with a bunch of smelly drunks. Everyone looked terrible, which is exactly how I felt. It was 5 a.m; I called my Dad. Naturally I didn't want him to know, but he was probably the only one who could bail me out. I must have called him thirty times before he eventually picked up. Twelve hours later I was out, on a crash course to reconstruct the pieces of my life laying on the ground. I was in debt from the bail and my grandmother had lent me $3,000 to pay for school, which I had spent on weed. I was ashamed I had let her down and lost my father's trust in one stupid moment of madness, or at least one stupid moment of madness where I'd been caught.

I began to question my motive for selling, namely money. Why the hell did I need it? To buy stuff because I thought it made me look cool which in turn, I thought, would make others think I was a better person? I thought that money and status should be my highest priorities; that's what we are led to believe anyway. The only redeeming factor was that I had no clue as to what I would have spent it on, let alone what I actually needed.

I began working in a burger bar, but apart from earning money, I questioned why I was working at all. As no good reason was forthcoming I became disillusioned and decided to escape from the frustration and the discontentment. I figured I wouldn't be angry about how much money I didn't have when I died, but I would care if I wasted my life making it my number one priority.

I began to approach life from the opposite angle: simplifying and abandoning all ambition to gain financial status. In retrospect, this was the period in which I acquired the knowledge that set me up for life on the trail. I read *Walden* by H. D. Thoreau and *Dead Poets Society* by N. H. Kleinbaum, to name but two. I found a one-room place with a shared bathroom. I made do with one fork, one spoon and one plate. Far from striving to have as much as possible, I sought to get rid of what I didn't need. It was fun, enlightening and even now, after the AT, I still try to live this way. It gives me a pleasant feeling as though I'm still on the trail.

I love the outdoors, so it seemed the best environment for doing something different. While I was planning the hike, I had the idea that I needed to escape from people. I soon learnt it was actually the people who made the trail in the end. Without everyone else, I couldn't have hiked the AT, nor would I have had such an extraordinary experience on it.

With all that time out, all that space to think, I believed that I would figure my life out — in fact, figure life itself out. However, does anyone really achieve this? Things ebb and flow but it's rare that we come up with any answers. All I wanted to do, at its most basic level, was to have fun. I knew that for the most part it would be great, but hard in places. I knew there would be tough moments, rough days. I knew it would be versatile and dynamic; at times it was to prove even hallucinogenic.

It was giddy groundlessness that kept me so alive. I knew that at any time I could meet anyone, from anywhere, and do anything. Everyone wants to get to the same final mountain on the same trail but everyone has different reasons for doing it.

I had figured out that conformity was dangerous and that the police, school and authorities had done me much more harm than I had ever done to anyone else. I did need to get away from urban areas so I could be myself and not be crucified for it. Call it hiding, if you will.

The only real dread I felt while I was out there was meeting someone else who was there for the same reasons as I.

John 'Thirsty' Beshara

A Bachelor of Arts, as far as I could tell, was a fancy piece of paper telling me nothing more than I had just spent seven years of my life and an obscene amount of money 'earning' it. Of course, there were great experiences and personal development along the way, but it wasn't nearly as satisfying as I had hoped. All that effort and I had no career prospects, which actually suited me, because the last thing I wanted was a career.

The only awakening that recognition impressed on me was that I desperately needed to do something different, maybe outrageous, and possibly even stupid. I considered several options: walk out of my front door with nothing but a little money and see where the wind blew me, devise some master plan to organise a criminal conspiracy, continue working my comfortable but insanely boring job, or go hike the AT. Option one lacked structure: there was a good chance I wouldn't even make it out of the city and the entire romanticised adventure would fail before it ever started. Option two was attractive but I had no real plan or experience in such matters. Work was definitely out of the question, as it didn't even come within the outrageous, different or stupid bracket. That left the AT.

I couldn't say for sure when the seed was planted. A guy at work had hiked for a couple of months on the AT. We talked about it occasionally and I kept toying with the prospect. Starting to do some research, I found that the more I discovered, the more the idea appealed.

Before I knew it, I had booked a flight to Atlanta and was working sixty-hour weeks to get the money together. I stayed up all night sometimes to fiddle with alcohol stoves and other homemade gear projects. I read everything I could find about long-distance hiking and began walking to work with a sixty-pound cinder block in my pack. In short, I was obsessed.

This carried on for six months. My buddy and I made weekend trips to every state park we could get to in a few hours. It was great luck that we got to experience just about every kind of weather on those weekend trips: the pouring rain at Lake Mariah, freight train winds coming off Lake Superior and a raging blizzard in Duluth to ring in the New Year.

The idea of hiking the AT appealed to me because it seemed so random, even pointless. I had spent the first twenty five years of my life doing more or less what my parents expected of me, because they had an eye on my future. In my estimation, thru-hiking was the direct opposite of that. It certainly wasn't, by any stretch of the imagination, required, and there was ostensibly little benefit to be gained from it that could have any bearing on my future plans. It was socially and professionally frowned upon by most people. I wanted to hike the AT for the sole purpose of doing it.

I flew into Atlanta with nothing, not even a small bag. I had sent all of my gear to the hostel I was staying at and didn't want to be burdened with shipping anything back. There were six other hikers in the hostel shuttle and a further sixteen at the hostel when I got there. The excitement and anticipation was huge, a culmination of all the training, the research and hard work was about to come to fruition. Sleep didn't come easily.

I elected to start my hike at Amicalola Falls, where many begin, as it is the official thru-hiker register point. On my way across the parking lot, someone caught my eye. A wide-eyed, cheerful-looking guy who was wearing a Packers hat and a University of Minnesota athletic shirt. I smiled, as I had just come from Minneapolis. Small world.

I didn't see that kid again until Fontana Dam, some 182 miles in. His trail name was Bush Goggles and we ended up becoming great friends, hiking a lot of the trail together. Holed up in the Fontana shelter with a couple of others, we enjoyed some beer and spoke animatedly about heading into the Smoky Mountains. We all partied that night and had a raging fire next to the reservoir. Bush Goggles left the next morning with a couple of other guys. I had some chores to do in town and didn't get going until the afternoon.

It rained solidly the next day so in order to get dry, a few of us decided to take an offer that the local church had posted on a tree for lodging. We stood around waiting by the road for a ride, wet and miserable, repeatedly failing to roll a cigarette in the damp conditions. Some British guy whom I had also met at Fontana called Fozzie came strolling by under his umbrella — casually smoking a cigarette, as if he was walking the dog on a Sunday morning — and headed off into the woods.

"Fozzie!" I cried after him.

"Yeah?"

"A guy called Bush Goggles is down the trail. We're staying at the church place. Tell him we ain't gonna make camp tonight!"

There was a momentary pause as if he was digesting my statement.

"Who?" came a muffled reply from the trees.

I shouted once more.

"Bush Goggles!"

"OK, I'll tell him!"

Dallas 'Bush Goggles' Nustvold

My Grandpa spent his retirement scrapping and junking, which meant he would get old lawnmowers, refrigerators, bikes and the like and salvage the valuable metals. Spending lots of time helping him as a young boy, I thought it was so cool, like finding old treasure in trash. Occasionally he would take me to one of his friends' houses, where we would go through their junk and sometimes find valuable antiques. It was this initial grounding that gave me an eye to spot 'treasure'. I used to watch shows like Time Team and nurtured the ambition to become Indiana Jones when I grew up.

I was also very adventurous and loved exploring the woods. Spotting animals such as a deer, watching an eagle soar or even just playing with plants were my other treasures. I was, and still am, awed by nature. When I was too young to get involved in any major adventure, I lived vicariously through some of the classics like *Robinson Crusoe* and *The Count of Monte Cristo* to feed my passion.

In high school my life changed somewhat after my Mum became sick. The doctors had no clue of a diagnosis for a long time but eventually they discovered she had lupus. It made me think about my life plans: did I just want to work until I became ill or died, or should I defy conformity and have some fun?

I read Bill Bryson's *A Walk in the Woods*, which introduced me to the AT. The seed was planted but not watered, as I spent most of my time in college with my friends experimenting with drink, dabbling a little in drugs but mostly chasing women. I was lucky to be one of those annoying students who could skip class, barely do any reading and still get an A.

Between semesters, I worked for my uncle's environmental contracting company as a general labourer, busting down walls with a sledgehammer, removing hazardous waste and making some money. As I had no idea what to do after graduating, when he offered me a supervisory role running jobs and managing workers for a better salary, I jumped at the chance.

It was like being a kid again sometimes. Often I was the first into old buildings that had lain dormant for years, like dusty time capsules. As the guys worked, I went off exploring and found old beer bottles, newspapers, pictures and great items like electric fans from the 1920s. I'd take out the scrap copper and aluminium to make some extra cash. After nine months, I'd had enough and the desire to sprinkle a little water on that AT seed crept back into my imagination.

I really had no idea what I was getting into. I was familiar with the woods, having camped on short trips occasionally but never for more than a week. As at college, I did little research; in fact, my only preparation was to buy the gear I thought would do the trick and then ask my Mum if she could drive me the eighteen-hour trip to Georgia.

Her lupus was under control but she still fought daily battles against it. She was a huge inspiration in my life, and I had always appreciated what she had done, especially the encouragement she offered me to walk the AT.

It was to be the start of the most extraordinary journey of my life.

Chris 'Juggles' Chiappini

It was August 3rd, 2000, and two minutes before I was due on stage at the World Juggling Championships in Montreal, Canada. My Dad was with me and I was nervous — of course I was nervous. I had competed the previous year at the same competition, hosted nearby at Niagara Falls, and earned bronze.

Part of my act was to close my hand around a juggling ball and wave a hand fan underneath, thereby releasing thousands of pieces of confetti. This entailed taping an extremely delicate cellophane ball filled with the confetti to the fan. It was ludicrously fragile; I felt that I needed only look in its vague direction and the cellophane would split, spilling the contents. I was sweating, shaking and aware that I shouldn't grip the ball too tightly, and yet I needed to or it wouldn't stick.

"Chris, do you need some help?"

"No, Dad. I got it!"

Eventually, with seconds to spare, I was ready.

I was ten years old when I first started juggling. I have no comprehension of what life can be like without this passion, it's so ingrained in me. As a boy, I soon glimpsed where it could take me and it became my identity. It's exceptionally difficult to learn but I picked it up quickly and realised that others enjoyed watching me. The praise I received made me feel great. Hearing applause as a kid feels marvellous, and the pleasure doesn't diminish as an adult.

My dad always encouraged me, I think because he is an artist also (a musician). He is aware how tough carving a career in the arts can be, especially doing something as out of the ordinary as juggling, but at the same time it's also hugely rewarding. Although he always inspired me, he never forced me to do anything, leaving me free to make my own choices.

Juggling is a solitary pastime. To achieve anything in the field requires thousands upon thousands of hours on your own, in a high-ceilinged room, constantly repeating the same trick until it becomes second nature. You have to push yourself mentally and physically to learn a new skill, or hold a trick for a long period of time. I never had a coach; I simply adhered to common practice principles and listened to those who were better than I was.

Josiah Jones finished his act and walked off stage towards me. He looked unhappy and rightly so, as his act had gone badly. In fact, it would have been better described as a train wreck: he dropped a lot of props. My name was announced and I looked at Dad, who just gave this smile that suggested he knew something that I didn't. My heart was pounding so hard, and my breathing quickened as I wiped away more sweat. The audience applauded and time seemed to slow down as I walked, confidently, on to the stage.

Dad and I had taken advantage of every trick we could to gain a head start, even down to my costume of polished black shoes, smart pants and a red sequined shirt. I looked like a young version of Elton John. He had hired a local dance teacher to choreograph my movements through the eight-minute routine to three different songs. She also taught me little tricks that could make all the difference, like taking a comb from my pocket and running it through my hair while winking at the audience. I worked with balls, rings and clubs and varied the quantity of each.

It went well, the audience responded and my Dad smiled as I walked off behind the curtain. I was confident but not blasé, feeling I had given a better display than all the other acts. I had the least number of drops (two) and the highest skill technique. It had to be gold.

It may seem like a strange comparison, but juggling has much in common with thru-hiking: it demands physical and psychological strength and dedication, hours of repetitive action to arrive at a distant goal and toleration of a solitary existence. I have always loved the outdoors but, to be honest, it was the chance to be alone that appealed. Dedication and repetition I had already mastered.

I lived thirty minutes away from where the AT wanders through Harriman State Park in New York State. I had walked some sections many times, as well as making a failed attempt on the Long Trail in Vermont, which is 272 miles long. The AT was familiar, close to home and on the East Coast. I just felt as though I would be safe there.

Several times in my life elders have said to me, 'Do what you want before you get married and have kids.' We're brought up to think that you can go on an adventure if you're still alive when the kids have grown up. I wasn't buying any of it.

I did win gold at the World Juggling Championships that year, and now I'm 28, juggling for a living. As much as I love what I do, I had never known anything else, never taken up any other passion and milked it for all that it was worth.

So in the summer of 2011, needing a break from throwing balls in the air, I made the decision to thru-hike the AT, and in the spring of 2012 I found myself looking at a bronze plaque embedded in a rock on top of Springer Mountain, the start of the trail.

I knew there were no medals for coming first. The only gold you achieve on the AT is for finishing.

Keith 'Fozzie' Foskett

The 1970s was a fantastic decade for interior design. Legendary wallpaper, majestic flooring and any item of furniture you longed for could be procured in bright orange. I was just a kid at the time but later in life, around 2008, I dove headlong into a 1970s revival for my lounge. The centrepiece was an old British Telecom phone complete with rotary dial, and even the small piece of card displaying the phone number and 'Dial 999 Fire Police Ambulance' was still intact. Pop a finger in the right hole for each number and push it round to an unassuming chrome lip, where it wound back to position with a hissing sound I remembered from my childhood. The two-tone chocolate-coloured body and receiver were immaculate. The phone lived on a white plastic table with an orange lamp, which completed my retro look.

The only drawback was that the ringing was incredibly loud; it used to startle the hell out of me and my cat absolutely detested it. Invariably he was asleep on my lap if someone called and in a nanosecond he would flip over, look at me with insane, crazed eyes, then glare at the phone and arch his back ready to pounce upon and subsequently kill it.

One afternoon I arrived home, walked into the lounge, and found him fast asleep. This was not unusual, as you can imagine for a cat, but his location was. To my surprise, he had snuggled up on my white table, lovingly spooning the telephone. Now, I'm an animal lover, make no mistake, but it was just too good a chance to miss. I quietly reached into my pocket, pulled out my mobile phone and dialled the house number ...

I'm telling you this to try and paint a picture, which in turn, I hope, will make a point. Great opportunities come along rarely. We don't necessarily have to grab them when they do; indeed, it may not be the right time and they may present themselves again later. More often than not, we don't take them because we are scared of what will happen if that path does not work out, despite somehow knowing that it will. Many of us go about our daily lives with no quibbles: we have accepted our lot, are happy with what we have and, fair enough, have no desire to change anything. On the flip side, many of us do feel stuck and lack the courage to change how we live. Paying a mortgage, feeding the kids and holding down a job are big enough challenges in themselves without taking the risk of attempting something that may not work.

Travelling, adventuring, undertaking an expedition, finding yourself, escaping, call it what you will, the number of people who are fleeing from the system has rocketed in recent years. The last generation's acceptance of how we live is now being questioned and many don't want any part of it. Thus, getting away from it, often into the wilderness, provides a chance for us to breathe, re-evaluate and make changes in our life.

Allow me to explain further. Let's assume that, when you pop out into this world, aged just a few minutes, you are able to read and possess the intelligence of an average adult. The swing doors of the delivery room squeak open and someone enters, dressed immaculately in a subtly-striped grey suit. I always imagine this individual as a woman. Her shirt is as smooth and white as copier paper, ironed to a crisp finish, with edges so precise you could cut a finger on them. Her hair is greased and visible comb lines appear like a furrowed field, which reflect the lights on the ceiling, before being pulled back hard into a tight ponytail, making her eyebrows lift somewhat. She wears little makeup save a weak, gothic white foundation and lurid red lipstick. Everything about this person screams perfection. Intimidated, you sense a feeling of authority that is about to impose restrictions on your life forever.

Instinctively, you accept the several sheets of paper she hands over and you notice the main header: Life Contract.

She places a clenched hand over her mouth and clears her throat delicately, a little apologetically.

"I'm from Life Planning. This is all pretty standard stuff. I just need you to read through it quickly and sign at the bottom."

She sits by your bed, a little too close for comfort, and shifts her stern gaze between you and the contract. You start to read, or rather to scan to get the gist of the content. You begin to feel uncomfortable and yet you start to presume it's all acceptable, like the terms of motor insurance. You summarise the content:

At five years of age you will start school, where you will stay until age 16. You may wish to choose further education, which we encourage. You will strive to achieve the best grades possible.

You will obey your teachers, peers and elders at all times.

Education complete, you will begin employment. This will last around forty-five years; however, there are concessions such as four weeks' holiday a year, a company pension and possibly other incentives such as a subsidised cafeteria. You are expected to work hard for your employer, be punctual, work late at your own cost and get along with your colleagues. Moving jobs is frowned upon.

The country where you live is under control of a government, which passes laws you are expected to abide by, regardless of whether you or anyone else think them fair or not. You live in a democratic society but will have little input into how it is run. Every four years, you may vote for the incumbent party or other options that will be presented to you.

The government will deduct something called tax from your earnings. Depending on your salary, this could be as much as 45%. Goods and some services are also taxed. You have no real say in how these taxes are calculated, invested or spent.

In your early to mid-sixties, assuming you have accrued enough pension funds, you may retire. It may well be possible that any annuity offered to you will not be sufficient to live on, in which case you will have to make your own arrangements to deal with the shortfall or possibly continue to work.

You are encouraged to get married and start a family. This will occupy a large proportion of your life, around twenty to thirty years as you bring up your children.

And so it goes on, and on, and on.

I ignore her eyes drilling into my side and her hovering hand offering a pen. I return her gaze, smile and hand the papers back.

"Nah, it's OK, thanks. I'll do my own thing."

And 'do my own thing' is pretty much what I have done. Of course I did my time at school and I have a day job when I'm not hiking. A lot of aspects associated with a conventional life I don't care for and have little choice in, but I make changes constantly. I do what I have to. Work, for example, is solely a means to earn enough money to go and get lost in the great outdoors.

Some years ago I discovered thru-hiking and a monumental void in my life suddenly filled. Almost instantly, I found a freedom that had been missing. I could travel to a part of the world that appealed and disappear into the wilds for a few months, with everything I needed strapped to my back. My concerns in life during those months faded to nothing; the rules and regulations that I had constantly endured and battled with vanished.

Away from civilisation, I discovered a new pathway. Far from being oppressive, my surroundings were invigorating. I felt no restrictions but revelled in immunity. I felt energised, my thoughts became clear and precise, my direction in life clarified and my goals focused.

I felt liberated.

Chapter 2
The Steaks are High

"Sir, would you like anything for lunch? Can I offer you a menu?"

"You actually have menus?" I replied, scratching my head, perplexed.

She giggled sheepishly.

"Yes sir, we have menus."

With that she handed me a leather-bound example and also a wine list. I couldn't believe it, a wine list as well.

"An aperitif, perhaps?"

That was far too much and I started laughing nervously. I turned away, momentarily embarrassed and looked out the window at the Atlantic some 35,000 feet below.

"A gin and tonic would be smashing," I said, smiling to dissipate any offence I might have caused.

I perused the options. Tender Fillet of Beef Steak, Dover Sole, Roast Chicken Breast and numerous other dishes were neatly presented, spaced evenly, with succinct descriptions on slightly marbled paper. I paused briefly as she returned with stainless steel cutlery cushioned in a navy blue napkin with 'Delta Airways' embroidered along one edge. She placed it delicately in front of me with a wine glass and my gin and tonic, ice clinking as it bobbed up and down.

"You have proper cutlery as well? None of that plastic stuff up front, huh? I'd like the steak please, medium, thank you."

Business class was a whole new world: an inner sanctum, an oasis in an aluminium cage, and something way beyond my previous experience. A good friend in the business had managed somehow to get me a discount ticket.

"Just ask for an upgrade when you check in," she had told me. "They always have room in Business on that route. You'll get it for sure."

At one point, I just had to take a walk back to the Economy section. I gently pulled the curtain to one side and peeked round. There they all were, livestock in an overcrowded pen, knees under their chins, looking somewhat cramped and prodding their catering option with puzzled expressions. I coughed loudly and some of them looked up. Smiling somewhat mockingly, I nodded a silent hello, coupled with an expression that said, 'I got a Business class seat, restaurant quality cuisine, a very quaffable Rioja, a better movie choice than the National Film Archive, a fully reclining option and more leg room than a ski lift'. Then I went back to my seat for a slice of chocolate cake.

***

In the spring of 1948, a 29-year-old carpenter called Earl Shaffer started hiking north from Mt Oglethorpe in Georgia, which in those days was the start of the Appalachian Trail. One hundred and twenty four days later he became the first person to complete the entire trail in one attempt and unintentionally coined the term thru-hiking. His journey and subsequent book *Walking with Spring* have since inspired thousands of others to do the same.

Taking just over four months to complete the trail is an admirable time, even by today's standards, but back then it was met with derision. Not solely because of the time itself but because someone had claimed to have hiked the entire trail in one attempt. It was unheard of. Even the Appalachian Trail Conservancy initially deemed his claim to be 'obviously fraudulent'. His feat earned him the name 'The Crazy One'.

Compared to the equipment we have today, his was sparse and inadequate. He carried no tent or shelter, no stove, wore simple boots that lasted until the end and an army rucksack. I sometimes wonder whether in sixty-five years' time others will look back on the thru-hiking gear of today in similar disbelief.

Shaffer was born in York, Pennsylvania, on November 8th, 1918. His family moved to a small farm near the village of Shiloh when he was five years old. His mother died when he was a teenager but had instilled in him an appreciation of poetry and literature. He graduated from high school in 1935 and during the Depression found work on neighbouring farms. In the winter he hunted and trapped for furs before eventually becoming a carpenter.

With his close friend and regular hiking companion, Walter Winemiller, he discussed and subsequently planned a thru-hike of the AT before their idea was put on hold by the outbreak of World War Two. Shaffer enlisted in 1941 and served as a radioman in the South Pacific until well into 1945. Winemiller was killed in action during a beach landing at Iwo Jima, a small island south of Japan. Shaffer's subsequent reasons to hike the trail stemmed from a desire to walk the army out of his system and to mitigate his feelings of sorrow at the loss of his friends who had died during the war.

The AT had been completed some eleven years before Shaffer's attempt but, owing to labour shortages and other factors brought about by the war, it was overgrown and neglected in many sections. With trail guides not yet in existence, he had only road maps and a compass, meaning navigation and bushwhacking were the order of the day.

In 1965 he thru-hiked again, this time starting from Mt Katahdin, the northern terminus, and travelled south to Springer Mountain, which had replaced Mt. Oglethorpe as the official southern start point. He became the first person to complete the hike in both directions. In 1998 he made another successful northbound hike at the age of 79, at the time the oldest person to do so. He succumbed to cancer and died on May 5th, 2002.

To this day, Earl Shaffer remains a hero and an inspiration to many.

***

Atlanta is the nearest major airport to Springer Mountain, but Delta flight 261 was bound for Miami. An hour or so south of the city lies a small town called Homestead, where I had spent three months volunteering on an organic farm some years before. I had kept in touch with the owner, Gabriele, who had kindly agreed to act as base HQ for my adventure. Essentially this meant somewhere I could leave gear that might be needed at some point, along with food supplies and other requirements to be mailed out should I need them. For example, the weather can still be cold when most start their AT hike, in late March or early April. A warmer sleeping bag is required until the weather warms and spring takes hold. A cooler bag would then be needed during the summer months. Food requirements vary for everyone; for me, most was procured from stores along the way.

However, some items I bought in bulk because they were cheaper or hard to obtain, in my case several kilos of my favourite chocolate protein powder to be mailed as I needed it.

A good HQ and someone who is willing to give a little of their time to help you out are invaluable when thru-hiking. I was also able to mail some new gear from American companies to Gabriele which saved on postage costs, as opposed to shipping them to England. In the coming months, I was to appreciate just how good a job Gabriele performed.

***

Amicalola Falls State Park is where most thru-hikers start their journey, following a nine-mile approach trail that links up to the actual start point of the AT on Springer Mountain. Getting to Amicalola Falls from Homestead involved a fifteen hour Greyhound trip to Atlanta, the prospect of which I wasn't exactly relishing. To tie up a few loose ends in Atlanta such as last-minute gear supplies, accommodation and a ride to the trailhead, I had emailed a thru-hiker distress call to friends I knew from my previous hiking adventures in the States. Hiker hospitality is amazing; American hiker hospitality is legendary. Within a couple of days of sending out my plea, I had offers of everything I'd asked for.

Keith 'Hiker X' Baitsell and his girlfriend Sarah 'Sami' Van Vliet both lived and worked in Atlanta. Keith had the 2,640-odd miles of the Pacific Crest Trail (PCT) already under his boots and understood the importance of offering assistance to hikers, especially those from a foreign country. My call for help had been forwarded to them via Kathryn 'Dinosaur' Herndon, also a PCT hiker whom I had met during my time on that trail, and they offered me somewhere to stay for a couple of days to get myself sorted. The delectable Lauren 'Swiss Miss' Moran volunteered as an excellent taxi service for the errands and a ride to the trailhead.

Nicknames such as 'Hiker X' and 'Dinosaur' are known as trail names. Not many use their real names on a thru-hike; most go by their trail name and often we still refer to one another by this name after the hike has finished. If you don't have a trail name, you can think of one yourself, but, more often than not, it is bestowed on you by another hiker. The name usually refers to your appearance, mannerisms or behaviour, and it is generally understood that if someone offers to name you, you have to accept it. However, this is not always so. My trail name, Fozzie, loosely derived from my surname, I had used since school.

I stepped off the Greyhound in Atlanta at 3.30 in the morning and looked around. I was hungry and secretly hoped to spot the neon lights of a roadside diner but it was not to be. A few passengers stood outside the terminal sucking on cigarettes, and warm air from the exhausts of a shallow queue of taxis rose up to meet the chill of late winter. A street light flickered annoyingly, revealing brief glimpses in the shadows of two men lurking underneath, occasionally glancing over in my direction.

"Downtown Atlanta at that time of the morning is not somewhere you should hang about," Hiker X had warned me a few days earlier. "Get a cab, come here and knock on the door. Don't screw around down there, it can be dangerous."

"But the Greyhound arrives at 3.30. I don't want to be knocking on your door at 4.00 in the morning!" I had replied, not wanting to impose even further.

"It's fine, I'll hear the door. I don't mind."

I walked over as the cab window slid smoothly down.

"You need a ride somewhere?" asked the driver, who bore an uncanny likeness to James Brown. I opened the door, got in and started humming Living in America.

I checked the piece of paper on which I had written Hiker X and Sami's address and repeated it to him. The cab lurched forward and we journeyed through empty streets that were barely contemplating waking up. He slowed to read the house numbers in a dim light and pulled over, offering a weak, "It's around here somewhere."

It was quieter away from the centre. I sat down on the doorstep and lit a cigarette, trying to delay knocking on the door to assuage my guilt. Bare trees were outlined starkly against a bright moon. A cat ran past, startling me, closely pursued by another. Finally I knocked gently on the door. No answer. I looked up; there were no signs of life. I knocked harder and then heard footsteps coming down the stairs and saw the hall light illuminate.

"Hiker X?" I asked, tentatively.

"Fozzie, come in."

"Look, I'm really sorry. I feel bad for getting you up. I really appreciate you doing this."

"It's fine, really. Sami is still asleep. Do you want a drink or maybe you wanna catch a couple of hours' sleep?"

"I could do with some shut-eye."

"OK, there's just the couch, I'm afraid, but it's very comfortable. You still want that breakfast?"

I'm a sucker for a good breakfast and nowhere delivers breakfast better than America. I had mentioned this to Hiker X in an email and was pleased he had remembered.

"Oh hell, yeah," I answered, no doubt with a greedy glint in my eye.

I slept for three hours, waking briefly as I found myself running through a planning list and final logistics. After a few minutes, the practicalities faded away and my mind settled, as it always did, on one, very simple question: why?

It is the standard query from people who don't understand the lure of thru-hiking. The stock answer you will get from most thru-hikers investing many months of their time, a few thousand dollars of their money and several thousand miles of walking is something along the lines of enjoying hiking and the freedom the outdoors bestows. Others may go into a little more depth but, to be honest, we tire of answering because one answer merely invites more questions. Most people cannot relate to spending around six months eating crap food, getting filthy, being too hot or too cold and smelling like an overburdened trash bin two weeks past a collection date in the heat of midsummer. Despite all of this, we live for it.

I spent many years trying to solve this question and it wasn't until I was writing this book that a definitive answer suddenly surfaced. Of course I love hiking and to be in the great outdoors is wonderfully nourishing. It is time-out from a conventional lifestyle that I don't particularly enjoy. I revel both in the solitude and the company on the trail and always return refreshed, recharged and energised.

However, when I really went into my reasons in depth, I discovered that I had felt the same need for escape many years before my first thru-hike, which was a thousand mile walk on El Camino de Santiago in 2002. But the appeal wasn't found in thru-hiking as such; this was just the means to try and placate a wanderlust. Even in my teens, I had a yearning — a deep-rooted desire to wander, to be nomadic. At first I thought there was something wrong with me. All my friends were concentrating on school, choosing a college or career path, debating where they would live and, later, in their early twenties, their thoughts turned to marriage and kids. All I wanted to do was get the hell out. I wasn't comfortable living conventionally and I'm still not.

I battled with it for years. I fought it, argued with it and became frustrated. Why was I different? Why couldn't I just get a decent job, find a house, make trips to IKEA, buy a better car than next door, get married and watch the wife pop out a couple of kids?

I finished education, dropped out of the extra year at school I had committed to and bounced around a series of jobs, none of which I enjoyed. I went into sales because I thought the meaning of success was having an office job. Back in the 1980s, if you had a white shirt with a silk paisley tie, a Prince of Wales check suit and a briefcase (even if it did only contain a round of sandwiches), everyone thought you had arrived. Appearance was everything. Surely if you looked successful, then that was the whole point, wasn't it? I was trying to conform, to fit in with a lifestyle that apparently we were supposed to follow because I didn't know any different or ask any questions.

In my mid-twenties during a stint as a financial advisor offering minimally shrewd advice to a lot of very boring people, I began seriously questioning my life route. Moreover, I was miserable and exhausted, constantly fighting my desires to travel and wander because they weren't accepted by the mainstream. I'd been led to believe that travelling was wrong, or at least spending more time travelling than working. Although travel was experiencing an upsurge, it was frowned upon as a way of life.

I loved praise, enjoyed being told I had done a good job, like a dog that comes when it is called, wagging its tail, and thrived on pleasing people and winning their approval. However, I also began to understand that receiving recognition for performing a meaningless job was a waste of a life. Surely, to go wandering without praise must be more rewarding than doing something I hated?

Disillusioned with trying to forge any career at all, I became angry with society, lost any interest with fitting in and instead I rebelled. I started smoking, drinking and chasing women to distract me from the urge to travel because, first, I didn't know how to escape the system and, second, I was scared that people would chastise me for being different.

To begin feeding my peripatetic desires while at the same time maintaining a semblance of being in the workforce, I joined employment agencies because I could work one job for a few months until the contract ran out and then escape somewhere. Being a temp didn't affect my CV (not that I really cared) and it was completely acceptable to work many jobs without any thought of future advancement. I made my first, tentative escape to Greece, where I spent a few months hopping round the islands by boat, testing my resolve. Even there, the drifter in me demanded further gratification by not staying in one place too long. A couple of days here, a short layover there, then move on — feed the craving, go somewhere new, anywhere. Keep moving, you must keep moving.

For the first time in my life, I felt peace during those times in Greece. I was happy because I was doing what I loved, roaming, but, more importantly, I was happy because I had stopped battling the desire and finally realised that wandering was what I was supposed to do. I didn't need to fight it any more. I embraced my life.

***

Dromomania, from the Latin dromas (runner) and mania (excessive or unreasonable desire, even insanity) is an uncontrollable impulse to wander, the kind that is appeased often at the expense of careers, relationships and maintains a blithe disregard for mortgages and pensions. When I first saw the word, though it sounded somewhat like an ailment, it struck a chord with me.

In extreme cases, a dromomaniac may have no memory of his travels. One such was Jean-Albert Dadas, a Frenchman from Bordeaux, who would suddenly start walking and find himself far from home in cities such as Moscow.

The fact that mania is tagged on the end of this word is unfair. Let's face it: most of us consider anyone with a mania to have something wrong with them. And yet, indulging dromomania, far from being frowned upon, should be embraced.

I don't care about the reasons for my wandering. I'm not one for understanding the mechanics of anything. I expect my car to start when I turn the key and I care as much about the periodic table as to why these letters appear as I type. Now, I cherish it. It is the one aspect of my life that takes precedence over pretty much everything. I deal with being stationary because most of the time I must, but I'm only truly happy when I indulge, and thru-hiking is my chosen method. The world is a wonderful place when experienced at walking pace.

Some say our desire to wander goes back thousands of years to when we had little choice in the matter. Seasonal changes drove us to the cooler mountains in the summer and back down to the plains in winter. We searched for more hospitable environments to live in. If food became scarce in one area, we moved on to where it was plentiful. In the Ice Age we fled south to escape; in times of drought we moved on in search of water. Cook, Magellan, Columbus and others were perhaps not so much mapping a new world as indulging their appetites to move ever onwards.

As far as romantic relationships go, forget them. My history of getting involved with women is not a happy one. It's not something that bothers me. I have come to accept it easily because, again, relationships don't fit with my wandering instincts. If I occasionally meet someone I like then I'm honest about my ways.

Most of my friends have accepted my ways and many admit to being a little envious, while others treat it with confusion or derision. Some people even become confrontational and demand to know why I should get six months out at a time. It's just not fair that I should be seeing this marvellous world when they are staring at a computer screen for eight hours a day.

Such reactions do puzzle me. I wouldn't aggressively challenge anyone who works a nine-to-five job. I struggle with their choice but respect those who have consciously made it.

For many it all boils down to fear. The standard life charter is comfortable for most, although an increasing number are beginning to cast it aside. We're an intelligent race but, for some reason, we choose to work for forty-eight weeks of the year and accept four weeks' holiday. Some, especially in America, don't even get that and are made to feel guilty for even asking for time out.

Many of you out there have dreams, a desire to do something different, but are perhaps hesitant to follow them because they are a little dangerous, perhaps risky. OK, some dreams fail, but I would urge you to at least attempt whatever it is you dream about. Persistence and desire can conquer any gaps in skill, knowledge and qualifications. If you want something strongly enough and are prepared to chase it as you've never chased anything before in your life, you can succeed in doing what you truly want to do. Whether that choice is hiking a few thousand miles in the wilderness or forging a career as a graphic designer, it makes no difference. Henry Ford once said that whether you think you can, or you think you can't, you're right.

There is another reason I thru-hike or, as I mentioned before, use thru-hiking as a means of escape. During my second walk on El Camino de Santiago, I met a French hiker called Pierre. He travelled with his delightful dog, Flo, and as we talked, the inevitable question of why we were walking naturally cropped up. One evening I ate dinner with Pierre and Patrick, from Belgium, whom I was walking with at the time and who translated for us.

Pierre said that he walked often and preferred to camp or sleep rough, partly because of limited funds and partly because of how he looked. The sides of his head were shaved and his appearance, which most would call scruffy, attracted the attention of the police. He had been arrested for sleeping in a park a year before with his previous dog, which, wanting to protect him, began barking and growling at the police when Pierre was placed in handcuffs. Much to his anguish, they shot his dog. Even now, a year later, his eyes welled up as he spoke and he pulled Flo closer.

He went on to explain his lack of faith in how we are governed, controlled, taxed and how he is treated unfairly by the police because of his appearance. His words resonated with me. Here was a man following a life he loved. Like me, he worked to earn some money and, when he had enough, he would take his devoted dog for a long hike, sometimes for months. Occasionally he slept under a bridge, discreetly, or camped out of view. He would perhaps stay in a cheap hotel once a week, get cleaned up and do some laundry. His appearance suffered, as does a thru-hiker's.

He disliked rules, regulations and hated being told what to do. He didn't understand why we need insurance and mortgages, why everyone's voice isn't heard; why the government doesn't really consult us, despite many people believing it does. He thinks we have lost our freedom and he hikes to gain his, and to escape.

Patrick stopped the translation. It was clear to us all that this dishevelled, wiry little Frenchman's thoughts had connected with me.

Was I an anarchist, as Pierre claimed to be? Do thru-hikers

and other adventurers undertake their long trips to escape the system?

I consulted the dictionary:

Anarchy:

1 – State of disorder due to absence or non-recognition of authority or other controlling systems:

2 – Absence of government and absolute freedom of the individual, regarded as a political ideal.

I wouldn't want a state of disorder but to have absolute freedom as an individual, if that is indeed possible in our society, is an idea I do relish. Perhaps there is a little of the anarchist in me. Perhaps there is a little of the anarchist in all of us?

***

Having finally understood and embraced my roaming ways, I turned from Greece to other destinations. After El Camino de Santiago, I began looking for longer hikes in remoter regions, in pristine wilderness, where it would be possible to walk further without encountering civilisation. I also wanted to experience solitude more. Solitude is a great leveller and I love it. Not that I don't enjoy company, but being on my own feeds the nomad.

My attention turned to America because they have an enviable collection of ridiculously long trails in remote regions. The three main routes are the Appalachian Trail (2,184 miles), running vertically through the eastern states; the Pacific Crest Trail (2,640 miles), which runs, again vertically, through the western states; and the Continental Divide Trail (distances vary as it is not yet fully complete, but the average is around 3,000 miles), following the Continental Divide along the Rocky Mountains and also south to north or vice versa, depending on your inclination. The AT is by far the most popular virgin hike, mainly because it is the shortest; it passes through many towns for re-supply and there is safety in numbers. It also has many shelters, usually simple, three-sided wooden constructions, sleeping on average around eight hikers, conveniently located near water sources and spaced along the length of the AT so you would normally pass perhaps three each day. Having completed a successful thru-hike of the AT, most turn their attention to the PCT and finally the CDT. Hike all three and you earn yourself the accolade of a 'Triple Crowner'.

Every autumn, the ALDHA West (American Long Distance Hiking Association) honours those who have walked the 8,000 or so miles to complete all three. As of October 2012, only 174 people had been successful.

Not one for conformity, I discounted the AT as a first choice, mainly because at the time, I thought I might get the chance to do only one of the big three and the other two appealed more. The AT has a reputation for being wet. It clings to the Appalachian chain of mountains, which receive more than their fair share of rainfall. Being English and familiar, if not necessarily comfortable, with being damp on hiking trips, my attention turned to either the PCT or the CDT. The CDT is a serious undertaking for which I wasn't ready: it's the longest, the most remote, has fewer chances of regular re-supply and skilful navigation is a must, as some of the trail is not yet complete. By elimination, the PCT was the obvious choice. It had a fantastic reputation, and encompassed a variety of geographical areas such as desert, high alpine mountains and dense forest. Moreover, it boasted a fantastic climate.

I completed the PCT in 2010, albeit taking slightly longer than I had planned for and developed an incurable case of the thru-hiking bug in the process. The AT was still in the back of my mind, along with the CDT, and in January of 2012 I had the possibility of taking on the AT that March, which is exactly what I did.

***

Long-distance trails are life-changing events. However, they're not easy. The impression most have of us thru-hikers is that we get a vastly extended holiday, eat only sweet treats, do lots of sunbathing, drink a lot, go wild swimming, smell terrible and generally muck around in the woods. Admittedly some of this is true but make no mistake: it is a huge physical effort and is about as far from easy as you can get.

If you attempt a long-distance hike, the chances are heavily stacked against you and there is a very real chance that you will fail. Most quit in the first month. They were not as fit as they thought, new gear is chafing everywhere, red-raw blisters make walking excruciating or it's too cold, too hot, too dry or too wet, sometimes for days on end. I always say push through that first month and if you come out the other side, chances are you will be successful. Above everything else, you have to be single-minded and totally fixed on your goal to succeed. If you are mentally strong, can persuade yourself that you're not in pain and can push another mile out, that your hunger and thirst are imaginary, that it really isn't the seventh straight day of being wet and the fact that you badly misjudged your food supply doesn't really matter, then you just may succeed.

The AT forges a path through fourteen states: Georgia, North Carolina, Tennessee, Virginia, West Virginia, Maryland, Pennsylvania, New Jersey, New York, Connecticut, Massachusetts, Vermont, New Hampshire and Maine. Just the prospect of walking through so many states may be enough to deter most, but a thru-hiker views this with a glass-half-full approach, seeing the crossing of thirteen state lines as an indication of progress. On the PCT you cross just two. Currently around 2,700 prospective thru-hikers set out to conquer the route each year, in addition to section hikers. These walk a piece of the trail each year, or perhaps may miss a year and take several years to complete a thru-hike. Then there are the day hikers, or weekenders, who make regular visits to the AT, usually living in the vicinity of it. Some day hikers will accumulate more trail mileage in their lifetimes than most thru-hikers. In fact some two to three million visit the AT each year. Virginia boasts the longest section, at 550 miles, whereas the trail in West Virginia just clips the state corner and is a mere four miles long. Maryland and West Virginia are considered the easiest sections, New Hampshire and Maine the hardest.

By the time a successful thru-hiker stands on top of Mt Katahdin (or Springer Mountain for a south bounder), he or she will have gained the equivalent altitude of climbing Mount Everest sixteen times, consumed around 900,000 calories and drunk approximately 600 litres of water. Most will have camped for more nights than in their entire life to date, and probably more than they ever will again. A few will have worn out just one pair of shoes; others will be finishing off their sixth. Many will have spent as little as a thousand dollars, others eight thousand or more. A small proportion will be injured and some, sadly, may even die.

Most hikers start the AT in Georgia and head north. They are known as north-bounders, or Nobos. A small percentage start later in the season after the snows have subsided further north and head south from Maine. These are the south-bounders, or

Sobos. North-bounding is by far the most popular, thanks to a thru-hikers' eagerness to begin earlier.

An average hike in either direction takes around four to six months, and in that time it is possible to experience all four seasons. Most start in March or April, just after the tail end of winter, and continue through spring and summer, finishing in autumn.

Spring is the logical start time; it makes best use of the impending finer weather. But a hike starting late March or early April means the seasons are not just times of the year, but an experience. Instead of getting out in the woods every weekend, or worse, not at all, we *lived* the seasons, which revealed themselves in ways we could never hope to see. We shared the changing face of the year every single day. We saw the trees change from emaciated skeletons to bearers of tiny leaves. We noticed those leaves become more abundant as time rolled on, watched them burst from their buds and unfold, splaying outward to catch the light, changing from a translucent pale green to an opaque depth, becoming the best they would ever be. And then we observed them attain middle age and decline to old age. Deep greens gradually lost their sheen and resignedly faded to yellows, reds and browns, clinging to their twilight years far from gracefully but more in a final, riotous flourish of an artist's palette. Then they died, fell and fed the children of the following season.

I felt privileged to encounter not just the leaves but the whole gift that the woods offered me. During the early stages of my hike, I would often stop at high points and look down. Up there it was still stark winter but witnessing the blossoming of spring in the valleys below and watching it slowly creep up the hillside was a season's tease. However dark and unfriendly my immediate surroundings, the energy of the changing season below me was abundant and unstoppable. Every day, as it grew warmer, that energy crept uphill to meet me, and every day I would look down to urge it ever upwards. I was completely in awe.

I watched creeks, streams and rivers burst from the snowmelt and, as the summer strode on, raging torrents weakened to calmer waters, rivers slowed to a more sedate pace, streams become shallower and creeks turned to mere trickles. Ponds and lakes receded, their banks becoming dry and crusty, emaciated weeds strewn on their shores.

I saw a damp, cocoa-coloured trail lighten to beige as a warming sun drew out the moisture. I observed snakes hesitantly checking the temperature to see if it was warm enough and then glissade back through dry leaves, unexpectedly silent.

I observed storms raging miles distant, gliding along the horizon casting rain shadows. Lightning forks cracked and struck the ground, followed by ominous rumbles. I felt the wind on my face to gauge its direction and sat, even longer, counting seconds between enraged flashes and angry claps. Holding up a dry leaf and letting it go, I watched it fall as the wind caught it. Sometimes I wished the storm would come to me so I could experience the anger right above.

I walked in downpours, snow, the unbearable heat of summer and sapping humidity. The roar of rain on foliage behind me was startling at times, and I would flee through the woods trying to outrun storms, giggling like a child at the craziness of it all. Paths became sodden until puddles formed, which in turn overflowed until trickles tumbled over tree roots and matured to streams themselves, soaking my feet.

I stood in silent forests late at night, trying to catch teasing glimpses of stars through branches. I strained my ears to hear nothing but absolute silence, waiting for a wind to travel up the west side of the Appalachian Mountains and censor the calm. Sometimes it merely stroked my face or ruffled my tent wall; at other times I would struggle to hold myself upright against it. Its energy was invigorating, so intense I felt as though it was filling me.

I sat on rock shelves, legs dangling over precipices, and peered down, feeling my stomach clench. Over a hundred sunsets gifted sapphire skies which melted into brilliant ambers, touched by rose pinks. And at dawn too, the sun first peeked shyly over distant hills, then worked a route through the trees around me until I felt its warmth on my grateful face.

I sat on logs around campfires with others who shared the love of this trail, and as we talked, their faces flickered in an orange glow, bright one second, dark the next. They spoke animatedly of their lives and what the trail meant to them, with moving honesty and authenticity.

I walked with children, the retired and every age in between. I befriended soldiers, conversed with teachers, laughed alongside builders, shared food with writers, drank in the company of artists, sang along next to musicians, enjoyed the scenery with truck drivers and camped in the company of forest rangers.

***

Dromomania. That's what I have, and if you're reading this, it's very possible that you do too. Don't fight it ...

Chapter 3
Privy Sitting

March 28th to April 1st
The Start - Mile 0 to 51

I have few expectations in life. A mandatory prison sentence seems only fair for those annoying individuals who insist on relaying their life story to the cashier whilst we wait patiently in the queue behind them. Secondly, it's obvious that *The Great Escape,* a 1963 movie starring, amongst others, Steve McQueen, should have its own dedicated TV channel and be broadcast on a permanent loop. Finally, coffee should be officially recognized as the saviour of the human race and be made accessible, mandatory and free for all. This is my world vision, and with it in mind I duly helped myself to a cup of joe and ambled over to the desk inside the Amicalola Falls Visitor Center.

Whilst filling in the hiker registry form, a man emerged from the back office.

"A group of British started about three weeks ago. You are British, right?" he enquired after noticing my passport. He was amiable enough, but his question annoyed me, as it always does.

"I'm English," I replied in a polite, but corrective tone.

"There's a difference?"

"Yes. England is part of Great Britain, and it is true that I am British but I'm patriotic enough to consider myself not British, but English. If the politicians have their way, before long I'll be known as European along with everyone else in the EEC. It's just my way of trying to save my nationality."

He looked at me somewhat confusedly, nodded, smiled weakly and wished me a good hike.

I circled the room once, checking information, looking at

maps and studying a stuffed snake, my nose pressed against the tank to get a better angle. It soon became clear that it wasn't a dead exhibit as it reared up, forcing me to fall backwards onto my arse in surprise. Quickly checking that Swiss Miss, who had given me a ride to the centre, hadn't played witness along with anyone else, I exited through the back door to save any loss of face.

Nice one, Fozzie. You haven't even made the approach trail yet, let alone the actual AT, snake encounter number one is already under your belt, and you've bloody fallen over. Great start mate, really. Way to go.

Swiss Miss followed me out and asked for my camera, suggesting I go and stand by the AT sign. I looked at the writing that I had seen countless times in photos:

Appalachian Trail Approach. Springer Mountain, GA, 8.5 miles. Mt. Katahdin, Maine 2108.5 miles.

She took a few snaps to ensure the second most important photo of the trip had been recorded, wished me luck, and gave me a hug and a peck on the cheek for good measure. This ensured I was grinning for the rest of the day.

I'm not an avid planner, so my hiking strategy was loose except for one aspect: begin slowly. The main intention over the first couple of weeks was to avoid blisters, which had plagued me on El Camino and the PCT. I figured a slower-than-average pace, regular breaks and short daily distances would be the key. I would doubtless have to reign in a little over-enthusiasm at times but the mileage deficit could always be turned around later.

The hum of the road faded and the visitor centre was gradually lost in a sea of trees. My environment had been simplified from a bustling, crowded and noisy town to the simple browns of late winter. A sand-tinted trail cut a clear path and was sprinkled with dry, crisp, umber leaves. I was surrounded by trees stretching upwards, attempting to touch a fading, weak mist. A clear sky was barely visible, and it was quiet, serene and already very, very beautiful.

The temperature was a surprise: unexpectedly warm. I peeled off my jacket. Amicalola Creek curved in to join me, offering a hushed gurgle as company, seemingly almost aware of the quiet. The falls themselves, at 729 feet high, were originally named by the Cherokee, 'Amicalola' meaning 'tumbling waters'. The ascent from the creek to the top of the falls entailed climbing up an impressive 604 steps on a wooden staircase. There was a smattering of overweight tourists in varying states of decay littering the climb, some grasping the handrail, bent over trying to catch their breath, others sitting on the steps chucking water down their throats wondering why they hadn't brought another six bottles. I felt good. I wasn't as fit as I could have been, but I had spent a couple of months getting into shape with several hour-long runs and a couple of fifteen-mile walks each week. I breathed easy and sped up all 729 feet like a sprightly teenager.

I knew Springer Mountain was a mere 8.5 miles from the visitor centre, but it seemed to take ages to arrive. A mix of anticipation and eagerness to sit by one of the most renowned hiking spots in the world forced my pace up. After each bend and turn in the trail I thought it would arrive, teasing me all the way until eventually, some ten years after I first promised myself to walk the AT, the climb mellowed and flattened into a clearing. A small gap in the trees facing north gave me what was soon to be a familiar view of round-topped, tree-cloaked hills fading away to the horizon. I set down my pack gently against a rock embellished with an embedded bronze plaque. A figure of a hiker stood proud and I ran my hands along the cold surface and felt my fingers ripple over the raised words:

Appalachian Trail
Georgia to Maine
A Footpath for Those who seek Fellowship with the Wilderness
AT 1934
The Georgia Appalachian Trail Club

I smiled. It was just a sign, but it could have been cast just for me, and indeed most attempting to thru-hike. The most significant words I had ever read about the AT sat right in the middle: 'A Footpath for Those who seek Fellowship with the Wilderness'. Just one line, but incredibly profound. I read the words again and again. I did seek fellowship with the wilderness: I wanted to be part of it again, to learn from it, to allow it to let me in and banish all the negative feelings and emotions that I was harbouring from two years spent in society since the PCT.

This was the moment I had dreamt about for so many years, a

scene I had pictured when my mood was low, a moment I longed for that had finally arrived. Content at last, I had around six months to follow a classic trail through prime areas of the American countryside. I was free to roam: there were no schedules, no phone calls or alarm clocks, and a collection of other like-minded people willing to indulge themselves for similar reasons with whom I could connect and share the experience. Again, for a few short months I had escaped from society, and the relief was overwhelming. I sat down, cupped my face in my hands, gave in to emotions and completely unashamed, I cried.

Voices signalled people were coming, and I hastily wrote in the register behind the plaque and left, partly due to embarrassment and partly due to my need to be alone. The path worked its way down from Springer and I passed Springer Mountain shelter, the first of many over the next few months, but felt no need to rest so early.

I did have a guidebook, but no map. The AT is so well-marked that a map is not really needed. Mine, written by a previous thru-hiker called David 'AWOL' Miller, supplied all the information I needed without one. It detailed mileage both completed and left to walk, an altitude graph, distances to the next shelter or campsite, water sources, other trails and notable features for positional reference plus town layout maps.

Further route clarification was provided by white blazes, or trail markers. These are thought to be scaled to the size of a dollar bill and regularly dot the AT. Most are painted on trees, some on rocks, fences or other mediums, and they signify that you are on the right track. Dinosaur had told me that apparently they are spaced so frequently that the next blaze should be visible from the preceding one. I didn't always find this to be the case but it was true a lot of the time. These simple white rectangles led all the way to Maine; one couldn't possibly get lost. They were even painted on the opposing side of the trees so those heading south were guided also. Side trails, such as those to shelters, water sources and other trails were painted in blue.

The trees narrowed. Clumps of rhododendrons encroached and formed tunnels around me: a small piece of green paradise breaking up the brown. I skipped and jumped over small creeks, sometimes using stones to get across.

I saw my first hiker up ahead: a thru-hiker for sure. Simple giveaways like the size of his pack and his short hair signified he was Maine-bound (many thru-hikers cut their hair short at the start and leave it untouched for the rest of the journey). I slowed and studied him; his gait and stride were different from normal. He trod carefully, seeming to concentrate on each step and foot placement. Walking on eggshells would be too strong a comparison but that's what it reminded me of. Occasionally one arm rose slightly to steady him as though he was balancing on a tightrope and he walked slowly. I caught him quickly, and before passing, so as not to startle, I spoke.

"You walk carefully. It's interesting to watch! What's your name?"

"PJ, and yours?"

"Fozzie. Nice to meet you."

Noticing my accent he asked, "Are you British?"

Oh crap, here we go again.

I slowed a little, intending to stop, but couldn't be bothered to explain twice in one day so I offered the simplified version.

"Yes, English to be exact. See you up the trail I expect?"

"For sure, it's all good."

After twelve miles or so it was already late afternoon and a blue blaze marked a side trail to Stover Creek Shelter. Hearing voices from that direction and eager to see my first shelter I veered off towards it.

With no plans to use the shelters that much, I had packed everything required to do without them: tent, sleeping bag, air mat, cooking equipment and the like. I had heard much about these simple, three-sided wooden constructions that dot the trail. Usually a focal point for hikers at the end of the day, they not only offer shelter from the rain and wind, but more often the lure of company. A wooden floor is usually built into the structure to elevate hikers off the ground. Simple additions like a fire pit, composting toilet or privy and perhaps a picnic table are occasionally found outside. There is no running water, electric, heating or plumbing. Shelters are purely that: sanctuary from the elements. They also help to minimise the impact on the environment; traffic is concentrated around one area instead of many tent sites so erosion is more limited, if somewhat heavy.

Occupied on a first-come, first-serve basis, they fill quickly, sometimes even by mid-afternoon. Hiker capacity is usually posted on one wall or by reference in our guidebooks but many times, especially in wet conditions, this is ignored and often exceeded.

The downside, for me at least, is that staying in a space with several others was not conducive to a decent night's kip. Snoring, passing wind, fidgeting, people holding conversations when others were trying to sleep didn't appeal. They are also renowned for sheltering other occupants: mice.

The main lure to our rodent friends isn't shelter, although that may be a bonus, but food, and plenty of it. Just above head height near shelter entrances are invariably several pieces of string or cordage, about a foot or so in length, with a stick tied horizontally at the bottom end. Most also have an empty food tin half way down, suspended by means of a hole in the tin and a knot in the cord. The purpose of the stick was to thread through the carrying loop on the top of backpacks and suspend them off the floor, away from mice. The can was there because although any mouse is capable of climbing down a line, they often find it difficult to negotiate the tin.

The food wasn't too much of a concern to me; at best, one could expect to find a nibbled pack of crackers, or perhaps some inroads into a loaf of bread. What worried me was the damage inflicted to equipment. It was not uncommon for hikers to wake in the morning and find several strayed holes in their packs or other accessories. With packs costing upwards of £100, you can imagine my concern.

I did stay in a few shelters, usually when they were quiet, and I became used to our little friends. Come sundown, the shelter would echo with the scurrying sounds of our guests, checking out what was on the menu, carrying out some route surveillance and holding planning meetings to discuss the best line of attack. I didn't mind; mice never bothered me. They were just like us, trying to survive and looking for something to eat.

As it transpired, I did usually home in on shelters come the end of day, purely for the company and in the hope that any bears would take a liking to another hiker before me. I'm quite considerate like that. They were great places to socialise when I was in the mood, catch up with whoever was staying there, get the weather reports from whoever had reception on the mobile, swap or share food and go sit by anyone who had dark chocolate.

Stover Creek was certainly one of the better offerings. It was actually split into two levels with a stated capacity of ten, although more could have comfortably slept there. Twelve other hikers were occupying themselves with varying tasks such as journal writing, cooking or setting up their beds for the night. I chatted to Eric, Bridget and Josh before heading over to a flat spot to set up camp for the night.

I was gone by the time the others were up in the morning, being keen to put in a good shift and get an early finish. I was amazed at how warm it was: I had been too hot in my sleeping bag overnight and, after a short-lived morning chill, it wasn't long before I was down to shorts and a T-shirt. Spring was waking up as if it had just realised that there was much work to be done. However, I tried not to become complacent about the weather. The AT has a reputation for changeable conditions, and apart from the rain, there are plenty of places, especially at higher elevations, where we could still get snowed on. The Smoky Mountains, some 165 miles down the trail, are famed for throwing in a little late winter snowfall. For the time being at least, I was relishing being out of the English winter and enjoying a premature start to the summer season.

I stopped to chat to a couple of guys carrying out some forestry work. They were eager to talk about their home state of Georgia and the woods. They pointed out the early flowers of the Trillium plant with its three virgin-white petals, and also Mayapple, sporting a simple, more delicate, single flower head. I asked whether there were any Ramps (wild onions) growing, but was disappointed when they told me that it was still too early.

I passed Eric sitting by Blackwell Creek collecting water for the evening camp.

"Hey Fozzie, the shelter is just up the way there. You staying there tonight?"

"Anyone there yet?" I enquired.

"Most of those from last night and some new faces."

"I'll see you up there."

Gooch Mountain Shelter signalled around thirteen miles for the day, pretty much the small target I had set myself so I took the side trail. Still hesitant to use the shelter, I found a suitable spot for my tent.

Bridget, Eric, Josh and another Josh were in the shelter along with PJ who seemed in a jovial mood. Noticing that there were now two Joshes and the confusion that this could cause, I decided that the bestowing of trail names should be implemented as soon as possible. For the interim period I referred to them as 'Josh Long Hair' and 'Josh Short Hair'. Highly unoriginal, I know, but I was taking the assignation of trail names seriously, and needed time to come up with some impressive suggestions.

I was surprised that everyone was still using their real names, but realised that the AT is the first route that many attempt, and trail customs were perhaps not yet familiar. Therefore, I made my feelings about trail names known to the group as we sat around the shelter, and the idea of bestowing them was proposed, albeit with a grace period for suitable names to be thought of, and either accepted or rejected.

I had chatted to PJ and Bridget, and I was curious about both of them. I'm not the most sociable person and I tend to reserve my communications to those with whom I think I would share an affinity. There are certain aspects of a person's character that suggest how devoted or focused to the adventure they are: from their hiking style, either lazy or purposeful, to whether they talk about the experience with excitement or an air of nonchalance, even to their organisation at camp, slapdash or orderly. All these aspects hold clues; indeed, I wondered how others may perceive my character.

Bridget was a classic example. She was 24 and hailed from Madison, Wisconsin. She had been making noises about hiking the AT for years, as she put it. After a year in the AmeriCorps (sort of a domestic version of the Peace Corps), she had done a little travelling down in South America, then returned three months prior in December. The next two months were spent as a special education assistant. With spring looming, she decided that career advancement wasn't at the top of her list. However, spiritual progression was, and the AT seemed the ideal place to nurture that desire.

She wore a grey T-shirt with 'Madison' emblazoned across the front and sometimes tied her hair back with a pink headband. Appearing much younger than her years suggested, a pair of oval black-rimmed glasses advanced those years somewhat, and she had a propensity to giggle, making her very endearing.

She was relaxed, but I noticed from day one that she was utterly focused on the task. Out for a month to see how she did was not on her agenda. Her short frame was not totally suited for hiking but just from the way she walked, how she went about her tasks in camp and from the positive way she conversed, I just knew Bridget would make it all the way to Katahdin.

PJ had quite possibly the shortest trail name I had ever encountered. A head of dark hair flopped around randomly but always seemed to look tidy, and he already sported a beard to get him into the thru-hiker spirit. He was 22, fresh-faced, and bright-eyed. I could tell by the frequency with which he smiled that already he was having the time of his life. He sounded a little effeminate when he spoke, and hugged the guys and the girls freely, but by the way he commented on members of the fairer sex, I figured he was straight.

I politely asked him about his character and he laughed, saying he preferred the description of avant-garde or eccentric. His character was, however, infectious, and would always brighten up any situation. He also confided in me that he had left his wife the day before travelling to the trail and how difficult it had been not only to tell her, but to pluck up the courage to actually do it. As he explained, he showed a little remorse and sadness as he stared off into space, then quickly snapped back to the present, smiled, and offered his usual catchphrase: it's all good!

There were bear cables some 200 feet from the shelter, and after dinner I went over to hang my food bag. Two new faces, Krista and her mother, were added to the list of those needing trail names.

Most shelters have bear cables somewhere in the vicinity. The idea is simple: after eating, pack all your food and smelly toiletries into a waterproof bag and hoist it up. Cables were usually stretched between two trees, high enough from the ground so as to be out of a bear's reach, with any bags at the two ends also far enough away from the trees themselves that they couldn't climb up and reach out to the bags from there either.

Apart from keeping a hiker's food safe and away from sleeping areas where a bear could encroach, the main purpose of these steel wires was to educate our furry forest friends. Bears are very intelligent wild animals with three main instincts: survival, eating and procreation.

Over the years they have learnt that humans, especially where they congregate, bring food. If these supplies are easily accessible, they make an association between people and an opportunity to eat. This is why there have been instances where bears have ventured into towns and usually, unfortunately, have been shot. Cables are simply a way of teaching bears that just because humans and food are in the same vicinity, it doesn't mean there is good eating to be had.

Black Bears are common on the AT and chances are a thru-hiker will at some point see one, if not several. They usually go about their business without bothering anyone, are reclusive and will keep away from humans. The best deterrent is to make your presence known; in a group this becomes easier because of conversation. Solo hikers generally take their chances, but may shout something every few minutes; I used to simply bang my trekking poles together once in a while.

If you find yourself in proximity to a Black Bear, first give it the chance to move away so it doesn't feel threatened. If that doesn't work, then the general options become numerous. Some say to back off slowly, still talking and avoiding eye contact. Others, including me, are a little more gung ho. If I see a Black Bear, I will give it the opportunity to move away, but I will make my presence known vocally. In my experience, most bears will run away when they hear us. Unfortunately, and I can vouch for this, some bears don't, and this is where potentially you could, for want of a better description, be in the shit.

As far as I understand them, a few, rogue bears share similarities with that drunk guy in the pub who just wants to have a fight. He'll glare at you for a while, and when he decides he really doesn't like you, may advance in a threatening manner, look angry and clench his fists. You then have two choices: stand your ground, or get the hell out of the pub. Fleeing is a sign of weakness; it displays vulnerability, fear, and is the only excuse he needs. It's the same with bears.

However, very rarely will a bear act aggressively. When it does, against all your natural instincts, you have to stand your ground. Run, and not only do they see you as a mid-morning snack but they get a game of chase to boot. Even scarier is what is known as a bluff charge, where a bear will literally charge to test you. Stay put, and this indicates that you are strong, which hopefully should do the trick. Bluff charges are exactly that: a bluff. Unfortunately, we have no way of knowing in such circumstances whether the bear is testing you or genuinely — rarely — intending to attack. Either way, don't move. Shout, hold your arms aloft, and pray.

I battled a phobia of bears for many years, to the point where I nearly decided not to hike the Pacific Crest Trail because of it. After a few encounters in California and Oregon, including two very scary situations in close proximity, I now hold a deep respect for them. The chances are a hiker may never see a bear on a thru-hike or be in a threatening situation. Encounters are uncommon, attacks extremely rare, and fatalities virtually nonexistent. Bears are beautiful creatures that are misunderstood. Having encountered them and experienced their behaviour, I now understand that they are not the problem. We are.

***

Ask a thru-hiker what they find difficult on trail and you will get various replies. Some may say they hate the heat; some can't deal with the cold. Others will complain about blisters, that their gear is not performing, or the lack of alcohol is too much. For me, it's an addiction to American cooked breakfasts. Reaching road crossings before 11 a.m. where a ride to town could be obtained always presented a battle of wills, and the AT, especially in Georgia, was riddled with roads. I always made sure I had enough food for the trail, but the lure of bacon and eggs was sometimes just too much to ignore.

For example, mid-morning on day three, I reached the road crossing at Woody Gap and my thoughts immediately turned to hash browns. I don't mean those triangular blocks of compressed potato we have in England; I refer to a pile of prime, shredded potato crisped up on a griddle. After only two-and-a-half days I considered this pretty weak, but in my meagre defence there were mitigating circumstances. Firstly, I was hungry. Secondly, rain was imminent, and thirdly, hitchhiking options were on blatant display in the car park across the road. Obviously, the situation had to be taken full advantage of.

Hitchhiking and asking for a ride are two separate skill sets. Some people who live near the major trails in the USA are used to not only seeing thru-hikers, but also being asked for a lift. Never one to assume this, I walked over to the car park and placed my backpack on the ground, near to a guy who had just arrived back at his car after walking his dog. I made sure I was in earshot and looked in his direction to obtain eye contact. Sure enough, he looked over, nodded and smiled.

"How's it going?" he enquired.

"Great," I said, casually strolling over. "Do you happen to know which town is near here?"

An open question generally makes an individual feel obliged to answer with anything but a "yes" or a "no". It also invites conversation.

"None of them are that close. Is there something you need?" he replied, towelling some dirt off his dog.

47

"Nothing more than a decent breakfast; I'm starving."

"The Wagon Wheel restaurant is just down the road. I'm heading down that way. Happy to give you a ride?"

With that, I thanked him profusely and climbed in the front seat of his ancient Volvo. Lucy the Dalmatian seemed somewhat surprised that someone got her front seat whilst she got relegated to the rear. I chatted with Jim during the brief ride to the Wagon Wheel, and he explained he was visiting relatives and taking time in the woods with Lucy. He decided to eat with me, and whilst declining my offer to get his bill, he in fact paid for both of us when I made a visit to the toilet. He even gave me a ride back to the trailhead. Southern Hospitality was alive and kicking in Georgia.

While I got over the shock of seeing my second snake that day, albeit a harmless rat snake sliding into a pile of leaves, I noticed two hikers approaching as I geared up to move from Woody Gap. They walked straight over to me and introduced themselves.

Thru-hikers look different from other hikers. Our gear veers more towards what we know works, as opposed to being slaves to fashion. You may see us walking in lime-green shorts with black tights on for warmth, orange running shoes and a light blue balaclava. Our appearance is often soiled, even filthy. The guys grow beards and have long hair (at least during the latter stages of a hike); the girls don't consider makeup necessary and sport hairy legs. This is how we distinguish ourselves from other walkers, and we tend to be drawn to other thru-hikers so we can share our experiences.

There was never any doubt that Phillip Colelli and Sam Ridge were thru-hikers. We had all just started so excessive hair growth wasn't yet apparent, but Phillip and Sam's equipment gave them away. They appeared more like a couple of joggers with tiny packs and we chatted momentarily before making inroads into the four miles to the campsite at Lance Creek. There was talk of a storm rolling in which made the shelter at Woods Hole more sensible, but it was seven miles further. We were all keeping our mileage low so Lance Creek seemed the better choice.

The site was busy. Bridget and PJ were setting up their tents, Krista and her mother arrived, and some new faces, Bill and Cassie, were cooking their dinner. Phillip and Sam had arrived just before me. AT campsites do not come equipped with such distractions as swimming pools, restaurants or bars. In fact the only facilities most laid on were level areas for tents and possibly a privy. Like the shelters, they were usually situated conveniently near water.

I looked up to menacing skies. The storm was not forecast until the early hours, but I decided to pitch my tent first, just in case. I was soon to discover that designated tent platforms, designed to conserve the surrounding area, left a lot to be desired. The obvious initial problem was the size. I grabbed one of the last plots and quickly realised that even my meagre one-man tent was too big for the space provided. I played around with various positions, but the best pitch I could muster involved hanging one side slightly off the edge. The guy lines stretched off the platform, which resulted in less-than-acceptable staking-out points. Then, I discovered the soil was rock-hard anyway, so had to resort to tying the lines to nearby trees.

***

Appalachian storms are legendary. Rain is common, and in the summer, fierce weather patterns scare the crap out of hikers. The other problem is the altitude of the trail. The highest point on the AT is Clingmans Dome at 6643 feet, but generally the trail merrily skips along at around four to five thousand feet, which coincidentally always seems to be the same height as the cloud level. Basically, if you're caught out in inclement weather on the AT, the chances are you're not under the storm, but actually in it.

For example, during Thanksgiving weekend in 1950, an area of severe low pressure pulled down a mass of cold, arctic air from the north whilst forcing warmer air up from the south. The result was catastrophic. One of the biggest storms ever along the Appalachian chain dumped several feet of snow in some parts whilst others in the warmer air suffered flooding. Wind speeds of 140mph were recorded on Bear Mountain in New York, and Mount Washington in New Hampshire, famous for documenting the strongest wind speed ever, anywhere, recorded gusts of up to 160mph. Extremes of temperature ranged from 50°F before the storm down to the teens behind it, and a low of -5°F was recorded. It cost insurance companies \$66.7 million (or, more than \$650 million adjusted for inflation) in claims, and was known simply as 'The Great Appalachian Storm'.

***

Mountain Crossings Outfitter at Neel Gap, thirty two miles into the AT, has a fantastic reputation amongst hikers and wasn't far from Lance Creek. Food is a big draw and I had heard great reports about the fully-stocked equipment store and hostel. It was regarded as the premier outfitter in Georgia and was right on the trail.

I climbed with Arne from Maine, Bridget, Bill and Cassie up the 1500 feet to Blood Mountain, passing a group of hikers at Slaughter Creek. We briefly chatted to one guy, and learnt that a bear had actually ripped down the cables near his camp and made off with his food bag. He had heard the commotion and said it was like being in the middle of a horror movie.

Great. Slaughter Creek, Blood Mountain and a rampant bear. How about being a little more positive with the place names around here?

We were looking forward to Neel Gap where Mountain Crossings Outfitter was situated, and we made light work of the seven miles before hearing the occasional vehicle somewhere on the road below us. We spilled out onto US-19, crossed over and entered the shop, eager for sustenance. Several of us also needed to dry out gear, so as the sun flooded the outside deck, wet tents, bags and waterproofs were draped about. When I heard that there was a tumble dryer somewhere, I took the opportunity to try drying out my sleeping bag. I enquired inside and was helpfully pointed to a flight of stairs up the front of the building where said dryer was located. Sam also needed to use the machine, and we found it easily enough. I was just about to place my bag in the top loader when I heard someone running up the steps. One of the staff appeared at the door and glared at me.

"What are you doing?" he demanded.

"I'm about to dry out my sleeping bag," I answered, thinking that looked plainly obvious.

"Do not put your dirty bag in the dryer!"

"Excuse me? My bag is not dirty." I was a little taken aback by his behaviour.

"I don't care; do not put your dirty-ass bag in the dryer!"

This offended me. Not only was I acutely aware that my bag was not dirty because it was brand-new, I knew my bottom was also relatively clean.

"My bag is not dirty, it's just damp. It's brand-new; I have only slept it in twice. I just need to dry it out."

"You are not putting your dirty-ass bag in the dryer!"

I was trying to keep my cool. At this point we were exchanging comments rapidly, and Sam's head was flicking back and forth between us quicker than at a Wimbledon final.

I was about to retort again when he interrupted me.

"Get out of here!" he demanded.

"Excuse me?"

"Leave. Get out."

"I'm not going anywhere; I haven't done anything wrong."

Sam's head, fatigued from the side-to-side motion, exchanged to nodding in agreement instead.

"You're not putting your dirty-ass bag in the dryer without a cotton cover bag!"

"Listen mate, do you want to tell me exactly what the bloody problem is here? I just want to dry my bag. It's wet, not dirty. If you want me to use a cotton bag over the top then I'm happy to do so. Where can I get one?"

"You can borrow one from the shop downstairs."

With that, Sam and I backed off gently, as one would with a bear encounter, and ventured back to the shop.

"Why didn't he just bloody say that in the first place?" I said to Sam as we went back to the shop.

"I have no idea," he replied.

I dried the bag successfully and bought a couple of snacks before returning to the deck, which had been transformed by a collection of thru-hikers drying out their gear. A few others had arrived, including Bridget, and I took the opportunity to return inside to buy her a little gift. Her preference for pink-coloured equipment was evidenced by various items hanging off her person and pack. I returned, and handed her a small karabiner in a subtle shade of flamingo.

"It will go with the rest of your collection," I pointed out. "By the way, I have your new trail name."

"You do?" Her eyes narrowed.

"Yep. In relation to your penchant for pink-coloured gear, I thought that 'Pink Bits' would be perfect." I raised my eyebrows in anticipation of her reply, and was convinced she would accept without hesitation. After all, it was a brilliant, amusing and highly original trail name.

"Pink Bits?!" she replied, in a tone which hinted she wasn't exactly enamoured with the suggestion. She repeated again, "Pink Bits?!"

"Yeah. It's good, innit?"

"No! You can't call me that!" She did see the funny side, but her refusal was firm.

"Why not?"

She paused momentarily with a slight hint of embarrassment.

"Because it's got sexual undertones."

This was a fair point. To be honest, I did realise that others could possibly perceive the name as having connections with various sections of the anatomy, but had ignored this slight problem in hopes that firstly, Bridget wouldn't catch on, and secondly, I thought the double meaning was kind of clever.

"So, that's a 'no' then, is it?" I sought final clarification, to which she merely raised her eyebrows.

"OK. I'll give it some more thought. See you later."

I packed and was making inroads into leaving with Sam when I spotted the same staff member who had confronted me by the dryer. A little despondent about the situation, which I knew would play on me, I took the opportunity to disperse any friction. I walked over and gently placed a hand on his shoulder. He turned around.

"Hey, look, sorry about the misunderstanding with the dryer," I said.

"Yeah, it's OK, but I'm ex-military. I tell people what to do and they do it."

On the defensive, and a little miffed that he still had an attitude despite my taking the initiative to approach him, I replied.

"Well I hate to state the bloody obvious mate, but you're not in the Army anymore. You're back on Civvy Street and serving customers. A little attitude adjustment would go a long way," and I walked off, back into the woods.

Sam kept me company, and we chatted away the seven-odd miles to Whitley Gap Shelter that afternoon. There were numerous others relaxing after the day's walk, most in the shelter or cooking on the table outside. I walked about a hundred feet away from them and noticed a faint trail through some trees, which lured me in. The woodland thinned and opened out to a narrow, flat area just before the ridge dropped away. The view was immense. I pitched my tent between two trees that creaked and groaned in a subtle wind, and afforded me a contemplative view. My short distance from the others meant the noise and chatter was less obtrusive but still comforting, and after setting up my camp I went over for some company and to eat.

Desperado, a new face, sat opposite me as I ate. It was refreshing to at last find someone who actually had a trail name, but our conversation seemed more like an interview. I enquired about her name and she told me it originated from the song Desperado, which she used to sing at karaoke. I tried to eat as she fired question after question at me, in between jotting down what I could only presume were my answers. She didn't participate nor converse a great deal, but merely muttered an 'um' after I answered each question. Then she let rip with my favourite.

"So, Fozzie, you're British right?"

I stared into my pot, seeking savoury rice salvation.

Please, not again.

"I'm English, yeah."

She nodded and scribbled on her pad whilst I tried to peek, unsuccessfully, at what she was writing. She cupped her hand around the notepad.

"Um, why do you say you're English?"

"Because I am English? Look, it doesn't matter. Are you a reporter or something? You ask a lot of questions."

"No, it's just for my journal."

With my hint received, she stopped. We made some small talk about the trail before my company fix for the evening was satiated and I sloped off to the solitude of my camp. I stood near my tent, just before the ground fell away, and let an Appalachian breeze touch me and lift the weaker branches of the trees, still bare. A Georgia moon picked out low clouds drifting lazily across distant mountains, white ghosts surfing silhouetted ridgelines. To the west, a faint yellow glimmer was the only reminder of sunset as it merged into a sombre sky. I crept into my little haven, wrapped my sleeping bag around me and gazed through the open door until, too weak to resist any longer, I shut my eyes.

Chatter floated over from the shelter, waking me in the morning. There were twelve miles to Blue Mountain Shelter and I decided again, on route, to address the lack of trail names.

Hiker names, Fozzie — you have to spread the word, get them named!

I arrived early, having eaten up the distance quickly, still keeping my daily targets around the ten to fifteen-mile mark. The place was empty. It seemed strange to have a shelter to myself, and the lack of conversation lent a solemn air to my surroundings: a solitary woodpecker made the only sound. I sat near the entrance and studied the data book, checked my day's progress, and looked at what tomorrow would bring.

After ten minutes or so, I happened to look to my left and saw Jerry sitting a mere ten feet away reading his Kindle.

"Bloody hell, Jerry!" I exclaimed. "How the hell do you do that? You scared the crap out of me!"

"Do what?" he replied, smirking.

"One minute you just appear out of nowhere; you're like some sort of Ninja! Wait a minute, that's it!"

"What's what?" He lifted his eyebrows.

"I got your trail name! People need to be named, dammit, and I got another one!"

He looked somewhat dubious, as most hikers do when someone informs them they are about to be christened.

"Go on, I'm listening."

"I hereby bestoweth the trail name of Kindle Ninja upon thee. What sayeth you?"

I had never given anyone a trail name that had been accepted, but I thought it was pretty damned good. His eyebrows rose contemplatively and he scratched his chin, smiling.

"Fozzie, I like it. Seriously, I do."

That was it. Confidence boosted, I set up camp whilst studying everyone's mannerisms, behaviour, appearance, and other important criteria for clues to trail names. This was no half-arsed effort: day five into my hike, and I felt I had accrued more than enough information. Slowly, the mob arrived, and Blue Mountain came to life.

I ventured off down a vague track in the direction of the privy.

"Fozzie, it's taken! Queue's here!" shouted Phillip from behind the shelter.

I retreated and sat to join him, Sam, Little Josh and a guy who actually did have a trail name called Central Booking. The privy occupied just one place so as people slowly emerged from the woods clutching their toilet paper, someone would disappear off for the next allocated spot. Occasionally others would join the line, so numbers remained fairly constant. Of all the places to get to know other characters, waiting in line for the toilet proved a priceless location, and privy sitting, as it became known, caught on.

Firstly, if you got bored with one person, it was only a matter of time before they left anyway. Secondly, the new arrivals changed the atmosphere a little and implemented subject changes, making for varied conversations. Time was limited in the privy queue so topics were discussed animatedly as people realised they didn't have very long, and the result was a little taster, a snapshot of the character. Plus, we jokingly chastised those who came back from their business that had either taken too long, or made impressive noises. One such culprit was Jonathan, whose faltering head torch heralded his return from the darkness some fifteen minutes after his departure.

"Bloody hell, mate," I began, "That must have been some dump."

Little Josh covered his mouth and giggled, I think a little embarrassed at my forwardness.

Jonathan paused just before us, and looking somewhat confused, said, "Man, you have no idea the amount of shi …"

Most of the group fell about in fits, and as I glanced over at Sam, it suddenly became apparent that trail name number two of the evening was beckoning.

"Phillip, I think I have Sam's trail name. You know that face he pulls when he's taken too much on a cigarette, and he doesn't want to breathe in case he coughs?"

"Yup?"

"Daffy Duck? It has to be Daffy Duck, doesn't it?"

Sam's lower lip receded whilst his upper lip extended somewhat, giving the impression of a beak. Phillip started laughing in confirmation, and Sam held no objections although we did shorten it to just plain Daffy.

Two new trail names out of three proposals; I figured that was a pretty good hit ratio. I chuckled my way back to my tent and knew I was happy. Not just at that precise moment, but my life in general thus far on the AT, and I still have fond memories of that evening on Blue Mountain.

Chapter 4
A Feast in the Forest

April 2nd to April 11th
Mile 51 to 153

One bonus of the AT, as opposed to other, remoter trails, is that it never warrants too much planning. As far as logistics go, or rather in my case, lack of them, it is a deliciously random affair to see what happens and deal with it then. The frequency of amenities along the AT's length means that if a food resupply is misjudged, it is only a matter of time before the next opportunity comes along. Apart from remoter sections found further up the AT, such as in Maine, towns are relatively frequent.

Organising overnight stops was easy, with a tent camping places were numerous and, if I decided to sleep in a shelter only to discover it was full, there was always another one a few miles up the track or somewhere to pitch in the woods. Apart from town stops, and getting to the roads that led to them, planning was loose and usually based on when food supplies would likely run out. Re-supply in town, check the data book, search for a road crossing three, four or five days up trail that provided access to the next town with decent amenities, confer with your buddies and the planning was complete. With logistics taken care of easily, I could concentrate on hiking and the trail was that much more enjoyable.

Planning and thru-hiking do lend themselves to each other, some hikers are diligent in their approach, others not so. Most have an overall strategy and some stick to it religiously but this, to me, defeats the overall objective. My planning arrangements for a thru-hike are usually limited to asking myself two questions: do I want to do it and do I think I can? If a hiker draws up plans for an entire route, pinpoints certain towns to resupply, allows a set number of days in between to hike those stages and other criteria then the very essence of why they are undertaking such an expedition is undermined. As the explorer Roald Amundsen once said, "Adventure is just bad planning."

Take a wrong trail for half a day before realising and the whole plan for the ensuing few months would then be out of sync, and it wouldn't just happen once either. Travelling through a country on a bipedal adventure should be primarily about freedom, an escape. Getting too involved with logistics hampers my enjoyment of the actual trip. I relish uncertainty and one should always be open to a little serendipity. Margins of error are not things I generally concern myself with because my overall plan is adaptable anyway — I can always readjust after. A lot of flexibility is demanded when a trip is several months in duration. I know the distance I ideally need to hike each day and generally that's what I do, but I'm not religious about it.

My scheme when researching a thru-hike is common sense and revolves primarily around the distance to be covered and the time available to do it. The rest of the plan happens when I start hiking. Most who attempt to travel north on one of the big three routes in America will be concentrating on one aspect: getting to the finish before the weather turns. The AT, PCT and CDT all run vertically through the country and most hikers walk south to north. It is only a matter of time before the wet autumn weather arrives, perhaps around September, and shortly after the temperature starts to decrease. That's when snow enters the equation.

My calculations focus on the distance required, the time span I have, factor in one rest day every week as a zero (a *zero* is a day when no walking is done) and perhaps one day a month off as a buffer. The buffer is there if I were to drop behind a little — a get out clause, but more importantly it's to indulge in a little randomness. If your schedule is too strict then when you pass that turquoise lake, cupped in a flower meadow between snow-capped peaks then you either have to pass it by, or at best have a quick dip, which then makes you feel guilty because you've stopped and are now behind schedule. Want a lazy extra couple of hours in your tent because you're taking in a view of the Sierra Nevada? Make your strategy adaptable. The strict planners will miss out but you won't.

The main culprits on the thru-hikes responsible for altering plans, and especially the AT, are events known as trail magic. Usually found at road crossings with vehicular access, trail magic consists of some kind-hearted soul, often an ex thru-hiker, who has surrendered their time and money to provide assistance to hikers. Basic trail magic could just be a can of pop and a bag of crisps left by the trailside. Others may have several tables and chairs under cover; kegs of beer, coffee, cooking equipment with fresh meat and vegetables, all the condiments one could ever hope for, electrical charging equipment and even rides to a local town. Thru-hikers would generally leave a donation to at least cover costs, or offer assistance where it is required.

Word normally spread along the route if trail magic was ahead. Sometimes we caught wind from a day hiker or a sobo and, conversely, us nobos would return the favour. The best encounters were the ones I didn't know anything about, perhaps because they had only set up that morning and word had not yet swept around about the location. Being blissfully unaware that trail magic lurked up ahead was my preference. There were few greater pleasures than catching a wayward waft of a quarter pounder grilling 200 feet below and looking skyward to pray that trail magic was imminent, then popping out of the woods to discover it. It was wonderfully ambiguous and one such example was *The Feast in the Forest.*

Deep Gap shelter was around sixteen miles from Blue Mountain shelter. I was starting to base most of my days around walking from one shelter to another. There was nearly always water available, sometimes a view, usually a fire and other hikers gathering promised company if needed. Sixteen miles was not a lot to walk in a day but keeping to my principle of starting slowly it made sense. There was also a 957 foot descent from Blue Mountain to Unico Gap, a 1068-foot climb to Rocky Mountain, a further 904 feet down to Indian Grave Gap and finally a three-mile, 1317-foot slog up to Deep Gap. Two months into a thru-hike and at peak fitness I could have knocked all of that off in less than a morning but I was determined to stick to my no blister plan.

As the day panned out, it became clear that Deep Gap was never meant to happen when randomness stole an opportunity. I walked on my own, revelling in the solitude and the chance to just think.

I descended steeply to Indian Grave Gap, turning and twisting down the bends, letting my legs go freely and then arresting the run. I thought I heard laughter and a few seconds later there it was again. I stopped, listened, and sure enough there were people below me and they sounded happy. A minute later and I caught wind of meat grilling.

Trail magic! Yeah! Trail Magic!

I broke into a jog, weaving around stones, hopping over tree roots and before long I was singing, then I started skipping. This merged into a jogging dance; two skips on the left foot with a right tilt of the head, two steps on the other side and an opposite tilt. My arms joined in and then an imaginary drum beat surfaced. I started giggling and singing.

Bacon's a'coming, it's not far below. Eggs? Well they're a'grilling, maybe hash browns to go? Coffee, oh coffee! I'm having some of that and ...

I rounded a corner to see a day hiker stationary in the middle of the trail looking at me strangely. You can always differentiate a day hiker from a thru-hiker because they look spotless and smell of shampoo. I pondered stopping but felt absolutely marvellous so pushed a little embarrassment of the trail and waltzed onward.

There's a day hiker on the trail. I'm in the groove, do you think he'll move? Maybe so, maybe so ...

"Bloody fantastic morning!" I yelled as I danced past taking full advantage of a banked corner and arresting a tad of over steer I careered past to take him on the outside. Open-mouthed with a deadpan expression, he raised his right hand slightly in recognition as his eyes followed me and then I was gone.

I bottomed out at Indian Grave Gap still laughing and sweating, although not, I hasten to add, still dancing or singing.

"Fozzie!"

I turned to my right to see PJ walking very quickly towards me.

"PJ!"

"Fozzie, it's so good to see you!"

He didn't seem in any rush to arrest his momentum, crashed into me, put his arms around my waist and there he stayed.

"It's so good to see you!" he repeated.

I'm not particularly forward with giving out love until I get to know someone so PJ's forwardness caught me off guard. I casually peered around me; no one was taking much notice except for two rather attractive women over by the fire pit.

This looks like we're lovers. Fozzie, I think you may have blown your chances with those two.

I would consider around two seconds more than ample for a man hug; anything longer makes me suspicious, and nervous.

PJ's hug tolerance was obviously far more liberal and there he stayed like a frightened bear cub stranded halfway up a tree. He eventually relinquished his grip after what seemed like an eternity.

"PJ, I only saw you the day before yesterday!"

"I know, but I missed you and everyone else. I lost all of you. Where are they?"

"I dunno mate. I think Phillip and Sam, sorry Daffy, aren't far behind. Sam's trail name is Daffy now by the way." I became distracted by people eating. "I'll explain later, I need bacon. And coffee, where's the bloody coffee?"

I wandered off with a vacant expression that only caffeine withdrawal could impart, homed in on the aroma of coffee and found Moo. Moo was running the show with a couple of helpers. The deal was eat and drink whatever you fancied and in return maybe wash some dishes, wipe a table, take some logs to the fire, anything to share the karma.

"Moo, hi. I'm Fozzie."

"Hi! What can I get ya?"

She seemed busy cooking but relaxed with it.

"Er, I don't s'pose there's any chance of some bacon and eggs, please?" I offered.

"Sure, hell yeah! You want some home fries with that?"

"That would be fantastic!"

Moo was an angel in the woods and thirty minutes later she handed me a plate dangerously overloaded with one of the best trail breakfasts ever. I had only been hiking for six days but my appetite was borderline dangerous. I went back for more and then spied the beer keg. Ever aware that my destination, Deep Gap Shelter, was still three miles up a 1317-foot climb, that I hadn't had a beer for about eight days, was probably a little dehydrated and tired, I figured I should take it easy and drink one or possibly two.

Daffy found me about two hours later lying down in the middle of a track which I had no recollection of going to.

"Fozzie? Fozzie! You OK?"

I heard him but couldn't move; despite the gravel it felt comfortable. I only drank five beers and being English, champion of beer drinkers, needed to sleep it off. I raised one arm weakly skyward in recognition of his concern and waved him on with a thumbs up. I just about managed a weak "I'll see you at the shelter."

Half an hour later I managed to get up, said a heartfelt thank you to Moo with a kiss on the cheek and stumbled my way up towards Deep Gap. A few cheers greeted my arrival and familiar faces were scattered in and around the shelter: Phillip, Daffy, Josh Long Hair, PJ, Bridget and some other new faces.

I sat resting against an oak tree and chatted to Phillip. He had the perfect build for a thru-hiker — a decent height and slim, some would say lanky. It was his first thru-hike but he had done his research, at least in terms of his gear which was super-light. His pack was so small that it if you faced him head on, you couldn't actually see any of it. Daffy and I joked about his pursuit of the ultra-light (even though Daffy and I were just as guilty), and teased him, suggesting he removed every alternate page in his data book, memorised it and threw it away to save more weight — the only repercussion being that every alternate day his chances of getting lost increased.

He was hiking with and had planned the trip with Sam although each had agreed they were free to do their own thing, such as walk alone or with others if they felt the need. Mild-mannered, he seemed a little quiet when we first met but even over the course of a day had opened up. I got the impression he needed a little time to get to know others, albeit just an afternoon. His southern accent hailed from Raleigh, North Carolina and after getting to know him, he too, along with Bridget, struck me as the sort of person who would make a successful thru-hiker.

Daffy offset him a little by being more of an extrovert. He, too, was 22 and had a fiery sparkle of adventure in his eyes, tinged with a little mischief. His hair sometimes flopped over his eyes so when he tired of squinting he'd flick his head to see properly. He had a propensity to sound like an unoiled door opening when he passed wind and his favourite sentences were "Yeah, I hear yer" and "Yeah, no, oh I dunno."

Talk turned to getting to town the following morning for a re-supply and the luxury of a shower and bed. Hiawassee lay eleven miles down US-76 which the AT intersected at Dicks Creek Gap. It was the first major stop since the start and hence others were also planning to get a ride, which meant hitching could be difficult. Josh Long Hair, Daffy, Phillip and I agreed to get an early start to beat the crowds.

"We could always call the cops," Daffy suggested.

"And?" I prodded.

"Just tell them something that will make them drive up so we can get a ride with them."

"Oh, I get it," I added. "Like telling them that all cops are corrupt and they can kiss my arse? By the way there's a gun fight at Dicks Creek Gap."

He laughed. "Dang, yeah, that'll do it!"

Josh Long Hair had suggested on several occasions that he needed a trail name but rejected our proposal of Tom Petty based purely on his similar looks to the rock star. He had voiced a preference for something connected to his profession (he was a writer and journalist) and a hiker called Rollin' had suggested *Byline,* which he duly accepted. This just left Josh Short Hair, amongst others.

"Oh, we got that," Bridget chipped in. "Josh Short Hair is now Chatterbox."

Josh Short Hair wasn't exactly renowned for being the conversationalist. Despite this I thought that he may find Chatterbox offensive.

I cringed. "You can't call him that!"

"Well we did and he's accepted it! He likes it!"

We managed an early getaway the following morning but despite this there were about twelve hikers at Dicks Creek Gap trying to look presentable for the passing motorists, which after a week in the woods was no mean feat. I wasn't in a hurry so sat on the grass enjoying the spring sunshine and smoking a cigarette. Slowly the numbers depleted until just PJ, Phillip, Byline and I were left. I decided to do a shift with my thumb raised and a police car promptly pulled in the layby.

Great, I stick my thumb out and the first car is a cop.

It is illegal to hitch in some areas of America. Because it varied from state to state I never bothered checking and, on the few occasions I had been questioned, I just put on a heavy English accent and played the dumb tourist. I prepared myself for a brush with the authorities but was pleasantly surprised.

"Howdy! You guys need a ride?" said Georgia's finest as he squeezed himself out of the patrol car.

I looked at the others, raised my eyebrows and offered upturned palms with a cheeky grin, revelling in my own success.

"We're heading to Hiawassee if you're going that way?"

"Sure am, I'll be five minutes, just need to check on something."

He walked a little down the road to check on a road sign and returned, requesting we all jump in. We got a guided tour of the local sights on route and thanked him profusely as he dropped us off at The Budget Motel, regarded by thru-hikers as the place to stay.

I did look forward to town stops but they usually ended up as rushed and sometimes stressful affairs, mainly because there was so much to be done. By the time a day was over I was glad to get back in the woods to chill out.

The process went along the lines of firstly, obviously, get a coffee. Then find a motel, preferably with another hiker or two to share the bill. Walk for ages to the launderette and back, take a shower, eat as much breakfast as stomach will allow and walk for ages to the supermarket to re-supply. Eat snacks, discard all food packaging and decant contents to zip lock bags, eat as much lunch as stomach will allow and walk for ages to find an Internet café. Check emails and update blog, eat more snacks, take power nap, eat snacks and find out who had the beer and where they had hidden it. Take an hour to chat to roommates, go to dinner and eat as much as stomach will allow, return to motel to eat ice cream, watch some TV, eat more snacks and then go to bed.

Calorie intake is the priority. It is rarely possible on a thru-hiker diet to replace the amount of energy expended. Trail food is limited to what is the lightest to carry, with some exceptions. Some sources state that thru-hikers eat 6,000 calories day (the recommended daily intake for a male is 2,500 and a woman 2,000). Although I have never calculated my intake, I would guess it is nearer to 3,000 simply because I never actually get that hungry whilst hiking.

However, by the time I hit town, I am starving and my body demands prompt gratification. During a day in civilisation I can quite happily eat up to 8,000 calories; I am constantly hungry and fat is the fuel of choice. Meat, eggs, ice cream, crisps, milk, cheese and oils are not the healthiest of foods but I have learned to listen to what my body wants on a hike, and bad fat is its preference.

My trail diet, on the other hand, is pretty healthy whereas most hikers suffer. I always try to leave town with an avocado, perhaps a pepper and a couple of bananas. My main evening meal is usually a dried rice dinner in various flavours. Snacks, which form the main calorific intake, consist of nuts, dried fruit, oat type crunchy bars and some granola for breakfast, possibly with some dried milk and a little sugar. Protein powder packs some good muscle repair and my drink of choice, apart from coffee, is some Earl Grey tea. I am English after all.

Having finally ticked off the chore list, the Budget Motel shrank as I sped away in the back of Andy's pickup truck the following afternoon. He had seen my outstretched thumb and pulled over. Phillip, Daffy and PJ had left in the morning but I had some errands to run around town. We had agreed a rendezvous at Plum Orchard Shelter for that evening.

Few leave for the trail in the afternoon so I had it all to myself for the four miles up a gentle 500-foot incline to the shelter. It was blissfully quiet. The hum of the traffic faded away and, enjoying my surroundings and the solitude, I took my time.

Tunnels of rhododendron bushes funnelled me through, sunlight catching the sheen of their leaves as rocks appeared randomly speckled with sage coloured lichen; they seemed out of place amongst a thousand shades of brown. It was strange being in the woods wearing light clothing as they still appeared to be in winter. The weather was still glorious and, although the sky was only just visible, again it shone blue. Birds chirped, perhaps my favourite sound of a new season, and I felt at home — not as in feeling close to England, but feeling as though the woods were where I belonged.

I do experience a deep-rooted sense of comfort when I walk through woodland, almost as though it is protecting me, and on the AT I was being well and truly spoilt. It is sometimes referred to as 'the long green tunnel'. It can be too much for some, months spent hemmed in on all sides by trees with little sunlight and no views but I revelled in it. I ran my hands along the bark as I passed; sometimes I stopped and placed my chin on the trunk to look skyward. Roots crossed the trail, worn in sections from millions of pairs of boots and all the while a sweet-smelling mustiness surrounded me.

In places young growth was splashing the ground with vibrant greens: grass, some young leaves and an occasional evergreen. Cooler air currents climbed up the Appalachians from the west giving me goose bumps and then vanished as I returned to the warmth.

Arriving at Plum Orchard, I opted to sleep in the shelter for two reasons. Firstly there was only PJ, Phillip and Daffy, along with section hikers George and Laura so it wasn't crowded and provided a good chance to experience one for the first time. Secondly, there was a note in the shelter logbook advising hikers to be aware of a Copperhead nest in the vicinity. The Copperhead is one of three venomous snakes found on the AT, the other two being various species of Rattlesnake and the Cottonmouth.

This was all the prompting I needed; I stayed near the shelter and kept a close eye on the ground in front of me when I went for a pee. Fortunately nothing slithered that night and I enjoyed a good night's sleep in my first shelter.

Another storm had been forecast the following day and I was due to spend my second night undercover at Standing Indian Shelter. I was still sleeping in my tent but if the weather was due to turn, and there was room, it made sense to sleep in a shelter. Good progress was confirmed as Daffy, Phillip and I posed for a photo at the state line between Georgia and North Carolina. We were already into our second state.

Phillip had gone ahead and I was enjoying some conversation with Daffy when we spotted a discarded bagel on the ground. We invented an imaginary scenario whereby they were in fact rare, wild animals.

We joked that these elusive creatures were naturally shy but renowned for being fiercely territorial and would attack if threatened or cornered. Daffy stopped dead in his tracks with his finger against his mouth as a signal for silence. We observed it for a good five minutes on the grass as it enjoyed a little warmth from the sun.

"I think it's the Plain White Bagel," he eventually whispered.

"How do you know?"

"Note the markings, or rather lack of them. It's the prominent breed in Georgia but there's also the Brown Bagel, no explanation needed, the Seeded Bagel with spots on its upper coat or the Spinach Bagel."

"Spinach?"

"Yeah, it's got a green tint."

Wild bagels were rarely seen but were, apparently, great eating: tasty raw, even better toasted over a camp fire and they had a natural affinity to spreads, particularly peanut butter, jam, or cottage cheese.

Sam, having hunted the Plain before, bent his knees slightly into a crouch and silently approached his prey. He somehow managed to get a mere forty feet before unleashing his trekking pole. I watched it soar in a perfect arc, like a flawless javelin throw, striking the ground directly in the Bagel's hole.

"Great Shot!" I cried.

Helpless and unable to escape, the Bagel was dispatched with a single thrust of Daffy's knife. He told me that anywhere in the main ring of the body will pierce the brain for a swift and humane kill. No gutting or skinning was necessary; every part of a Wild Bagel was edible and, hunger getting the better of us, we built a fire and toasted it right there and then with some peanut butter. I have to say it was delicious.

Standing Indian Shelter heralded my second night under a roof in a row but, again, there was good reason. The forecast storm was a sure sign that the shelter would fill quickly so in the company of PJ, Daffy and Phillip we arrived at 3 p.m. The middle of the afternoon was a little frustrating for me because it was simply too early to stop. I then had around six hours to kill before hiker midnight, as it was called, otherwise known as sleep.

I looked forward to a couple more weeks when my body would be in good shape, particularly my feet, and I would be capable of pushing out twenty or twenty-five mile days, even more. These normally meant a finish of around 6 p.m. which left an ideal space of three hours to set up camp, cook diner and update my journal. For the time being I was sticking to my no blister regime which still seemed to be working well.

An older lady called Susan had already staked a claim to one corner of the shelter, Bill showed up citing a case of flu for his recent absence, and with Eastwood as well the shelter was up to its capacity of eight hikers. Ninja and Shakespeare arrived and shared the fire with us before announcing around 8 p.m. that they were going to push on to Carter Gap shelter, some seven miles further on. Despite our best efforts at trying to convince them otherwise — due to the imminent storm, the fading light and the fact that the shelter would probably be full as well — they enjoyed the fire for a little longer but took off about 9 p.m.

Hiker midnight is whenever the sun goes down and, generally being a courteous bunch of people, thru-hikers would tend to get in their sleeping bags so others could get some sleep. Some may read by torchlight and perhaps some may stay by the fire, talking quietly.

I sat in the undercover lean-to area because I could sense the rain was imminent and wanted to experience my second, legendary, Appalachian storm. The wind had intensified, there was a damp smell to the air and, well, just that sense you get that it's going to rain. All hell broke loose about 9.30 when the skies erupted in a torrential downpour and the noise, oh my god, the *noise!*

I stood and surveyed the carnage from my haven, in awe of the deafening roar as rain tore through the trees and smashed into the ground. I would have been unable to hold a conversation with someone right next to me. Despite a fading light the wall of water obscured everything, and the trees disappeared in a silver deluge as the fire remnants hissed and spat in one last, brave effort. The wind slammed into the shelter. I looked back to see head torches flicker on and the rest of the group sat upright to experience the anger. The tin roof shuddered and cried a metallic shriek as it fought back against the elements. We all became concerned about Shakespeare and Ninja but there was nothing we could do. Eventually the cacophony subsided and we all got some sleep.

***

The 100-mile mark was heralded by a few whoops the following day as Daffy, Phillip and I made short work of the 1000-foot descent before pulling into Carter Gap shelter for a rest. It was the middle of the morning so we were a little surprised to see two hikers still wrapped in their sleeping bags. One of the lumps stirred and Shakespeare's familiar features appeared from the depths looking a little the worse for wear.

"Did you get caught in the storm?" I asked.

"We got about a mile from here when it started. We were soaked." He said, rubbing his eyes to get accustomed to the light. Ninja woke up and confirmed this, adding that they also got cold and were sleeping late because they didn't get any rest when they reached the shelter — partly due to the noise of the storm, but mainly because the shelter was full and they had to squeeze onto an uncomfortable dirt floor. They looked pretty miserable as we left them to catch up on some sleep.

Becoming increasingly frustrated with fifteen-mile days and finishing in the middle of the afternoon, I was eager to stretch my hiking muscles a little. Convincing Daffy and Phillip to also follow suit, we covered the twenty miles to Rock Gap Shelter which was located four miles from the US-64 road crossing. There we planned to get a ride to Franklin, some ten miles east for a decent meal and quick re-supply the following day.

It was April 6th, the day before Easter and as we unwound at Rock Gap a steady dribble of familiar hiker faces rolled in. Shakespeare and Ninja arrived, now dried out and joking about their damp adventure. A straw cowboy hat bobbing down the track signalled Eastwood's entrance and before long, the ambience of the shelter was transformed by laughing, conversation, steam rising from meals being cooked and also the arrival of the Easter trail angel. The local Ranger had taken it upon herself to boil enough eggs to feed an army, decorate them with bright paint, carefully place them on a cotton towel in a wicker basket and come up all the way from Franklin to feed us, as well as walking the four-odd miles from the road. She was greeted with obvious good cheer at the unexpected protein treat and chatter subsided as we stuffed eggs into our mouths with vigour and made repeated enquiries about second helpings. The net effect of our unexpected feast was that the shelter and immediate surroundings resonated rudely for a couple of hours to the tune of hikers passing wind. I was glad I was in my tent.

Phillip, Daffy, PJ and I were eager to get to Franklin quickly — not, as you might think, because of the lure of good food, coffee or perhaps even to see a little of the town, but because we needed to get back out the same day. The reason was our first *bald* (a high point clear of trees, affording great views) called Siler Bald, where we had decided to camp.

Catching a ride quickly but only to a junction outside of the town, we opted to walk the remaining two miles and pulled into the first, and most important, port of call, the Motor Co. Grill. Goose bumps had us reaching for warmer tops as we entered the air-conditioned chill and we cordoned off a large circular table in one corner. I offered an apology to the waitress for our slightly less-than-savoury aroma after a few days on trail with no shower. Most eating establishments along the AT are used to hikers and the waft of sweat, filth and general unpleasantness that follows them but she took it in her stride.

Having eaten, I left with PJ to search for an Internet facility, our stomachs groaning, and quickly realised we had both been caught off guard. After only eleven days and 114 miles, already we were becoming detached from society. Everywhere seemed alien; our wooded sanctuary was now concrete. The path was hard with traffic to our sides, not soft and shaded. This is common on trail. Experiencing the outdoors for even that amount of time, let alone several months, changes your perception of society and towns suddenly become unfamiliar.

I quickly became uptight — there was only one Internet café which was closed, people got in my way and the noise and general mayhem annoyed me. I retreated to Ingles, the supermarket, re-supplied as quickly as I could and got the hell out. It made me even more aware of my difficulties living in society and after enjoying the solitude of the woods, my problems seemed magnified.

Siler Bald, almost sensing my mood, did its best to calm me. We made short work of the 1000-foot climb from where our ride back dropped us and ignored the sign to Siler Bald shelter. The woods thinned; we stepped out into a clearing and made a short final climb through grass to the summit. We had high expectations of our first bald and Siler didn't disappoint.

The grassy dome peeked out from the woodland below us. Alone and isolated, this was our hotel for the night. An emerald desert island lost in a vast ocean of trees.

I had heard that the Appalachian balds, more common on the southern part of the trail, were originally cleared by the Cherokee or early settlers, but subsequent research makes this theory unlikely. It is argued that man may have been responsible for some, and it is accepted that isolated trees on the summits were cleared and further felling around the tree-line provided materials for fencing and pens where livestock were grazed, but the actual reason for their presence still remains a mystery. Cattle or sheep herds would be driven to the summits between early April and May, depending on the weather. In extreme years snow could still fall during this period and some herds would move back down to the relative safety of the woods and lower, warmer elevations. Even so, some animals, hot from the journey up, died from the sudden, cold exposure. Bone Valley creek, a branch of Hazel creek which drains off Siler itself, is so named after the bones of cattle that died there in the spring of 1902.

We loved the open air and wide space on Siler. We pitched our tents, played a little Frisbee and made friends with a family who were camping there for the night. We enjoyed a second hearty meal of the day as they were kind enough to share some of their food with us.

360-degree views of the land surrounded us. Gentle, round, tree cloaked hilltops stretched away to the horizon in every direction. A two-toned land of green down below ascended to the browns of the higher ground, still waiting for spring to creep up.

As dusk fell we stood and watched the sun sink and an orange sky gradually succumbed to darkness. From our perch and with no obstructions we gazed at a star-splattered canvas above us coming to life. I felt miniscule, humbled to accept my small seat in an infinite theatre. The universe was putting on the show and I was merely content to just sit, be silent and study the extravaganza.

Up above and all around me the play unfolded and the storyline began, changing by the minute. Clouds drifted past in no hurry, lighting varied, shadows stretched and, gradually, North Carolina turned silver as a rising moon chased away the remnants of reds. Subtle breezes stroked my face and the trees rustled. I stayed awake as long as I could muster the energy but eventually closed my eyes, sighed and drifted off, only to wake several times during the night to experience it all again.

Several encores didn't disappoint and although I now had a small idea of what the AT was capable of, that night was a mere prelude to the ensuing months. A canapé if you will to the feast, the prelude to the main show that had yet to unfold.

***

The Nantahala Outdoor Center, or NOC, situated on the Nantahala River itself, is a mecca for outdoor enthusiasts. It attracts hikers, bikers and those keen to learn rafting, canoeing as well as other diverse subjects such as wilderness medicine. It is a draw to AT hikers. The trail itself goes straight through the centre and what with the promise of some cheap accommodation, a decent restaurant and other amenities, it is on everyone's to do list. Dinosaur had also been kind enough to mail a package there for me to collect containing what she promised was a load of goodies.

I continued to walk with Phillip, Daffy and PJ as our pace was similar; we had also gelled well and were relaxed and loose with planning. That said, we often spent most of the day on our own, albeit a short distance apart as we settled into our own pace and rhythms. Meeting up at the end of the day we would usually camp together, discuss the day's events and make arrangements as to where the next day's destination would be. It was the perfect arrangement and just how I liked hiking: a little solitude during the day and the pleasure of some great company in the evenings.

The temperature had cooled somewhat, which wasn't unusual. It was that unpredictable no man's land between the end of winter and the beginning of spring. Couple that with the AT's changeable elevation and unsettled mountain weather, and we were constantly either adding warmer clothing or peeling off a layer. The Great Smoky Mountains — perhaps one of the best-known sections of the trail and home to Clingman's Dome which at 6643 feet was the highest point on the entire AT — was around eighty miles ahead and famed for its changing weather patterns, especially at that time of year. Once through the Smokies we hoped winter would well and truly have given up.

Spring was not the only thing blossoming; it had transpired that there was a little romance doing the same. PJ, having become used to a little affection during his brief marriage, was now suffering from a lack of it and it appeared to be hitting him hard. His testosterone levels were running riot and cracks in his celibacy, albeit not voluntary, were surfacing in frustration with a lack of female tenderness. Struggling to deal with his rampant hormones he confided in me as we approached the NOC.

PJ had started to leave notes announcing his undying affection for a hiker known as Firefox in the trail registers. These were books left in the shelters, and other places where hikers left notes on anything they felt like writing. They also made great communication tools and messages often reliably worked their way back to the intended recipient.

I never did read any of PJ's remarks and he was a little shy about revealing his comments. Despite them being public and the ease of reading his notes, he often only revealed he had left Firefox a message the day after so his declarations of love were all behind us.

Conversely, remarks and rumours also found their way back up the trail and when it transpired that Firefox had no intention of catching PJ, or indeed pursuing any romantic liaisons, he spent a day in a slight love depression but quickly moved on.

I had never thought to ask how Firefox had earned her trail name, and subsequently never did. I assumed it was connected to the Web browser and her ginger hair. After all, Google Chrome, Safari or Internet Explorer didn't have quite the same ring about it.

Trail romance isn't unusual and, indeed, some hikers who meet on the trail go on to get married and start families. If you're single, however, being out in the woods for months on end naturally can become a little frustrating. My sex drive could never be described as exactly raging. Sexual abstinence was not something that really bothered me so I just dealt with it. In fact, I did my best to steer clear of romantic liaisons, or a little fun, because of the complications that could arise in the aftermath of such encounters.

A little harmless trail fun between two consenting individuals quite often turns sour post encounter when one subsequently demands more than the other is prepared to give. Intimate misunderstandings, as in real life, create confusion whereby one individual is under the impression that a quick foray into the bushes, or testing the overnight condensation capabilities of their tent interiors, is mistaken by the other as the beginning of a relationship.

Arguments quite often ensue and accusations of being used, betrayals of trust or worse are levied. The situation rapidly turns sour and one of the party may storm off, suddenly increasing their mileage and speed to escape the situation.

For many the appeal of trail sex is tempered by the thought of what happens to the body after a few weeks on trail. The most off-putting aspect is bodily deterioration. Many male hikers complain that the sweet-smelling females they encountered at the start were now sporting hairy legs and armpits. On the flip side of the coin, the ladies struggled with guys who looked well-groomed and clean-shaven on Springer Mountain, but now had lips that had vanished from sight behind an unkempt beard harbouring various food debris. Bodily odour from both sexes and soiled clothing didn't exactly grease the wheels of romance either.

***

We camped at Cold Spring Shelter, leaving a brief twelve miles to the NOC the following morning. This became common practice the day before a zero or a *nero* (a nero is a day where little hiking is done), because it meant we could get into town early. Arrive in the evening and most motels state you have to vacate before 11 a.m., leaving little time to run the errands demanded. Arrive in the middle of the day however, and full use of the room could be utilised for most of the day.

Phillip disappeared behind some bushes and busied himself with erecting his tent, sounding somewhat like a burrowing creature as he cleared away the leaves. Daffy was sitting down scraping the dirt out of his toenails and PJ was trying to decide whether to sleep in the shelter or pitch his tent.

Phillip's tent wasn't in fact a tent at all — it was a poncho that could be erected by means of a trekking pole into something resembling a tent. True to his lightweight philosophy, this piece of gear not only doubled as rain wear and shelter meaning he saved weight by not carrying both, but it weighed around the same as a pair of socks.

The only problem was that one side was open to the elements so critters and mosquitos had free access, not so much a problem during the early stages of the hike as our blood-sucking friends didn't really wake up until the weather warmed. What it did mean was the rain could work its way in if Phillip gauged the wind direction incorrectly, or if it changed. We had been lucky with the rain so far but I remember talking to him at our previous camp at Lance Creek when a little rain had started to fall in prelude to the storm. Phillip had to gradually wiggle his way to the back of his shelter as the rain made inroads under the tarp until he was wedged somewhere in the depths at the rear, desperately trying to keep dry. Not surprisingly the conversation had centred on a new shelter, possibly a hammock so he could look forward to a decent night's rest.

***

The trail plummeted sharply from Cold Spring shelter and, despite a little 1000 foot ascent from Tellico Gap up to Wesser Bald, it was a knee-jarring 4200 feet drop all the way down to the NOC. With a mile to go we passed the A. Rufus Morgan shelter and spilled out onto the US-19 just in time for lunch at The River's End Restaurant.

Steep descents on the approach to towns were common on the AT, and indeed other trails. Because of the inhospitable climate in the mountains, the lower elevations were deemed more friendly and, especially during the early settler migration stretching west in the States, most towns sprang up around these locations, often known in America as 'gaps'. More often than not they were in the proximity of rivers to supply water. Roads and train lines could be constructed taking advantage of the kinder terrain.

Phillip, Daffy, PJ and I managed to rent one of the cabins for a night. The rate was very reasonable and, as usual, split between the four of us it proved even cheaper. I sat on my bed eagerly ripping open Dinosaur's care package which, being a thru-hiker herself, contained a well thought-out array of goodies such as sachets of electrolyte drink mixes, necessary to replace the salts and minerals lost during sweating, some sweet treats and a very welcome addition of some Earl Grey, luring me into making a quick brew.

We only managed a few chores in the afternoon so agreed a zero in the morning made sense. I watched a brown swirl of water disappear down the sink and shower as I washed both my clothes and myself. I updated my journal and secured a few supplies from the sparsely-stocked store to see me through to Fontana and the guys occupied themselves with similar tasks.

An alarming number of tourists disembarked from the morning train and suddenly the NOC was brimming with camera-laden, sunburnt day trippers who — from their appearance at least — had no intention of even getting in a boat, let alone learn the relative merits of healing with wild plants. I did what I could to scare them off by picking my nose, coughing loudly and plucking imaginary fleas from my beard to eat.

There was no computer to use at the NOC so I spent some time wandering around aimlessly waving my phone about trying to locate a decent Wi-Fi signal. I managed to order a power pack which would allow me to recharge my phone on trail, a poncho and a Sawyer water filter. The poncho also doubled as a groundsheet for my tent, saving me some weight as I could also send my rain jacket back home.

Phillip and Daffy set off at 6.15 a.m. but after giving into temptation for a decent breakfast I started making inroads into the 3000 foot climb to Cheoah Bald which seemed surprisingly easy.

Having gained a respectable altitude on the climb up to Cheoah Bald, as usual the AT rewarded me by promptly losing it all on a 2000 foot descent to Stecoah Gap. It was like being handed a bag of sweets which was then promptly snatched back again before you could take one. This was to become standard practice on the AT, and the constant dipping and diving caused frustration for some.

There were a few hikers enjoying some simple, but welcome, trail magic at Stecoah Gap where a cooler had been left stocked with cold drinks. As I sat down with a Coke, a truck pulled up with Eastwood yelping for joy in the back as he emerged clutching a triple cheeseburger and onion rings from a diner a few miles down the road.

Eastwood made me laugh. Even his name made me think of cowboys and what with a deep southern drawl and his cowboy hat, the image was almost complete. All that was missing was a couple of gun holsters and a horse, and every time I saw him I half expected a procession of wagons and early settlers to arrive behind. I never saw him down or unhappy; he always seemed to be smiling, cracking a joke or two and lifting the spirits of those he was in the company of. He was also tremendously thoughtful, especially with food. If eating, or preparing food, I lost count of the times he offered me a share and this was no exception as he wandered over stuffing his burger on one corner of his mouth and his outstretched arm clutching his onion rings in the other offering me a couple.

"Got a quick ride, Fozzie," he said, waving his burger in circles and struggling to speak as his triple cheeseburger took up most of the room in his mouth. "Great diner just down the way there, couldn't resist a burger. Here, have an onion ring," he offered as we hiked up to Brown Fork Gap Shelter.

Fontana Dam and the small store lay a few miles ahead and marked the start of the stretch which went up into the Smoky Mountains. I was relishing the prospect. One of the highest sections of the AT and famed for its scenery, abundance of shelters and fantastic reputation, I had heard much about it during my research.

Despite the chilly night at Brown Fork Gap Shelter, spring was slowly making inroads and the weather had been great up to that point. I had not experienced the famous Appalachian rains I had been expecting, except for a couple of nights, so if anything I was looking forward to warmer climes. Perhaps I had become a little complacent towards the elements.

Little did any of us know that the weather, and Mother Nature, had other ideas in store.

Chapter 5
The Smokies

April 12th to April 23rd
Mile 153 to 309

Most Americans I meet on my travels admit, when they discover I am English, to being a little jealous of our European history and wished their country boasted a similar heritage. They mostly refer to our visual architecture in Great Britain and Europe, the old castles, cathedrals and other such examples — even further back to periods thousands of years ago have left us wonderful reminders such as Stonehenge.

However, I would have to disagree with them because America does have its own, enviable history. Visually perhaps we are more spoilt for choice but indigenous people lived in the US for thousands of years before the first European settlers arrived. They may not have left much evidence but they have made their mark in the history books. It wasn't until Christopher Columbus's arrival in 1492 and his subsequent trips that buildings started to materialise which still serve as a reminder now.

Columbus's claim to be the first European to land in the US is debatable. Research and theories now suggest the Vikings may well have been before him. Bjarni Herjólfsson, a Viking sailor blown off course on a voyage to Greenland around 985 could have been the first to sight America, although it is thought he didn't land but headed to Greenland when the winds allowed him to do so.

Herjólfsson described his trip to Lief Ericson who set off around the year 1000 to see for himself. He did land on American soil and is thought to be the first European, some 500 years before Columbus to do so. Spending the winter of that year as well as 1001 and 1002, he then returned to Greenland. Several more forays ensued until he attempted to establish the first settlement in 1009. Accompanied by around 200 men, women and livestock, initially amenable relations with the Native Americans broke down and they were driven back out of America.

In 1960 a site now known as L'Anse aux Meadows in the northern tip of Newfoundland was discovered. It has been suggested that this site may have been Ericson's first settlement. It shares similarities to Viking sites found in Greenland, Iceland and remains the only non-indigenous settlement in America. Of course there are more, we just haven't discovered them yet.

Despite North America having a lack of ancient architecture compared to the rest of the world, they are fiercely proud of what they do have. The AT does have a wonderful sense of history behind it and passes through many historical sites especially those associated with the Civil War of 1861 to 1865. Harpers Ferry, considered the half-way point of the trail is a classic example, having some poignant old buildings and reminders of the war.

The Smoky Mountains are home to some seventy-eight structures within the park, remnants of bygone Appalachian communities. Even out in the middle of the woods, miles from anywhere, I passed old stonework — perhaps a ruined building or wall that once served as a livestock enclosure. Many places have historical associations and their names have wonderful stories behind them, hinting at an even greater sense of mystery, interest and curiosity. Much has long since gone but these names serve as a lasting reminder that rouses the curiosity.

I have mentioned Slaughter Creek which is so named after a battle between the Cherokee and Creek Indians during the late 1600s. Near to Slaughter Creek is Blood Mountain which some say is named after a bloody battle between the same two Indian tribes; others say it is the red-coloured lichen growing near the summit that is responsible.

Recent history has also left its mark on place names. Charlie Connor who, along with his friend Horace Kephart, were out hiking when they rested on a rocky outcrop then known as Fodderstack. Connor, upon removing one of his boots discovered he had a bunion which shared similarities to the shape of the rock. Kephart declared he was going to get the place on a government map and subsequently did. It is now known as Charlie's Bunion.

Lost Spectacles Gap, approaching the 700-mile mark in Virginia, is named after Tom Campbell, a member of the Roanoke Appalachian Trail Club who misplaced his glasses there on a work hike.

The recent past also served as a reminder. I was following the writers that had trodden the path I was now taking: Earl Shaffer, David Brill and David AWOL Miller to name just a few. I wondered if, in a hundred, or maybe a thousand years' time that these inspirations would be remembered, preserved for eternity as a name associated to a part of the trail.

These legends had all thru-hiked here and I had devoured their words in gusto as preparation for my hike, and years before when I had first heard of the AT.

All the mental pictures they had given me — their thoughts, observations and feelings that were up until then, just images — were now unfolding. Now I was sharing their experiences, thinking the same thoughts, seeing what they had observed and feeling what they had felt.

I knew now what Miller meant when he described how his calves became caked in dirt because his boots brushed against them. When Shaffer observed how the rain rolled in, how the mist was dense and muggy in the low spots but shifted and swirled further up, I now saw in front of me. The emotions that Brill had struggled with when saying farewell to his injured friend, Victor, who left the trail, I was also to share.

Even my friends who I had met on the Pacific Crest Trail two years earlier also inspired me. Dinosaur, Pockets, Grey Fox, Texas Walker Ranger, Swiss Miss and more had all shared their AT memories, offering me guidance and painting their own pictures.

As I passed certain points on the trail, I, too, was to feel what they had. Like the ruined homestead where Pockets had collected water from a well. He had expressed to me his unease with the place, almost a fear that although he was alone there; a bad presence lurked. I was also to feel it.

When Swiss Miss described the freezing rain, that intolerable point just before it turns to snow and soaks through your jacket to the very core, my body had also experienced.

Or the delight that Grey Fox had revelled in when he described how he had crested a hill in Maine and finally seen

Katahdin for the very first time.

How Dinosaur told me that I should take the time out to contribute to some trail maintenance, and imparting in detail the planning and physical strength it takes for two people just to move a boulder two feet I would soon be able to relate to.

I held onto moments like those, passed on by my friends and tales from many years ago. They pulled me onwards, the anticipation building the nearer I got, almost to the point that sometimes I screamed for them to arrive so I could finally see, or feel, what others had.

All the history, stories, legends and myths, all the way back to Lief Ericson and up to haunted homesteads were nestled in the back of my mind. The little nooks, crannies and crevices that filed those thoughts away, some place safe where one day I would unlock them were now, piece by piece, being opened.

And what of my memories? I viewed the trail in three perspectives: the past, present and future. The past was gone, from Springer Mountain to a point a fraction of a second behind me where I had taken my last step. The present I observed as I watched my foot fall on the precise part of the trail between those two roots that I had hoped it would. And the future was the next step, visible but unknown, all the way up to Mt Katahdin.

As I walked, my memories were being filed away. Some would be more vivid than others, some I would look back on with happiness, others with sadness. They would remain with me for the rest of my life for me to share with others. As Grey Fox had shared his vision of Katahdin, as Shaffer had observed that fog, I would also reminisce and pass on. I hoped that my passion, shared with others, would spur them to come and walk in these woods and up these mountains.

And what of my words? As you read them, what do you picture? I hope you take them, tuck them away and at some point in your future you place your foot in that same spot between those roots on your journey to Katahdin.

***

I hovered along the trail from Brown Fork Gap Shelter at about 3800 feet, the trail swapping constantly from the chilly west side where the sun had yet to make any inroads and spots of ice mirrored the trail, over to the east where it was noticeably warmer as sunlight found a way through the trees. It had been a

cold night and I had slept wearing most of my clothing. My down bag wasn't performing and it wasn't until closer inspection revealed that most of the down had migrated to the bottom of the bag that I spent a good hour, on Daffy's advice, impatiently trying to ease the insulation back to the top. The fact I had run out of coffee hadn't helped until Eastwood jump-started me by brewing and handing me a mug of his.

I topped up with water at Cody Gap, sped up the 800 feet from Cable Gap shelter and let gravity ease me down the 2000 foot descent to bring me out on the NC28 road crossing. My data book advised that this was the place to get the required permit for the Smoky Mountains ahead which I duly did and just over a mile later I pulled into the Fontana Dam shelter, affectionately known to hikers as the Fontana Hilton.

With an impressive capacity of twenty, plus nearby toilets and a shower, the Hilton earned its reputation from the relative luxury and amenities it afforded to us hikers. It was, however, brimming — and unable to decide whether to stay there or not with the crowds, I spent another hour continuing to fluff up my sleeping bag before hunger got the better of me. I caught a ride to the Fontana general store a couple of miles up the road to stock up with food for the Smoky Mountains. The Pit Stop restaurant dished me up a generous portion of nachos before I managed to get another ride back to the Hilton.

Even more hikers had arrived, and beating a hasty retreat, I took a quick shower before bumping into Phillip who shared similar concerns about the full shelter. He had performed a quick scout of the area and found a small island just opposite the dam which he showed me. It looked perfect for a little stealth camping, as we called it, so suffering from slightly wet shoes crossing the few feet over, we settled down to sleep.

The Smoky Mountains, or Smokies as they are known, are one of the most renowned and revered sections of the AT. So named after the natural fog that hangs over the range which commands views of the Tennessee and North Carolina border, they are also home to the highest point of the entire trail, Clingmans Dome at 6643 feet. Designated a UNESCO World Heritage Site, they are home to 187,000 acres of old growth forest and, somewhat worryingly, the densest black bear population in eastern America. I had been told by several hikers that my chances of seeing a bear were far greater in the Smokies than any other part of the trail.

I left with this firmly on my mind, unable to decide whether it was a positive statistic or not. Eager to get up there and experience it all, I made a good start at 7 a.m., albeit an hour after Phillip who was becoming fond of his early departures.

The trail joined the road over Fontana Dam itself which sits at an elevation of 1864 feet and shortly after, I began to climb into the Smokies. Despite the usual up and downs of the trail in between, the climb carries on pretty much all uphill to Clingmans Dome which means an AT hiker has a 4779 feet ascent stretching out over thirty-three miles. This is the literal difference between the two points, when the dips and dives are taken into account; you can easily throw in a few more thousand feet. Further progress was confirmed as I crossed over into my third State, Tennessee from North Carolina at mile 174.

Despite gaining height and cooling, the Smokies were alive with the new season. Flowers splashed colour everywhere. Sarvis trees had blossomed and were cloaked in tiny, white flowers. When I saw my first one I mistook it for a layering of snow. The ever reliable rhododendron bushes were yet to flower but their buds appeared to be at bursting point, poised to unleash their purple, white or pink blooms in a few weeks' time. Laurel bushes were also eager to please, the buds firm to the touch and seemingly about to explode.

I reached a small break in the trees and peered back at the Fontana Reservoir, already a tiny speck lost in the green furrows and folds of its surroundings. Although this stretch of trail was still covered in trees, they appeared less dense, almost thinned out. Regular gaps appeared offering far reaching views. Seemingly the AT was compensating me for the thick forest I had experienced up to that point.

I was feeling at ease with my world and starting to become accustomed to the AT, its whims, moods and habits. The trail rarely routed around a mountain, or cut along the side, but took a far more direct approach usually straight up and over. A flat, three-mile section would take most hikers an hour to complete. Straining up and down the various peaks often meant it took two hours to do that distance. My natural hiking speed is between three and three and a half miles an hour, but after a few days on the AT it was hovering around two to two and a half. I had been warned not to get complacent by other hikers who had already completed the trail. They advised that just because I had a few thousand miles under my belt, and the PCT, not to consider this trail as easy bagging. I was beginning to understand what they meant.

Statistics for the total amount of elevation gained on the AT are not definitive and vary from source to source but it is considered to be around 464,500 feet. To provide a comparison, Ben Nevis, the highest mountain in Great Britain, and no mean feat to summit, is 4409 feet which means you'd have to summit Nevis just over 105 times to achieve the same elevation gain. If you thought Everest a tough prospect, by the time an AT thru-hiker finished their mission they would have climbed Everest sixteen times. Some sources even claim that the altitude gain on the AT is greater than the Continental Divide Trail.

Many hikers, after the initial romance of the trail has subsided, become frustrated by the AT, especially the pointless ups and downs (known as *puds*). I often joked that when the AT was originally constructed, they chose the hardest route possible. In the vast majority of cases, the trail would always climb up and over an obstacle instead of skirting around it. It annoyed me sometimes, usually at the end of a long day with just a couple of miles to camp when I'd notice the elevation graph showing a 1000 foot climb. In the main it didn't bother me, I had done my research and knew, roughly, what to expect.

The AT is shorter than the PCT by around 462 miles. However, even after just a couple of weeks in arguably one of the less demanding sections, physically at least, I already considered the AT tougher.

***

"Do you snore?" enquired Bridget as she squeezed into the gap between PJ and I in Spence Field shelter. Heavy rain was expected so it was full.

"Sometimes, yes. But only when I sleep on my back. On the occasions I have slept with someone else …" She interrupted me with a mild glare.

"Sorry, *near* to someone else, then I make sure I sleep on my side."

When I accused her of snoring in the morning, an accusation she firmly denied, I felt rather smug when both PJ and Beacon backed me up.

Phillip had run out of food so was making the best of a tortilla with no filling for breakfast. I had food but had run out of alcohol for my stove. Dreading the thought of starting the day with no coffee, everyone had kindly chipped in with a few dribbles each after seeing my onset of mild panic. Eric informed me his trail name was now Bowser, and no one had seen Daffy for a few days although Phillip informed us that he was a few days behind walking with another group.

"Daffy likes to change those he socialises with sometimes," he explained.

Misjudging a re-supply and running out of food or fuel was common. The great thing about hiking the AT and the amount of hikers on trail meant that it never proved a problem and, in fact, was a wonderful lesson in camaraderie. If someone had run out of oats for breakfast, was short of a main meal, didn't have any sugar or was despondently shaking their gas canister with a concerned look, then someone would always offer to help. Without asking, we could always count on someone to offer an item from their supplies to make up the deficit. In true outdoor spirit, something was usually offered in return, but often declined because we knew that at some point, we would be in the same situation and the karma would return full circle.

***

After a sixteen-mile uphill slog I arrived at Clingmans Dome and sat with PJ, Phillip and Bowser. I didn't really know what to expect from the highest point on the trail except a decent view but I was sadly disappointed. As is common with our infatuation towards high places, some idiot had deemed it necessary to celebrate the location by cutting a swathe through the trees, laying down a road and building what I can honestly say was the ugliest structure I had ever witnessed — not just on a trail, but anywhere, period.

The tower on top of Clingmans Dome, built in 1959, was at the time probably a much-praised example of modern architecture. Unfortunately, as with most of these eyesores, it now resembled something like a concrete, spiral car ramp often found by the side of multi-storey car parks. Half a mile down the road, hordes of tourists on their annual vacation would park their cars, kit themselves out with their Walmart hiking accessories and plod, out of breath, up to this monstrosity to lay claim to standing on top of the highest point in Tennessee.

Kids wailed, adults complained that there wasn't a coke

machine or a McDonald's, others posed for photos whilst the rest of the area was littered with out of breath, dehydrated holidaymakers. Some even asked us to take photos of them so I quickly resorted to my habit of picking imaginary items of debris from my beard and eating them whilst Phillip and PJ removed their shoes and socks to act as a deterrent. We sat at the base of the tower resting and at one point a Japanese man walked cautiously over to me as if I were some sort of wild animal who had just emerged from the woods after a few weeks. Actually his observation bore some credit. He hesitantly handed me his camera.

"You take picture please?"

I finished wiping my nose on my left sock and took his Nikon, whilst he walked to the base of the tower. This I just found puzzling and hilarious, although with a little restraint I remained relatively polite. Instead of climbing up the spiral walkway to the top of the tower where the view was, he merely stood at the bottom and requested I include the tower in the shot.

"Why would you walk up here and not actually go to the top of the tower?" I asked Phillip. "And, why the hell would you want to include that hideous thing in the photo? What the fuck?"

Phillip, PJ and Bowser looked as puzzled as I was and just shrugged their shoulders.

We relaxed for an hour until early evening and the last of the mob had disappeared down to the car park. Phillip proposed that it would be a great idea to actually sleep at the top of the tower which didn't exactly excite anyone's wild camping instincts but as it was a pretty original idea, and something we could potentially get into trouble for, I was all for it. It was under cover after all.

Clingmans afforded a vast view from the top of the tower and we spent a good hour taking it all in. The wind started to whip up just before sunset and the temperature dropped alarmingly. We were high up and exposed so had expected a chilly night, although not as windy. A three feet high wall circled the observation platform which provided a wind break as we hunkered up next to it. I made a brief effort to move more down insulation to the top of my bag but became so cold that, eventually, life preservation instincts got the better of me and I retrieved every item of clothing out of my bag and pulled it on. I abandoned my sleeping bag revival once more but Phillip came up with the obvious, interim solution.

"Fozzie, turn it over!"

***

Newfound Gap, where the AT intersects US-41 is a renowned spot for trail magic. A large parking area provided ample space for vehicles coming up from Gatlinburg, a large town fifteen miles down the road, to park and set up welcome refuelling spots for hikers, as well as rides into town.

To add to my sleeping bag woes, my air mattress had sprung a leak. At 3.30 a.m. on Clingmans Dome, I was roused by a weak hissing sound somewhere near my right ear and shortly after, my comfortable perch was reduced to an airless strip of plastic. Not only that, the air chambers inside had deteriorated and I was forced to get a ride into Gatlinburg to buy a replacement as well as a food re-supply.

The AT lifts a hiker's expectations of their world. We become used to seeing magnificent views, towering mountains and serene surroundings. When we have to leave the trail for town, our hopes continue as we dream of old, quiet, historical settlements rich in history where we can re-supply and take it all in over a civilized meal.

As if I had written these wishes down, Gatlinburg glanced momentarily at them, smirked rudely and scrunched them into a tight ball. Tossing them onto the ground, and for good measure, it jumped up and down on them and then set them alight.

I didn't know what to expect of the place but as soon as I arrived, I made plans to run my errands as quick as possible and make for a quick escape. It was busy with holidaymakers and Gatlinburg was well set up to cater for them. Tacky shops lined the main street, selling everything from overpriced T-shirts to ice cream. Spotless cars and motorbikes cruised up and down just for show in between long periods of gridlock, whilst I became frustrated trying to weave a route along the crowded sidewalk. The supermarket was way out of town so I had to settle for the meagre supplies offered by Walgreens — which meant no fresh food, a limited display of boxed, undesirable stock such as Pop Tarts and an uninspiring selection of main meals. The only saving grace was the NOC store which was well-stocked and I managed to buy a respectable brand of sleeping mattress. The NOC shuttle even took us back to Newfound Gap where I quickly disembarked and ran for the cover and solitude of the woods.

I passed Bowser quickly and although he tried to stick with me, my momentum, need to escape civilization and a desire to get to Pecks Corner Shelter before sunset meant he gave up after twenty minutes. The fact that I covered the eleven miles to the shelter in less than three hours I put down to the psychological damage that Gatlinburg had inflicted on me. Pecks Corner shelter was busy and as usual I pitched my tent before chatting to Phillip and Fonsworth, who was taking his choice of a trail name very seriously. He explained his intention to think of an extended title which he hoped would result in a somewhat posh sounding air.

"You could put a Horatio in there," I suggested. "Nice ring to it."

"I like it, Fozzie."

"By the way, did you know, back in England, that you can buy a Lordship title?"

"You can?"

"Yeah. Don't quote me on it but I'm sure I read it somewhere. Pay whatever organisation is responsible a few bucks and you can legally start your name with Lord."

The ball was rolling and Fonsworth, subject to further elaborations, was now Lord Horatio Fonsworth.

My main source of food for the next few days consisted of oats, which had been the only edible option available at Walgreens. As I forced down the apricot variety over breakfast, in between re-packing, I opened my pack to see a mouse curled up at the top. He yawned, appeared even to rub his eyes and nonchalantly climbed out to disappear under the shelter.

The trail bobbled along around 5500 feet for a few miles and I pulled into Tri-Corner Knob Shelter for lunch. Bemoaning my lack of dinner supplies, Walking Man and his nephew, Ninja Turtle, handed me a generous bag of homemade dried chicken and vegetable casserole. Along with two packs of Beef Ramen Noodles that someone had left in the shelter, my stomach quit complaining at the prospect of a good feast that evening.

Cosby Knob Shelter was also crowded and despite my chilly night at Clingmans Dome, I hoped the lookout tower on top of Mt Cammerer would provide more sheltered accommodation. Situated half a mile off the AT, it had been built in 1937 by The Civilian Conservation Corps and was manned by a fire ranger up until the 1960s.

I caught up with Phillip and PJ and the tower proved to be a real gem. Not only did it have a far more luxurious wooden floor, even a roof, but it was fully enclosed on all sides and sported several windows. It is amazing how trail life simplifies our expectations of what makes us content. Forget whining that your smartphone is out of date, that your car is too old or the coffee you just bought is too weak, we were over the moon at the simple prospect of having somewhere to sleep with a roof, walls and windows.

Mary Poppins, so named because of his umbrella, sprung through the door shortly after and introduced himself, further helping bulk out my food supplies by handing me half an avocado. I offered a pack of Beef Ramen as an incentive for further bartering but not surprisingly, he declined.

The preference to shelters and other under cover buildings was becoming the norm during this stretch because of constant bad news on the weather front. We had somehow managed to miss the rain that had been forecast during the past few days, save an occasional shower — but on pulling into Standing Bear Hostel it finally caught us up.

The place was busy, understandably, as over the course of the day the sound of rain on the roof became louder until that corner of the Appalachian hills sat under a constant, heavy deluge. We were thankful for the shelter.

I decided a little trail magic of my own was called for at breakfast. The rain was still downing spirits so I figured a good old cooked breakfast would go down well with Phillip, Daffy and PJ. Taking hiker appetites into consideration, I calculated twenty-four eggs would suffice for the four of us plus an alarmingly high stack of bacon. No sooner than it had hit the plates, it was devoured with much lip smacking, finger licking and approving nods.

The rain was still falling mercilessly the following morning. The usual train of thought is to sit out inclement weather because it's obvious that it will never last that long. Phillip and I stared out at our soaked environment from the seclusion of an overhanging roof and discussed one of two options: either go or stay. The problem with waiting is that it could go on for days and those are then days wasted being stationary.

It's not particularly pleasant starting out in the rain but waterproof gear is pretty efficient these days and once you're warmed up it's actually quite a novelty. I looked at Phillip; he looked at me. We shrugged our shoulders, hoisted our packs and I popped the umbrella up.

The steep climb from Standing Bear Hostel wasn't helped by a slick surface coated with wet leaves, which stuck in several layers to the points of our trekking poles. We brushed past wet bushes and contorted our bodies around poison ivy.

We warmed on the five-mile, 2500-foot climb to pop out of the woods onto the lovely sounding Snowbird Mountain, and then bounced along the top to Max Patch Bald. Up there I felt like I was in my home county of Sussex. It looked just like the downland near where I grew up, played as a kid and still go now. A low hanging cloud added to the similarity and occasionally a weak, yellow sun tried in vain to break through making us squint. The rain stopped but our feet remained wet as they brushed through the wet grass.

Continuing to Roaring Fork shelter, I counted twelve hikers inside and another five brushing away leaves to make space underneath. Phillip had secured a new hammock and was extolling its virtues as I tried in vain, again, to fit my tent onto one of the designated tent areas. I eventually crawled in, pulled down a rain flap at the front for use in bad weather and commenced a gear drying operation. When I tried to exit I discovered I couldn't. The release clip for the beak was by the tent peg, beyond my reach. It was like being locked out of the house, except I was stuck in a tent.

I peered under the flap and saw Bridget strolling past through the trees.

"Bridget! Help!"

She stopped and cocked one ear, looking around aimlessly trying to fathom out who was calling her.

"Over here!" I implored.

"Wassup? What are you doing?" she said whilst crouching down and trying to peer under.

"Look, don't take the piss but I can't get out. I'm stuck."

She started giggling and after pausing for what I thought was a few seconds more than necessary, just for a little self-satisfaction, she eventually released the small karabiner and I was a free man.

The rain lashed down all night and constantly smacked on the tent. Unable to sleep I rose and was gone by 6 a.m. Phillip caught me mid-morning as we summited Bluff Mountain and then sped down the 3500 feet to emerge from the woods at Hot

Springs. As usual there were a few errands to run in town but none were as important as the Smoky Mountain Diner, conveniently one of the first stops. We ate like bears, tearing at steaks like wild animals between forkfuls of vegetables and gravy, our plates wiped clean with bread rolls.

We secured a cabin at The Hot Springs Resort and Spa, taking one which slept four in anticipation of Daffy and PJ arriving, which they duly did. The bench outside of the laundrette seemed a good place to watch the world go by as my clothes dried.

"Are you Fozzie?"

I looked up to see a guy around my age (but with a far superior beard) and a young girl who I took to be his daughter.

"Yes, that's me?"

"I'm Balls; this is my daughter, Sunshine. I bought your PCT book."

"Ah, so you're the one!" I replied, smiling. "Thank you very much. You two are going for the Triple Crown right?"

"Sure are, it's going well."

Sunshine peered round her Dad and said hi, all freckles, red hair and a huge smile. Even at the end of the day she appeared to have enough energy to walk further. I relayed the conversation to PJ later to which he replied that he had bumped into them the day before and heard her say to her dad: "Come on dad, let's do a twenty-five!"

We spent a day in Hot Springs. I liked the place. It was a compact town with all the amenities lined up along the main street. Red brick buildings flanked the railway line and it was a short walk from our cabin in the woods squeezed between Spring Creek and the imposing French Broad River. The trees had sprung to life down from the mountains in a vibrant chartreuse. The calmer waters by the river bank, sheltered by half-immersed boulders soothed my tired feet as I dipped them and I spent time reading, occasionally swapping boulders for those bathed in the early spring sunshine. Children screamed as they played by the campsite and the occasional waft of meat grilling on barbecues made my mouth water.

I collected my new water filter, poncho and power pack from the post office then ventured into the library to take advantage of the free Wi-Fi and to update my blog. Krista was doing the same and we chatted briefly about our progress.

She was due to travel to Japan for work so only had a few

weeks to enjoy the AT. Her mother had since returned home as she was only joining her daughter for a week. Krista was the focus of most of the male hikers' attentions. She was attractive and initially reserved, because of the attention she was receiving I think, but after we had spoken a few times she opened up somewhat. She explained that her new trail name, Pork Chop, had come about because she had recently packed out an impressive supply of meat to the trail. She dealt with the male attention she was receiving nonchalantly, often ignoring it. She smiled as she spoke, slightly embarrassed and she was very endearing. I joked that as she hiked with a blithe disregard for the guys, most of them were left in her wake in varying states of love-struck despair, littering the trail. Frankly, I just thought she was a goddess.

The community centre was packed that evening after news that an AYCE (all you can eat) was up for grabs. Tables lined the room, and dishes of pasta, garlic bread and salads disappeared quicker than the staff could replace them. Chatter was minimal — hikers were occupied with fuelling up and made several visits to satiate their appetites.

I bumped into Bridget who declared she had given herself a trail name and was now to be referred to as 'Lady Forward'.

"How did that come about?" I asked, confused and eager for an explanation.

"Well, it's the name of the statue on top of the capitol building in Madison. The motto of Wisconsin is forward, for whatever reason and as I'm a lady who's planned on moving forward for 2000 miles, it seemed appropriate. And, there is the added bonus of fending off any unsavoury names that could be given to me by, say, a creepy Englishman."

"Ouch. It's nowhere near as good as Pink Bits," I retorted.

PJ was immersed in his guidebook in between shovelling pasta into his mouth.

"We've done 274 miles," he announced with little emotion, easing an escaped segment of pasta back into his mouth. I couldn't tell if he was impressed or disappointed.

"It's progress, mate," I offered. "Just don't look at the bigger picture too much."

We were often reminded of the bigger picture by a renowned map of the AT, produced by The Appalachian Trail Conservancy. As it follows the trail northward, it is, understandably, not so wide but quite long. I regularly saw it displayed in restaurants, libraries and other establishments but tried not to pay much attention to it because it was daunting. I had checked it at the Smoky Mountain diner with Phillip, who had proudly declared that we had completed just short of the width of a little finger. In other words, after three weeks on trail, we were just 12% done.

I had learnt on the PCT, and other hikes, never to look at the bigger picture because progress was slow and could wear you down psychologically. Despite doing an activity that we love, focusing on the distance covered can make a hiker a little despondent.

I take each week at a time, manageable chunks to concentrate my efforts on and when I complete that section, I give myself a pat on the back and look at the next one. Even those sections are broken down further by looking at each day and then split again into hours. Two to three hours, or six to ten miles, and then I would take a break. Do the same again, have some lunch, look at possible options for a camp and then repeat the process in the afternoon. Slowly, day by day, week by week and month by month, the bigger picture gradually reveals itself.

***

It had started raining and the temperature had also dropped. I worried about how cold it would be up at the higher elevations. Hot Springs sat at just over 1300 feet and as I left with PJ and Pink Bits — sorry, Lady Forward — it became colder as we climbed. By the time we pulled into the Spring Mountain Shelter after eleven miles, thankfully, the rain had stopped. Wet gear hung from every available space as hikers blew into cupped hands, pulled on extra layers and stomped their feet to try and warm up. Everyone had become a little complacent after the great conditions we had been blessed with and the Smokies were living up to expectations. I pitched my tent on a little section of raised ground commanding a good view of the shelter to watch the evening's events.

The Smokies continued to play a guessing game with the weather over the next few days. Dry, wet, hot, cold; we never knew what was around the corner.

Earthling was huddled in the Little Laurel shelter trying to keep warm as we arrived and Pops turned up shortly after. We all remarked on how the weather seemed to be turning for the worse and even stopping to rest was becoming difficult because all our body heat drained quickly.

PJ stopped briefly before we both left to climb the 876 feet to Big Firescald Knob before descending to our destination for the day at the Jerry Cabin shelter. The further we climbed the colder it became. The main problem was the rain which seemed undecided as to whether to remain be, or change to sleet. It soaked us, seeming to leach through our waterproofs and chilling our very cores. I couldn't feel my hands despite my gloves and straining on the incline, I just couldn't warm up.

The shelter appeared in the gloom as a fine mist engulfed us. A wisp of smoke spluttered from the chimney as a blue tarpaulin stretched across the front. I entered and as my eyes struggled to see in the darkness, I made out several hikers wrapped in sleeping bags or sat by the fire rubbing their hands. The place was full. A meagre pile of wet firewood promised little and after spending a few minutes trying to wriggle nearer the heat I retreated back outside to set up my tent in the rain.

My hands, now numb, struggled with the guy lines as I tried to push the tent pegs into a sodden soil. Forsaking anything else I quickly blew up my sleeping mat and climbed inside my sleeping bag where I lay for an hour until, slowly, my body eventually warmed up. Rain continued to hammer on the tent and I cooked a warming meal before darkness forced me to sleep.

Overnight, as the temperatures had dropped further, snow had fallen and I woke to a world of white. I peered out, coloured tents dotted the area, lightly coated with powder. I reached for my shoes which had frozen; my waterproofs were stiff with the cold and a chunk of ice slid down my water bottle as I tried to drink. I had to place my socks into my sleeping bag to defrost them. After three days without washing them, this was none to pleasant an experience.

I jumped over frozen puddles and followed footprints in the snow down the 1000 feet to Devils Fork Gap which shivered under the snow line but was, at least, dry. The sun fought a battle with the rain and every time I looked up through the canopy it was difficult to fathom whether the next few minutes would be wet or dry. I repeatedly changed my layers to keep a constant temperature.

In a matter of a few days, I had gone from the relative warmth of Hot Springs back to what seemed like midwinter. The trail fluctuated so much between different elevations that the weather was a constant puzzle. Up high was cold, down in the gaps it was bearable and anything in between was pure confusion. It started to affect me and play games with my head. Coupled with the dense woods my mood slumped and although there was little I could do about the weather, I longed for a bald where I could have some sense of space as compensation and occasionally the trail obliged.

Once in my sleeping bag at night I warmed for the first time that day. I often left the flaps of the tent open so I had wonderful views stretching to distant mountains.

The Appalachians are essentially one long, wide ridge. Because of the abundance of woods and forest, a hiker rarely actually sees the surrounding landscape, so balds, or gaps at the edge of the woods, made wonderful surprises, an escape from the sometimes claustrophobic environment of the woods. I frequently took breaks there to survey a blanket of trees stretching as far as I could see.

Often, in the fading light of early evening, those distant hills — sometimes one, more often two, three or more, peeking up from behind each other — took on varying tones of blue. Like gentle waves in shades of beryl, azure, cerulean and sapphire fading away to merge into the sky. I used to wonder if someone, somewhere out there, was also sitting down and looking back at me, wondering exactly the same thing.

At times the mountain tops narrowed to a rocky ridge a few feet wide, where I felt as though I were balancing, edging along with my arms outstretched as a counterbalance. Occasionally, I lost touch with my feet as I focused on the trail in front, becoming mesmerised and detached, almost in another world. I forgot the ground under me and floated, gliding without any sensation, just balancing on blue.

Chapter 6
Throwing down the Gauntlet

April 24th to May 8th
Mile 309 to 523

I wear a leather strap around my neck with three silver pendants. The first is a St Christopher, the patron saint of travellers, given to me by my boss at the time in 1994 before I left on a cycling trip to Israel. I'm not a religious person but I do like to think that Christopher looks over me on my travels.

The second is a cedar tree, symbolic of the country of Lebanon. On that same cycling trip, during a harsh winter in early 1995, I stayed overnight with a family in a simple, three-roomed house in Syria. It was basic to say the least as they clearly had little money, but they gave me shelter after seeing me in town one afternoon, trying to warm up in a snowstorm. When I left, the son handed me the pendant. At first I refused because it had some value and they had already shown me enough kindness and generosity. I felt somewhat guilty accepting it but he insisted.

The third is a small Celtic cross, synonymous with Galicia, a province in North West Spain. Monica, a cook working at the Refugio Ave Fénix, in Villafranca del Beirzo, a small town on the Camino de Santiago, gave it to me after I had rested there for a few days.

I like to think of them all as my lucky charms. In twenty years of travelling since being given the first one, I have stayed out of trouble. I always hike with them and even if I am out for a day's walk, a week's cycle ride, or indeed a few months on trail, I do not feel safe without them.

Sometimes I touch them where they hang, halfway down my

chest. I rub them between my fingers and even place them between my teeth. I wear them when I sleep and I keep them on in the shower. They are as much a part of my travels as the associated memories.

They also serve a double purpose, being a great indicator of my walking posture and rhythm. I don't like to mess much with the mechanics of my walking because I believe it is a natural process that we are born with. However, having read a few books on the subject such as *Chi Walking* and *Born to Run*, I have become curious about how we actually walk.

Both authors advocate making changes to various aspects of the body whilst hiking and running to encourage landing on the forefoot, the theory being that a lot of injuries associated with walking and running are caused by striking the ground, incorrectly, on the heel. A forward strike of the foot makes one less susceptible to injury, increases speed and means a hiker can cover more miles in a given amount of time. These advantages are not deliberate, merely an unintentional influence of making these changes

I made two main adaptations to my walking after reading, in particular, *Chi Walking* by Danny Dreyer. These were to shorten my stride and to lean forward. A shorter stride encourages a forward strike of the foot. Leaning forward, not from the waist but from above the heel (imagine a hinge at the back of each ankle), whilst keeping the body straight also promotes a forward strike.

When I first started to change the way I walked two years ago, it took a little getting used to. My body's natural reaction was to revert to how I had walked since I could first stand upright. I had to constantly remind myself to implement both changes — but slowly, with much practice, I have now reached the point where it is just about becoming natural and I don't have to think about it.

As well as watching over me, my neck pendants are a great indicator that I am walking correctly. As I lean slightly forward, they swing away from my chest; as each trailing leg comes forward to strike the ground, the momentum of my body comes forward and these pendants hit my chest, resulting in each pendant chinking an audible reminder. As the next foot reaches forward, they swing forward and then return again.

Once I'm walking, regardless of how fast or slow, they stay in rhythm as long as my body is hinged forward and each foot strike is accompanied by a clink of silver. If I become lazy and revert to my walking style of old, I lay back somewhat, resulting in a strike nearer to the heel but more importantly, my pendants fall silent. They sound a little like loose change in your pocket when you're running for the bus and it's become a very reassuring sound.

Others carried similar lucky charms or items they felt incomplete without. Kori 'Rocket' Feener from Topsfield, MA, had a propensity to fall. In fact, she fell or rolled her ankles every single day up until the last sixty miles. She put this down to losing focus, getting lost in her head and not concentrating on what was actually on the ground in front of her. "The Trail doesn't like multitasking," she told me.

When she first saw Mt Katahdin, visible from miles away because of its sheer size, she stopped to take in the view. As she geared up to go, she noticed a hawk feather on the ground which wasn't there when she sat down. "It looked beautiful," she said. "Grey with white stripes, it was soft and something about it made me feel like I needed to hold onto it. I ended up tying it in my hair and, for the last sixty miles of the hike, I didn't trip or roll my ankle once. I still have it — it hangs in my apartment and it can be seen in my summit photo, poking out of my pony tail."

***

PJ and I emerged from the woods onto the I-26 somewhat sodden from the trees dripping on us. It was a further five miles to Bald Mountain shelter and as we looked up, moody clouds raced overhead. The Little Creek Café was three miles down the I-26 although we didn't know if it was open and Wolf Creek Market store was a further half mile.

As we sat by some rubbish bins contemplating our options, and our hunger, Trooper David L Buckner from the North Carolina Highway Patrol pulled up. His window slid down which gave me the opportunity to ask a question I had been dying to know the answer to for thirty minutes.

"Morning, officer," I started with. "You see that sign up there?" I gestured to my right.

"Yes?" he replied with a curious and confused expression.

"Well, what does it mean? Read it, it makes no sense does it?"

His head turned to face the sign which read 'Permitted trucks not allowed'.

I continued. "If a truck is not allowed down that road then how can it be permitted to go there? Conversely, if a truck is permitted to go down that road, how can it not be allowed?"

He scratched his head, smiled and looked at PJ who just shrugged his shoulders and offered, "He's British, I apologise."

"PJ, English mate, please," I corrected.

Trooper Buckner could not offer an explanation but it was a good way to open up a friendly conversation, and in turn, perhaps get a lift. PJ knew this was what I was gearing up for and whispered discreetly "Fozzie! You *can't* ask a cop for a ride!"

I carried on. "You don't, by any chance, know what time the Café shuts do you?"

"I do, yes. You've missed it by a few minutes."

"Damn, I'm starving. How far is the store?"

"It's about three miles. I can take you there; I'm not busy, happy to help out. I can only get one of you in the car though, it's full with gear."

I had a quick debate with PJ and we agreed I should go.

"What do you want to eat mate?" I asked.

"Chicken, Fozzie. Anything with chicken, I need chicken."

Not only did Trooper Buckner take me down to the store, he waited and gave me a lift back as well. We even discussed the relative merits of wild food foraging in the patrol car as he flicked through pages on his laptop showing me different plant species. As I left he handed me a badge with 'North Carolina Highway Patrol' embroidered on it.

I have always had good encounters with the cops in America. I think the English accent works wonders, especially when partnered with a little ignorance about local laws. Play the dumb tourist and all sorts of avenues open up.

I do, however, have problems with those in positions of so called authority. Where it stems from I don't know. Subsequently, I am generally not too fond of the police because of some past experiences in England where they abused their authority and assumed they were above me. I didn't like being told what to do by my parents, bosses, friends or my teachers and I still struggle with it.

Immigration and customs are my worst nightmare, especially in the States although my passage through Miami airport was, for once, smooth because of a genuinely smashing officer who let me through with two months over my visa allowance when he found out that I was hiking the AT.

In the most part I find immigration run by a rude bunch of individuals who, having seen my backpack, assume I am just bumming around the country for a few months with little money. They are more often than not impatient, intolerant, ask stupid questions, don't wait for an answer and act as if they are better than me because they wear a uniform, which they falsely believe puts them in a position of power.

I do not, and never will, consider anyone to be above or below me. And correspondingly, I do not consider myself above, or below, anyone else.

Trooper Buckner was an absolute gem, wished us well and sped off. As we stood under a bridge where highway US-23 went over us it became clear that bridges made excellent shelters. The I-26 was a small country lane with few cars and the traffic noise on the busy freeway over us was dampened by the actual structure itself.

A hiker called Honey Badger arrived, also a little on the damp side and after a quick check to make sure no one was looking, we scampered up the concrete embankment and found a flat platform completely sheltered from the rain.

The only apparent hazard of bridge life was taking a pee which entailed walking sideways along the steep slope in a crouched position aiding a lower centre of gravity, to avoid slipping. This was not made any easier wearing Crocs and by the time I reached open air and commenced operations, a strong wind blew most of my bodily fluids back up my shirt and into my face. Despite this — and the occasional vehicle hissing past below us on the wet road — we slept well, no doubt relaxed at the thought of a dry night. Bridge life held much potential.

Now out of the Smoky Mountains and, except for some parts where the elevation went up to 6000 feet, we were enjoying warmer conditions down around the 3000 feet mark. I continued to walk with PJ and Phillip. Sometimes we travelled within earshot of each other, but in the main we walked alone and teamed up in the evening to camp or to share a motel room in town.

The familiar faces I had become friends with popped up and crossed my path every once in a while: Bowser, Byline, Fonsworth, Mary Poppins, Pink Bits, sorry, Lady Forward, Pops

and Earthling to name a few. Daffy tinkered with his alternative socialising habit, made appearances now and again and a constant stream of new faces entered my world.

***

Despite my inability to spot wild ramps, Phillip became very excited one morning after passing the Clyde Smith shelter. We had both been preoccupied admiring the golden ragwort, whose golden yellow flowers often carpeted sections of the trail, when he stopped dead in his tracks causing me to bump into the back of him.

"Fozzie, are these ramps?"

We sniffed, prodded, stroked, observed and studied the possibilities. Slender, vibrant green leaves thinned into red stems before changing to white just before they disappeared under the soil. We pulled one out and smelt it; undeniably it was an onion. A couple of minutes searching on our phones for images and we both agreed we had found the elusive source of food. The identification was positive which was ideal, because we were bloody hungry.

Pulling out probably more than our fair share, we toiled up the steep, 2000-foot climb to summit Roan High Knob. Finding the spring and addressing the immediate problem of borderline dehydration, we gulped down water as though we hadn't drunk for days.

Peering into the depths of our respective food bags, we took stock of the culinary opportunities. I had several of my usual rice meals and Phillip produced not only a bag of sliced salami but a sachet of olive oil as well.

Before long our pots were brimming with handfuls of wild ramps as the salami sizzled and spat in the hot oil. A wonderful aroma of fried onions acted as a homing beacon for the few day hikers spread around the shelter. We handed them a few of the surplus stock and devoured our new found source of fresh, wild sustenance with gusto, licking our lips.

For a few miles after Roan High Knob the AT opens out briefly and entertains the claustrophobics. The trail twisted, turned and I bowed to its every whim, revelling in the wide, open spaces. I passed the imposing Overmountain shelter, dipped into short sections of thin woodland which opened out into vast, green, boulder speckled moors. I crossed over into

Tennessee which at times looked and felt like the Yorkshire moors, Dartmoor, or the South Downs. I felt the sun on my back and ran my hands through bushes, which were now bursting with vivid green leaves, alive and thriving in the warm sunshine.

The contrast of an occasional ivory cloud against a deep, electric sky was highlighted by rounded hills intense with deep greens. It was early May and winter had been defeated, stubborn to the last but now behind us. The mornings and evenings were brighter; hikers could start their days in the light and enjoy extended, warmer evenings. Summer was looming and although every AT hiker was relishing the prospect of hotter days, little did we know at that point just what it had in store for us.

Phillip was a day ahead with PJ as I had decided to take a zero at the Mountain Harbour Hostel. Departing I was soon joined by a hiker called Nito. He had short, curly, black hair and spoke with a Latin accent that made him sound somewhat like a gangster. He made good company and we sped easily along, enjoying the flatter section between Bear Branch Road and the Kincora Hiking Hostel at Denis Cove Road.

**

After leaving the Smoky Mountains the talk turned to a man called Bob Peoples. Hugely respected by hikers for the work he has done maintaining a long section of trail around where he lives at the Kincora Hiking Hostel, he is a legend in hiking circles. So much so that quotes often appear scribbled onto shelter walls in the area.

'When Bob Peoples stays in a shelter, the mice bring him *their* food.' Or, 'The bears hang Bob Peoples's food bag for him.'

Since 1988 he has logged several thousand miles of hiking just to maintain the trail and every May around a hundred past and present thru-hikers join him for a two-day intensive trail maintenance event known as 'Hardcore Kincora'. His hostel, set back from Denis Cove road, asks for a mere $5 donation which includes a bed, shower, laundry, use of the kitchen and rides into town.

Unfortunately I never got to meet Bob. I arrived late evening and he was out on a shuttle run. Byline and PJ were sitting down looking ill with upset stomachs claiming a pizza from town was responsible. Phillip was checking on a lasagne in the oven fit for five people but had plans to consume all of it and Fonsworth was cooking the healthy lentil option with Margaret. Cats were everywhere; postcards from previous hikers covered the walls and I sat outside after enjoying a shower, relishing the quiet around Kincora.

Phillip seemed a little despondent that evening. When I enquired why he looked so glum he simply explained he was tired and a little fed up with the rain. He continued.

"They should put Wi-Fi in all the shelters," he began. "And electrical outlets. The path should be cleared five feet wide and there should be an awning over the entire trail."

Well rested I left the following morning as the trail descended sharply from the hostel down to Laurel Falls, which at eighty feet high is so named because of the laurel bushes in the area.

It was hot and very humid, seeming to sap the very strength out of me. I toiled up the 1659 feet towards Pond Flats where Deep, a German hiker, and Fuurther, who pointed out his trail name was spelt with two u's, sat by a fresh spring drinking the cool water. Deep's name had come about literally because he spoke with a deep voice. We had tried to name him Arnie, as in Schwarzenegger, because of the similar tone but he had settled on Deep.

He left before Fuurther and I but returned a few seconds later looking shaken.

"What's up mate?" I enquired, seeing the ashen look on his face.

"There's a big snake on the trail," he replied, stony-faced and deadpan.

Fuurther cautiously walked up the trail as I tucked in behind him, peering over his shoulder. He was a local so snakes were nothing new to him. Just off the trail a large rattlesnake basked in the sun with a bulge halfway down its body, no doubt the remnants of lunch.

"God dang!" exclaimed Fuurther. "Biggest god damn snake I ever saw!"

As we crept closer it let off a warning rattle but seemed docile, possibly full from its meal, so I approached slowly to take a photo. Snakes are the main reason why manufacturers install a zoom function on cameras and after getting closer than I should have, I quickly fired off a couple of shots and retreated hastily.

I passed Iron Mountain shelter and a concrete structure caught my eye. I had been coasting along enjoying the flatter trail which bumbled along around 4000 feet when over to the left, just by a wooden seat, stood a stone pillar with what appeared to be a gravestone embedded into one side. I went for a closer look and read the inscription.

Uncle Nick Grindstaff
Born
Dec 26, 1851
Died
July 22, 1923
Lived alone, suffered alone and died alone

The inscription sparked my curiosity and I took a photo but was unable to find out any details surrounding this man until I returned back home and did some digging around. Nick lived alone on the ridge between Stoney Creek and Doe Valley for forty years. He was orphaned as a child and raised by relatives until he reached adulthood, when he married and inherited part of the family farm.

He made a living farming for a few years but suddenly moved to Missouri for reasons that are unclear. Some stories say his wife died, others say she left him. Further accounts detail him being robbed of everything he owned. He eventually moved back to Iron Mountain where he lived out his remaining years as a hermit with his dog Panter, a horse, and some say a pet rattlesnake.

In July 1923, his friend Baxter McKewen stopped by to check on Nick but found him dead with Panter guarding the body. The dog had to be prised way from its vigil. To his day, no one knows how Nick died.

Relatives constructed the chimney shaped structure we now see on Iron Mountain a couple of years after his death. To add to the sense of mystery, years after the AT was constructed, hikers camping near the spot reported hearing the howls of a dog through the night.

You've got to love a good mystery ...

***

I had only managed sixteen miles in eight hours and was sweating copiously. The air was oppressive and, suddenly, shelters were not the targets that many were aiming for — it was the water sources too. Over the course of a summer, especially a hot one, some creeks dry up and the chances of obtaining water become slimmer. It was still only May but temperatures had shot up and everyone was complaining. Instead of fantasising about food, our attention turned to our favourite cold drinks. PJ told me he had been dreaming about an ice-cold cranberry juice for days and as he walked away from the TN-91 road crossing, I couldn't resist getting a lift to the charmingly named town of Shady Valley, just over three miles away.

A local called Kirby dropped me off at the General Store. A couple of Harleys were propped up outside, the doorbell tinkled as an occasional customer walked in or out and I looked at the signs above the door offering a deli, fuel, general merchandise, restrooms and 'Home of the Shady Dog', whatever that was.

A can of Coke settled the immediate thirst crisis and I ordered two hamburgers whilst picking up a few items for the food supply, including the coldest carton of cranberry juice I could find.

I was back on trail in an hour after another quick lift back to the trailhead by Joe, a local section hiker. Lord Horatio Fonsworth passed me as I was gearing up by the roadside and commented on the cranberry juice, still ice-cold with condensation bubbles forming on the outside as I wrapped it in my jacket for insulation.

"Man that looks good!" he said, whilst walking off with his head turned back.

"It does dunnit! I'm going to surprise PJ with it," I explained. "He's been hankering after one for days."

It was only four miles to Double Springs shelter and I walked through pleasing, yellow-coloured meadows splattered with buttercups and dandelions whilst catching glimpses of the agricultural landscape back down in the valley. A collection of hikers had congregated to sit out the afternoon heat and take advantage of the cool spring water by the shelter. I figured word may have reached PJ about my purchase and sure enough when he saw me approach, he got up and came swiftly over.

"Fozzie!" he exclaimed with a desperate expression that only the thought of a chilled carton of cranberry juice on a hot afternoon could bring on. "I heard you went to the store and got me cranberry juice!" Saliva was almost dribbling down his chin.

Alas, for poor PJ's salivation at least, satiation salvation was not imminent.

"Yes, PJ, I did."

He looked excited and his eyes opened wider in anticipation, looking like they would pop out.

"The problem is," I added, "I drank it all."

His expression changed in a millisecond to a mix of shock, disappointment, anger and possibly a small smattering of hatred.

"I'm really sorry mate but that last three miles was stinking hot and what with all the salt from the burgers, I just … well … I just couldn't resist it. PJ, I'm really sorry, I'll buy you another one."

He stared at me, gormless, and said nothing.

"PJ, Come on! Don't make me feel guilty! I may have drunk it but at least I bought it for you in the first place!"

This explanation, admittedly, didn't offer much consolation.

Lord Horatio Fonsworth chipped in. "Fozzie, I can't believe you drank it."

There was an uncomfortable silence for a few seconds, during which I feared PJ would grab my throat and try and throttle me. I felt I was being cross-examined in a court room after a very weak defence. Eventually he started laughing, along with Lord Horatio Fonsworth plus a few others and a strange feeling that I was now on the end of a wind up surfaced.

"Fozzie, I'm just messing with you! It was nice of you to buy it, even if you did drink it. Don't worry, it's all good!"

I spent the night camped near the Abingdon Gap shelter, waking briefly at 4.30 a.m. when a small group of hikers woke me as they left early. I couldn't get back to sleep, especially after hearing what sounded like a large animal around camp. Too scared to peer under the tent to be confronted by a bear, I pulled my sleeping bag over me and prayed.

The chatter was rife in the morning when several others also recounted hearing similar sounds during the night. One was Margaret who, having pitched near me said:

"I heard it too and spent most of the night with my knife ready, just in case."

"Blimey!" I retorted, "Remind me not to creep into your tent during the night!"

I talked briefly with a new face, Cheddar, so named after his fondness for my native English cheese.

"It's a good cheese with a great reputation," I said. "But, I have to say that my personal favourite is Stilton."

"What's that like?" he enquired.

"Completely different. Softer, creamier, smellier and it has blue veins of mould running through it which some people dislike. As far as English cheeses go, I think it's the champion."

"Really?" His curiosity seemed aroused so I took the opportunity, instead of trying to give someone a trail name, of improving the one they already had.

"Far superior to Cheddar in my opinion. I think you should consider changing your name to Stilton — I think it will command a lot more respect, enhance your reputation and show off your cheese knowledge."

I left him to ponder the idea and headed off with Phillip who informed me he had given himself the trail name of Lazagne, which he purposely spelt with a z. He had reached the decision after his mammoth portion of said dish at Kincora.

We walked with excitement, and for good reason. Damascus is quite possibly the most famous and revered town on the entire Appalachian Trail, and it lay just a few miles down the trail. It is renowned for an annual event known as 'Trail Days' where thousands of hikers both past and present converge on this small town in Virginia, swelling the population from around 1000 to 20,000. Most camp a short way from the centre of town and enjoy huge campfires, food and drink, foot washes, medical check-ups and a host of other services often laid on free by the local community.

Unfortunately, we were too early by about ten days for the event but the plan was to carry on north and hopefully hitch a lift back for the experience.

It was a small, cute town and I liked it immediately. Old, timber-clad houses lined the main street in subtle, pastel shades. Gardens were well kept and spring flowers danced by picket fences. The local trails were busy with people jogging, cycling or walking the dog and a collection of local shops catered for everyone. Damascus nestled in the green folds of the surrounding hills as cloud shadows passed over creating occasional respites from the heat.

We camped in the grounds of one of the hostels run by the local Methodist Church which was known simply as 'The Place', and took a zero the following day. I shared a room with PJ, Lazagne and an English hiker called Chez 11, spending the day relaxing. Chez 11 was the first English guy I had met so it was good to catch up on some news, especially our respective football teams' performance.

He was 20, and had worked, amongst other places, for the railways at Leeds train station as well as Debenhams department store. He supported Everton, which I didn't hold against him and spoke animatedly, with great fondness about his brother, who suffered from cerebral palsy. He was always relaxed and spoke slowly, choosing his words carefully.

Our room was positioned directly in front of the stairs which gave us a good view of who was coming up and if we fancied a chat, or they did, we'd call them in. I started to think of our little room as the reception.

Pink Bits, sorry, Lady Forward, was one such example who popped her head around the door after hearing us discuss who would be the first to summit Katahdin. The AT was never a race and most of us really didn't care who would be the first to finish, but egos defend themselves rigorously when provoked. The finishing point, and which one of us would get there first, was always on our minds.

In a good-humoured, brief discussion, she claimed she would be there before all of us.

"Are you throwing the gauntlet down?" I probed.

"Perhaps, but whichever one of us two is behind has to carry it."

"It's a done deal," I confirmed.

She approached, smirking, and handed over an imaginary gauntlet. Obviously, being a heavy, armoured glove, its weight caught me by surprise.

"This thing is heavy!" I exclaimed. "Whoever is behind and has to carry this thing will be at a serious disadvantage."

"I know," she replied. "That's why you have it now because I'm leaving. See you up the trail."

"You can count on it."

I left Damascus with Chez 11 in the afternoon with aims to reach Lost Mountain shelter, fifteen miles away. Nito was loitering outside the store and offered me a shot of bourbon for the trail which I duly accepted. We generally didn't carry alcohol into the woods because of the weight so opportunities to indulge had to be grabbed without hesitation.

"I have too much weight," he said. "I need to lose some. The bourbon is yours if you want to carry it."

It was a fair sized bottle and, as much as a wee tipple in the evening for the next few days appealed, I thanked him but declined.

The rain started again and, feeling stubborn, I delayed stopping to don my waterproofs until it approached the downpour stage. Eventually and reluctantly, I removed my pack, put on my poncho, put up the umbrella and started to walk again. One minute later I rounded a corner to see the shelter right in front of me.

Daffy rolled in to everyone's surprise and dispensed some decent hugs. When PJ realised he was back in the fray Sam was on the receiving end of his frightened bear cub up a tree hug routine.

I saw Nito approaching out of the corner of my eye as I was erecting my tent. A mixture of urgency, impatience and inquisitiveness creased his furrows.

"Fozzie, you got any TP?"

"Any what? What's TP?"

"Toilet paper."

He looked a little embarrassed and spoke softly so no one would hear. He was also grimacing, walking around a little agitated and kept crossing his legs.

"Nito me old mate, do you need the bog?"

"Yes, I'm a little desperate. I can trade you, I've run out."

Now, I was more than prepared to offer a few squares out of kindness; I didn't expect anything in return and knew the trail would return the favour at some point when I needed something. However, Nito was obviously desperate for the toilet and as he had mentioned the 'trade' word, I thought, shamelessly, the opportunity should be taken full advantage of.

"Well, Nito, let me see. I could do with a generous dram of that bourbon for this evening and what's that you have in the bag there? Is that a pack of dehydrated veggies? How many squares do you need?"

I started to rummage round in my bag for the paper.

"Six will do it," he implored.

"Six? Just six squares?" I offered in surprise. "That's impressive, mate. I'd struggle to get by on six squares. I usually double up as well, you know, just in case of tearage? And what about tomorrow? You may need to go then as well."

Nito's expression was now borderline panic.

"Fozzie, that's fine! Bourbon is there, here's the veggies."

I counted out six squares, possibly slower than I should have done, and handed them to him as he raced off to the privy. TP was not an item that thru-hikers buy in stores because of the bulk of two roll packs so usually we procure it in public toilets. I had a few squares of inferior quality which I hadn't used since picking it up at the diner in Hot Springs. The thickness was concerning and its texture reminiscent of baking parchment. I was pleased to get rid of it although did feel a little guilty and fully expected a little bad karma in return for my greed. Especially, even though Nito was unaware, as it was only one-ply as well.

Lazagne sauntered over as I was cooking my dinner.

"Chess, Fozzie?" he enquired.

"Sure, take a pew."

We had both discussed bringing a travel chessboard on the trail but discounted it because of the weight, when he came up with the bright idea of downloading the game onto his phone. Subsequently, the England vs. America competition had been underway for a couple of days. If a game went on too long, perhaps past hiker midnight, then we just picked up from where we had left it the next time.

We were both around the same skill level — that being poor amateurs — so the games were fairly well balanced. After two games we were drawn level at one game each. As I checked my meal cooking, he made a move and handed me the phone. I perused the possible options as he chatted to Daffy or quickly started pitching his hammock. The entire game would usually stretch over the course of an evening or two.

The annoying aspect of the game was that when one person won and checkmate was reached, a deadpan, computer synthesised voice exclaimed *checkmate!* Either Lazagne or I, having just made the killer move would still be holding the phone and simply smiled smugly, holding it aloft near the other's ear to announce our victory. Tonight was his turn and, having finalised his options, he sat back confidently and held his phone aloft. It was 2-1 to the States.

Checkmate!

Lazagne's playful ego, and desire to rub his victory in, continued the following morning as I woke, rubbing my eyes at 6 a.m. As I lay there contemplating the day ahead, I heard footsteps creeping up to my tent. They paused a couple of feet away and as I cocked one ear to try and find out what was happening, the immortal, electronic voice wafted through the woods.

Checkmate!
Promptly followed by Lazagne giggling like a school kid.
"See you up the trail Fozzie!"

***

Once in a while, the AT breaks out from the seclusion of the woods and, for anything from a few minutes to perhaps a day, a thru-hiker suddenly revels in a new found freedom. These open spaces were little treats along our 2178-mile journey and offered rare glimpses of the landscape surrounding us.

It was a new playground and as simple as it might sound, always exciting. Suddenly we could see our surroundings, feel the sun on our backs, and hold our face against the wind. A clear pathway cut over the landscape, sometimes visible from miles away: either a bare dirt track or silvery grass that had been flattened by the boots of others. We could see if the trail was going up or down, if it skirted a mountain or climbed deliberately up and over it. We saw thru-hikers ahead and behind. The sudden, new-found freedom of these open spaces had us giggling and behaving like school children.

One such place was the Grayson Highlands in Virginia. Regarded as a highlight of the trail, it leaves a lasting memory with most thru-hikers. The 4522-acre area passes near Mt Rogers and Whitetop Mountain, Virginia's two highest peaks.

Grayson, as with most areas where I broke out of the woods, caught me by surprise. First of all the sun blinded me, then the heat hit me and I dropped my pack scrabbling around for my sunglasses and cream.

This is fantastic! Look at all this space!

I had lost track of Daffy again, hearing through the hiker grapevine that he was a couple of days back. I had no idea of Lazagne's location and rumour had it that PJ had slowed down drastically because of some sort of foot ache. It didn't bother me; I enjoyed their company but to be honest, sometimes the nomad kicked in and all I yearned for was space, solitude and quiet. I had all three in abundance.

The light was mesmerising. Early morning sunrays spliced through a low, weak mist like probing searchlights. Dew glistened on wet grass, infinite clusters of sparkling jewels — and clouds drifted lazily across the landscape as the sun lifted higher, their shadows speeding over me. I could see weather

112

patterns miles distant. Brooding clouds tormenting the land, toying with it until the storm unleashed its anger.

Grayson is home to herds of ponies introduced to control the grass and most are used to humans. Stop for a break, rustle a food bag and before long a curious few will wander over hoping for a titbit and some even demand a few strokes.

I reached the Wise Shelter and pitched my tent nearby. After tallying up my mileage for the day, I was pleased to see another hundred miles had been passed, bringing me up to 500 in total. I was just under 25% done.

Rain fell overnight, perhaps seeming heavier because I had no trees for protection and after lying in my tent watching tiny explosions of water erupt as the rain smacked into the ground, I decided it wasn't going to stop and set off. The trail was transformed into dark mud and large pools had formed. Some sections had become creeks in themselves and I squelched through, the dirt muddying my shoes before being washed clean by the torrent further on.

I reached the Scales livestock corral and made a beeline for the only sheltered area, a roof overhanging the privy. Snot Rocket and Anchor joined me as we peeled off waterproofs, steam rising from our bodies in gratification for the release.

I walked with Tripping Yeti in the afternoon and, after the rain had finally stopped, spent time observing how my environment came back to life.

After the noise of the rain gradually subsided, little changes happened around me. Where the tree canopy thinned, the residual drips stopped; and once back in denser woods, water plopped with a satisfying smack onto my head. It became quieter, the sun emerged and started to dry the land out, steam rose making the air humid and wet plant leaves appeared polished. The birds chirped, sounding like an orchestra and slowly, the insects emerged and buzzed around me. Just like us thru-hikers after hiding from a storm, we tentatively peek out from our shelters and gradually venture out once more.

Chapter 7
The Wapiti Shelter Murders

May 9th to May 16th
Mile 523 to 620

Infatuated by the prospect of pizza and lost in thought, I sped along an easy trail towards the Partnership shelter before stopping abruptly in mid-stride, alarmed at the cacophony behind me. For a few seconds I dared not turn around, confused and afraid of whatever was responsible for the deafening roar that was rapidly closing in on me.

Eventually, cautiously, I turned around to see a wall of water speeding towards me through the woods. I was on the very front edge of a rainstorm and it was coming right for me. In panic, I reached for the side pocket where I kept my poncho and umbrella. They both snagged on the pack strapping as I desperately tugged to release them. I looked up — so heavy was the downpour that it appeared like a waterfall, bearing down on me with frightening speed.

Shit! SHIT! Fozzie! Do something and make it quick!

Of the limited options available, I chose to run. I realised as I sped through the woods that the whole idea was just plain ridiculous.

What are you doing?! You can't outrun a storm!

Like a frightened hiker running from a rampaging bear, I continued to flee. Focusing on the immediate trail ahead, I quickly scanned the ground for obstacles, jumping over tree roots, leaping for boulders before springing off into mid-air and landing, the momentum making me slide on the slick ground. I darted from side to side avoiding obstacles whilst occasionally flicking my head around to see if I was making any headway.

Unfortunately I wasn't.

Oh crap! Go faster! Run you bloody idiot! Run for fuck's sake!

I started giggling like a child, laughing at the absurdity of it all. The mad turmoil was gaining on me and eventually, after a couple of minutes, I could go no further. Collapsing in a heap of sweat and gasping in air, I watched as the wave raced the final few feet towards me like a surfer might study a breaker and I braced myself.

The dispersed wind hit me first, smashing into me, almost knocking me over. Then the torrent engulfed me and within a minute it had passed. I sat there soaked, drunk and intoxicated by the sheer energy of the elements that I had been fortunate enough to witness. It was unbelievably invigorating.

***

The abundance of time that a thru-hiker is blessed with means thinking becomes a novelty. During our normal lives we believe we do have time to think but, actually, we merely skim the surface. With not much else to do except walk, we become lost in our own thoughts, almost meditating. We can study any topic with a depth of detail that is hard to explain. Instead of spending a few minutes trying to solve a problem before something interrupts us, on the trail I used to spend days pondering various subjects — and not just the usual, boring topics such as finances, or work, but a host of diverse areas as simple, even, as the rain. And boy, when it rained out there, it really rained.

The physical side took care of itself and left the mind free to wander, so once the legs were warmed up the mind started to drift. I pondered what I was doing and how lucky I was to be experiencing it. Would dinner be rice or pasta? Would I camp that night or sleep in a shelter? Or I got the chance to spend time studying everyday things like the weather, or as I liked to call it, precipitation observation studies.

It's not that I got bored, far from it. When life was simplified, the grey matter spent valuable time exploring subjects that we didn't normally bother with because we think of them as mundane and not worthy of focus in our busy lifestyles. However, even areas that we perceive as possibly boring, or unworthy of our attention, can prove fruitful.

Rarely did we get a light shower; more often than not it was a torrential downpour. We had been lucky: the first two weeks were amazing weather, a couple of nights a storm passed over but during the day I had only been rained on, briefly, about five times. Thing is, those times had all been in the last week. Because I was enclosed by the forest most of the time, it was difficult to see the sky for a clue as to what was coming. Occasionally I glimpsed a dark cloud, or just overcast skies through the foliage so I began to employ my other senses for clues. The wind picking up was often a sure sign that there may be a storm blowing in, and if the temperature dropped that backed up the assumption. There was another sense which I couldn't put my finger on — it wasn't a smell or taste, more a sensation that rain was imminent, this I referred to as the 'Alert Stage'.

During the alert stage I looked up, checked on the clouds and if a few tiny droplets brushed past my cheek, this put me on 'Red Alert Stage'. I stopped and listened. Sound was the biggest clue to what nature intended. If I heard the rustling of water as it hit the leaves and undergrowth then a decision had to be made. Did I stop, don my poncho and have umbrella at the ready? Or did I, often foolishly, kid myself into thinking it would stop and I didn't need to bother?

The pattern was similar every time: the droplets became heavier, increased in frequency and then, reluctantly, I stopped to prepare. All hell usually broke loose during the procedure of wrapping up. The thunder roared, fierce winds whipped through my surroundings bending over tree limbs and it was a race to weatherproof myself. During an Appalachian storm the roar of water cascading down through the canopy onto the forest floor was deafening. The path was transformed into a torrent, cascading down the trail as if it owned it. After five minutes or fifteen, maybe an hour, the deluge abated and for another half hour I kept the umbrella up to see off the last of the droplets spilt from the trees. Then, the amazing experience was the birds, signalling that it was all over — quiet one second then an avian orchestra filled the air and told me it had past, everything was safe.

Apart from the initial warnings and using my senses to gauge if it would rain, I also spent time observing the rain itself. First was the temperature of the water, which was often cold during the first month, the tail end of winter — especially at the higher elevations. Exposed skin such as hands, and my lower legs

which my poncho didn't cover, became numb in minutes. Also, my arms, protruding from the poncho, became goose pimpled in retaliation and, eventually, my hands ceased to function properly. As the elements warmed, so did the rain but even so, it was often an invigorating experience to be cooled.

Velocity also came into play. Sometimes, at one end of the spectrum, I experienced just a fine spray, almost a mist, that gently stroked over me and caused me to wipe my face, eyes and the droplets that collected in my beard. At the other end were the angry torrents which were sometimes so heavy that it felt as though I were underwater. Appalachian storms were often so intense that it was a battle to stay dry; hikers were beaten into submission and we longed for a shelter to escape the anger.

Then there was the angle of onslaught. In the woods the trees sheltered the winds somewhat so the rain often hit the west side of the Appalachian hills before being subdued and falling vertically. However, in the rare open spaces, such as meadows, it slammed into me from one side. I pulled my umbrella down to my side, bracing it against me from a near-horizontal pounding. Coming from the front, there was little I could do. The umbrella would obscure my field of vision so I had to hold it slightly aloft and study the ground just visible in front of me. Often resigned that the rain had gotten the better of me from a headlong attack, I merely let it slam into me and scrunched my eyes nearly shut, bowing my head down to escape the stinging on my face.

These storms did follow similar patterns. I knew, roughly, what to expect taking in all these factors so I knew how to deal with them. Thankfully, save a few days when it rained for hours, the storms eventually passed over, chased by the wind — and there were long respites to dry myself and keep an eye out for the next one. For the most part I enjoyed the novelty of them. The forest was spring-cleaned, the air became fresher and the experience was invigorating.

***

I reached the Partnership shelter quickly, chatted to Tyvek who was breaking camp and reached the Mt Rogers Visitor Center shortly after. Several despondent hikers including Snot Rocket and Anchor informed me that a pizza delivery was out of the question because no one was answering their phone. I called Dinosaur.

"I'm at the Visitor Center, just got in!"

"OK, I'm on my way!" she replied.

Dinosaur had already walked the AT in 2006 and I had met her on the PCT in 2010 with Swayze, her boyfriend at the time. Our paths had crossed several times on the journey. She had always taken the time to chat and her infectious personality shone through. Her trail name came about after lack of funds for the AT meant she had to use her Dad's forty-year-old Kelty backpack from his days in the Scouts, which managed just over 600 miles and several dental floss repairs before giving up. She called it her Dinosaur and subsequently took the name for herself. A true outdoors lover, not just content to spend time in the outdoors whilst thru-hiking, she carried this passion over to her work as a member of the Konnarock trail crew based out of Sugar Grove. This group did a lot of work in the Grayson Highlands but co-operated with several other trail clubs, the Appalachian Trail Conservancy and the US Forest Service to look after sections of the trail from Rockfish Gap, near Waynesboro, Virginia, all the way back to the start at Springer mountain itself.

I had never done any trail work but Dinosaur had suggested a little food and lodging in exchange for a couple of days' work which I had jumped at. The Konnarock crew hosted several volunteers each week who gave a week or two of their time to maintain the AT and stay at the Sugar Grove premises.

She pulled up in an ageing '93 Toyota Corolla which squeaked when she went round corners, gave me a hug and off we squeaked. Stopping briefly, so I could solve my hunger crisis with a huge sandwich, we arrived at Konnarock where I was introduced to Dave Hebert, AKA Czar, or the Louisiana Bear who ran the show.

The original building of the AT was only part of the story. The trail is subject to constant wear and tear, not just from hikers but more often from the weather. Maintenance involves surface repair in high traffic areas and protection from the elements. Water will always follow the path of least resistance and often it's the trail itself that unintentionally acts as drainage. Water bars, which are designed to direct water off the trail, consist of either wooden or stone barriers built across the trail to divert water off to the side. Steps are often built, especially in areas of high traffic such as trailheads near roads where day trippers also use the trail. Then there is the clearing of undergrowth encroaching onto the trail, removal of fallen trees and a host of other areas to contend with. It's a constant battle to keep the AT open and the hard, physical work is untaken by a dedicated band of maintenance crews working long hours in all sorts of conditions: rain, snow, cold and heat. Their toil is appreciated, but often taken for granted. Not only was I looking forward to the experience but, as with a lot of thru-hikers, giving something back to the trail which has been a big part of their life is something they do gladly.

We worked for two days in the Grayson Highlands on a section of steep trail suffering from erosion. A series of steps had to be constructed mainly from incredibly heavy boulders, utilised from the immediate area. It was hard work; the logistics and sheer physical effort required just to move these beasts were huge. An approximate hole was excavated by eye according to the size of a nearby boulder and then, using a series of straps and several volunteers, it was hauled in short bursts over to the site where it was manoeuvred into place. Adjustments were carried out such as filling in the hole to accommodate the stone so it became stable and didn't rock, and then we moved onto the next one. With around twelve of us on site, I received some small insight into how much work must have been required for the whole of the AT when it took most of us the whole day to install just two of these blocks.

Apart from the exhausting but rewarding work, the other great part of my experience was the food. Dave usually stayed at base camp dealing with the office side of things but also cooked an absolute feast for us every morning and evening.

Appetites were borderline dangerous and as we patiently queued through the kitchen, each edging closer to the pile of food awaiting us, lips were licked, stomachs rumbled and excitement grew. Slowly, each one of us edged closer to various dishes until we were able to pile our plates high, retire to the canteen and placate our hungers. Then we returned for more.

I always voiced my appreciation, as did most thru-hikers, when we walked through a trail maintenance area and after my time at Konnarcok, I had a new found respect for these people that do such a wonderful job of keeping the AT open and usable. My hat is bowed not just to Dinosaur, Dave and the rest of the Konnarock crew but to all the maintenance teams who toil tirelessly.

***

It's not often during my life off trail, when I work my day job that I wake up in the morning with a smile. The prospect of another mundane day rarely excites me so it's with reluctance that I tip myself out of bed and head off to work. On trail, however, once the sun has woken me, smiling is the first thing I do. The prospect of lying in my tent for a few minutes, gearing up to move and planning out the day visually always makes me happy. It's where I'm content in my life at that moment.

More often than not I'm smiling during the day as well and as I reached the Lindamond school, part of an early settlement built in 1894, I ventured inside to view a bygone era and check the visitors book where Lord Horatio Fonsworth, having clearly done some homework on extending his title, had signed off his message as 'Lord Horatio Fonsworth Belvidere Bentley Tiberius III, Esq.' I was smiling for the rest of the day.

The trail left the school through a meadow, one of several that dotted Virginia. A silver, flattened line of grass wove through, snagging my trekking poles. I often caught a tantalising glimpse of these open spaces from the confines of the woods above as I descended. Farms dotted the area and as well as the teasing little views from the hills, there were audible clues too: the distant hum of a tractor or mower, dogs barking, livestock, or perhaps a car engine humming along a narrow country lane.

The plan, loose as always, was to put in five, twenty-mile days to get to Pearisburg. There I hoped to catch a ride back to Damascus to experience Trail Days.

I passed Pops and Apollo sheltering from the fierce sun in the middle of a meadow under a giant oak tree. They invited me to sit with them and as I lay down my pack and took a rest in the grass, Pops handed me a cold beer fresh from a recent resupply. I felt no urge to move; the heat was intense and the beer refreshing. We all stayed there for a couple of hours, relaxing, catching up on the trail gossip, watching birds soar above us and taking in the sounds of a quiet afternoon in the Virginia countryside.

Pops was highly respected on the trail. 53 years old and with long grey hair tied back into a ponytail, his beard reached his chest and he was tanned from a life outdoors. His lean frame suggested he looked after himself, and often he would hold court in a conversation, delivering his own insights, thoughts and views on all manner of subjects wisely and with great insight. Everyone loved Pops.

It wasn't until after I returned from the trail and was watching a film called *Hard Way Home,* made by Kori 'Rocket' Feener who had hiked the AT that same year, did I realise how wise Pops was. Kori filmed him on a few occasions and one of the lines he delivered had me nodding in agreement.

And those great souls that have learnt to let go, out here like us we let go, we put on packs, we hike in mountains. We've let go of the TV, the illusions, the jobs, the insurance and all these other concepts that have been holding us into this man made world, instead of being lifted up into God's creation in this life we have.

So, let go.

***

The overnight weather didn't bode well. I had camped in the woods, miles from anywhere after coming up just short of my twenty-mile target with a nineteen. As my water boiled ready to make coffee, I packed up my stuff, occasionally grabbing a handful of granola. Enjoying the caffeine rush, I sat and watched my world slowly wake up. A stream quietly gurgled to my side as it weaved through rhododendron bushes, the sandy bottom clearly visible through its waters. The woods were silent save the birds heralding another day and a weak mist occasionally floated past only to disappear, letting the sun warm me once more.

I had earmarked Chestnut Knob shelter to escape the rain. Despite its meagre capacity of eight, I figured arriving mid-afternoon would secure me one of the spots. AWOL's guide also promised that the shelter not only boasted four concrete walls but a door as well. Time spent outdoors has a wonderful way of teaching us what we perceive is important and it puts our lives into perspective, reminding us of how little we need to be content — case in point that I was excited to be spending the night with the bonus of four walls and a door. Life couldn't have been much simpler.

There were eighteen miles to Chestnut Knob but also around 4500 feet of climbing to get there. A clear sky and piercing sun suggested the weather forecast may have been wrong as I watched emerald leaves turn silver with light bouncing off them, and chinks of sunlight blinded me as the leaves occasionally lifted in the breeze, providing a clear passage through.

Relishing the meadows, I followed blazes painted on posts driven into the ground, sentinels pointing the way. My shoes and trousers became soaked from the overnight dew which coated the grass and glistened in a low sun. Virginia rolled casually, somewhat easier than the previous states and although it boasted some big mountains, the climbs seemed gentler. I crossed wooden stiles over quiet, potholed country roads as an occasional tractor bumped along. Deer bounded away as I startled them and cows eyed me curiously from a distance. I longed for the shade of the woods when out in the open and, conversely, looked forward to the warmth of the sun when walking through the woods. At the top of each hill, I stopped and looked back at where I had travelled. I was once told that the best views are sometimes behind, and more importantly, it would probably be the last time I ever saw them. Then I turned away, held the image, stored it somewhere safe and carried on towards Maine.

I took a break by some unexpected trail magic just off the small country lane left by Lumberjack and Labrat who were previous thru-hikers. Two coolers excited me as it was another hot day and I longed for a sweet drink; anything else was a bonus. Sure enough, one was brimming and unashamedly I took the last cold Coke, opening the other to see what goodies it contained. Joy of joys! Peanut butter and jelly sandwiches accompanied by a note saying they had been made just that morning. There was even a piece of paper detailing the latest weather forecast, confirming the news I had heard from others that rain was on the way. Thirsty, a thru-hiker who I had met briefly at the Fontana Hilton arrived and lived up to his trail name as he gladly popped open another can. We subsequently spent fifteen minutes belching and laughing at our good fortune.

He left just before me and I spotted him half a mile ahead as we finished off the final four miles. A pond two miles before the shelter signalled our water source and several other hikers were filling up. There was a queue of about six before me on account of the limited space around the shallow stream. I looked back to see more hikers approaching and, concerned that I would miss a place at the shelter, I scrabbled through some undergrowth. Further upstream a small pool emerged and I dipped my mug in the shallow water and poured the contents into my water bag. By the time I had finished I had bypassed the line and nipped out before those coming up the hill.

Chestnut Knob shelter sat in a clearing commanding fine views back down the trail. Not only did it sport four walls and a door, but also a couple of windows as well. I grabbed a bottom bunk closest to the door as slowly, a steady stream of hikers dribbled in and the shelter filled.

With a recommended capacity of eight, after everyone had squeezed in, the number rose to twenty. Far from being cramped, everyone took care with their space and it was surprisingly comfortable. Some sat on their bunks, like me, cooking their evening meals, writing their journals and other tasks, whilst Pops took a place at the small table and made hot chocolate with bourbon for everyone who wanted one. Laughter filled the air, conversation was animated and good cheer echoed around.

As each of us slowly succumbed to tired limbs, Chestnut Knob quietened until the last light went out and Pops blessed us all.

"Good night my friends, be safe and God bless you. I love y'all, you hear? I love y'all."

"Night Pops."

The woods were a murky, damp world when I left Chestnut Knob. A mist hung low and intermittent rain fell for most of the morning. There was no wind, and it was eerily quiet save the gentle plopping of water on the sodden ground around me. I made my way down a slick trail onto a dirt track, just off the VA-623. Thirsty was huddled under some trees with Embassador and Flint, trying unsuccessfully to roll a cigarette and debating taking up an offer of lodgings posted on a tree by the local church. I nodded a greeting and, eager to keep warming up, I carried on into the trees.

I paused momentarily, thinking I had heard a cry from behind me.

"Fozzie!"

I had; it was Thirsty.

"Yeah?" I called back.

"A guy called Bush Goggles is down the trail. We're staying at the church place. Tell him we ain't gonna make camp tonight!"

I caught the gist of what he was shouting but misheard the

name.

"Who?" I called.

"Bush Goggles!" He cried.

"I'll tell him!"

I didn't catch him up until some four miles later at the Jenkins shelter. There was no one else about and Bush Goggles sat on the edge of the sleeping platform, swinging his legs and taking a rest from the rain. I sat beside him, keen also to spend a few minutes out of the damp.

"Are you Bush Goggles?" I asked.

"Yup, sure am," he replied.

"I have a message from Thirsty. They're gonna stay at the church place tonight."

"Oh OK, thanks. Where you heading?"

"Dunno. Helveys Mill shelter looks good for the mileage I'm doing."

Dallas 'Bush Goggles' Nustvold was 23 and came from Minneapolis, Minnesota. He grinned a lot, mischievously, as though he had just played a prank on someone and was anticipating the moment they found out. His hair was short but his beard was sprouting proudly; in fact he had more hair on his face than his head. He was so named after casting some admiring glances at a member of the fairer sex one day in Gatlinburg. When she turned around and wasn't as attractive as the rear view had suggested, Trevelyan 'Walkabout' Edwards, an Australian hiker, chastised him.

"Christ mate, you got your bush goggles on!"

Bush goggles is an Australian slang term describing someone's attraction to a — let's say — *homely* person of the opposite sex caused by isolation, such as working in a mine, or in this case, too long spent in the woods.

He was young, in good shape and eager to put in some miles. Walking quickly, perhaps a little above my normal pace, it was like walking behind a pacemaker. I could stay with him but it was a decent workout. His official employment title was an environmental contractor site superintendent. This was far too much of a mouthful so I decided to refer to him as a builder to simplify things.

Chez 11, Deep and a few others were spread about Helveys Mill shelter. Bush Goggles preferred to sleep in a tent, a bright yellow tunnel model which was unusual in that the entrance was on the top; instead of crawling in, it was more a case of stepping in.

Gear hung from every available hook drying out. Seeing the privy a way off in the trees, and eager for a visit, when I opened the door I discovered there was no roof so I went back to retrieve my umbrella. I had several unusual experiences on the AT but sitting on the bog, with my umbrella in the rain was a first.

***

I planned to return to Damascus Trail Days for a weekend so I had put in a couple of twenty-five-mile days to make up for the mileage deficit that Trail Days would incur. I had also passed the 600-mile mark and was into the fourth state of Virginia. Fighting fit, I had not suffered from any blisters. My legs felt strong, my head in order and despite the AT still proving difficult in terms of the ascents and descents, I was hiking well and confidently.

Daffy had dropped back again and although I hadn't seen him, Chez 11 said he had seen a couple of messages in the trail registers from him. PJ had disappeared and I hadn't seen Lazagne for a couple of days. When I checked my email, a message from Lazagne solved everyone's whereabouts, advising they were all in Bland. The bad news was that PJ had suffered a possible stress fracture in his foot. Although I hoped he would be OK to carry on and the diagnosis was wrong, I knew deep down that he had a problem.

Injuries, depending on the severity, can and do end thru-hikes. Most of us are a stubborn bunch, and despite what the doctors or physios tell us (on the rare occasions when we actually bother to see one), we usually ignore it. Some carry on with injuries, and it is possible to do so depending on the type, but the risk is that the repercussions later on can be more serious.

The standard joke on trail about doctors is that whenever a thru-hiker pays a visit, regardless of the problem, the advice is always 'get off trail'. Therefore we usually don't bother making an appointment. A few may rest for a day or two if something hurts and then carry on ignoring the problem, hoping it will go away. If I'm not thru-hiking, the advice I remember from a physio a few years back is to wait for the pain to stop, then rest for a further two weeks without exercise. Invariably, the pain usually takes ten to fourteen days to stop, meaning an injury can mean taking a month out. If I'm hiking and somewhere starts hurting, I may slow down but normally I hope, pray to the god of muscles and injuries, grin, bear it and carry on.

Stress fractures are common to the feet where repetitive stress over long periods of time mean the muscles, unable to cope, transfer the load to the bones which results in hairline fractures. When I read about PJ's problem in Lazagne's email I feared the worst. I had full faith in PJ — he was focused, determined and intent to finish the trail. However, stress fractures aren't something to be ignored, thru-hiking or not. PJ, for the time being at least, appeared to be out of the hunt.

Hikers, runners, cyclists and most sportspeople have experienced injury and it's a huge disappointment. Even with drugs and remedies it is often weeks before they can return to training. Rest is the only sure fire method to cure most problems. Not only do you have to rest, but most of the hard work spent training is then subsequently lost.

I have been fortunate, except for one occasion on El Camino, not to have been injured on a thru-hike. Pushing hard one day in Spain I pulled my right calf. I slowed my pace somewhat but carried on to the end in Santiago. Twelve years later and it still aches if I ask too much of it.

Six weeks before I was due to travel to California to start my Pacific Crest Trail hike, whilst out running, I pulled up quickly with a sharp pain in my right knee. The diagnosis was runner's knee, a common injury with sportspeople, especially, unsurprisingly, runners. The prognosis was not good; my local physio advised it could mean up to eight months of rest. I looked at him in horror, said I had six weeks maximum and asked him to do everything he could to fix it. A week before my departure it still hurt, albeit only a fraction of the original pain. It was a risk, he admitted, but advised that I go and hike. If anything, the actual exercise would strengthen the surrounding area and support the injury. Thankfully, it was fine although as with my ankle, it still twinges from time to time.

On the North Downs Way, a 140-mile trail local to where I live in south east England, I was into day one of the hike when my right extensor digitorum longus, a muscle running down the outside of the lower leg, began to ache. I ignored it but later the same day, I rolled my ankle on a right hand camber which pulled it sharply and a pain shot up my leg. I foolishly carried on and amazingly, given that I rarely roll my ankles, I did exactly the same thing later.

The pain did subside but I was hobbling for a week after returning home when I had finished. The physio ordered rest, which put me out of hiking for three months. The result is that now, although it never hurts, I can only describe the sensation of a Velcro strip running down the outside of my leg — which, on a bad day, feels as though it is constantly being pulled away and stuck back repeatedly.

The drug of choice for thru-hikers is Ibuprofen. Although now associated with stomach ulcers, it is the preferred pain reliever and also reduces swelling. I always carried it but used it sparingly, usually when I was flagging in the afternoon and the legs started to ache a little. Most took 200 mg — although some thru-hikers became immune to the lower doses with constant use and would take up to 800 mg, sometimes even more.

I also carried caffeine tablets. Due to an unfortunate lack of coffee bars in the middle of the Appalachian woods, I enjoyed the hit. The energy boost was almost immediate and come the middle of the afternoon, along with a couple of Ibuprofen, my body reacted gratefully. For at least two hours, the aches subsided, the energy rocketed and if I had a flattish trail, I could quite happily cover eight miles in less than two hours. The negative side of this was that I increased the chances of injury by pushing too hard so had to reign in my enthusiasm.

Often it was the easier, flatter sections of trail where I got injured because I could push harder. Virginia was a classic example and kinder — the severe ups and downs had subdued somewhat. Bush Goggles and I enjoyed a more relaxed hike, thankfully without aches and pains. We passed Jenny Knob shelter, scampered down the hill to the wonderfully-sounding Lickskillet Hollow, cranked out a further five miles to the Kimberling Suspension Bridge and shortly after, popped out on the VA-606.

Trent's Grocery was a mere half-mile west. I turned to Bush Goggles.

"Hungry? Burger?"

He merely grinned and shortly after, re-fuelled, we sped along the eight miles to the Wapiti shelter, dodging and running scared of thunderstorms. The small shelter sat just off trail, and a faint track wove down to a creek through thin woodland. The rain had stopped and sunlight filtered through the canopy, dancing on the ground. There was no wind and only birdsong broke a still, quiet evening.

Its beguiling atmosphere offered no clues to the bloody events that happened there in May, 1981. Or perhaps the ethereal woods were still in mourning.

Robert Mountford Jr. and his hiking companion Susan Ramsay had pulled into the Wapiti shelter to stay for a night during their thru-hike. They had befriended a local, Randall Smith, who had charmed his way into their trust and also stayed at the shelter. Smith lived nearby in Pearisburg and knew the area well. Having a fondness for the woods he made regular trips there. A welder by trade, he worked occasionally when he needed money.

After they had settled down and were sleeping, Smith shot Mountford Jr. in the head with a .22 calibre handgun. Having woken, Ramsay was then repeatedly and violently stabbed. Post mortem reports revealed her hands had received injuries, suggesting she was awake and had tried to defend herself. When both hikers failed to turn up in Pearisburg, police first searched the Wapiti shelter as it was the nearest one to town. Blood was discovered between the floorboards and a search of the immediate area revealed both Ramsay and Mountford Jr. buried in the sleeping bags.

Smith was arrested a few weeks later, subsequently found guilty and sentenced to thirty years in jail. There are numerous theories about why he carried out the killings, one being that he had made a pass at Ramsay which Mountford Jr. had intervened in. Some say the killings were revenge for Ramsay's rebuke and his dislike for Mountford Jr. Unfortunately Smith, despite his incarceration, didn't change.

He was released on parole in 1996 after serving just fifteen years. He caused no trouble in jail and was in fact described as a model prisoner. Over the subsequent twelve years, he scraped a living from welding and, when out fishing in 2008, had camped in the woods again just a mile and a half from the Wapiti shelter.

He befriended Scott Johnston of Bluefield, VA, out on a fishing trip with his friend Sean Farmer of Tazewell, VA. Smith chatted to Johnston, complaining that he had caught nothing and Johnston, feeling sorry for him, opened his cooler and handed him a bag of his fish. Johnston told him where he was camped with Farmer and invited him to dinner that evening.

Smith spent several hours with the two men that evening after they cooked trout and beans for him, even feeding Smith's dog.

He eventually got up, and having walked a few paces, pulled a gun from his pocket, turned and shot Johnston in the neck. He then turned the gun at Farmer and shot him point blank in the chest. Johnston, despite his injury, fled into the woods as Smith let off another volley of bullets after him, and one hit him again in the nape of the neck.

Farmer struggled to his truck a few yards away as Smith caught him and pointed the gun at him once more, but it failed to fire; he had run out of ammunition. Farmer drove off. His headlights picked out his friend staggering into the road and he swung the door open for him. They both escaped.

They received treatment for their wounds and lived to tell the tale. Smith fled the scene in the vehicle that Johnston had abandoned, but subsequently crashed and was picked up quickly by the police, to whom he was well known. He was taken to the police cell where later, an officer knocked on his cell door to bring him food and received no answer. He knocked again to no avail and Smith was discovered dead in his cell. It is believed that he died from his injuries sustained in the crash.

I never found out about the killings until after my return from the AT and realised I had not only slept in the shelter where the murders had taken place, but quite possibly slept in the same spot that either Ramsay or Mountford Jr. had met their demise.

***

Just over six miles from the Wapiti shelter a thru-hiker meets a dirt road at Sugar Run Gap. Half a mile east lays Woods Hole Hostel, a place previous thru-hikers had recommended I stay. Set down this quiet road, amongst the surrounding woods, Woods Hole was opened in 1986 by Roy and Tillie Wood; their granddaughter, Neville, continues to run it with her husband Michael.

I crunched down Sugar Run Road, walked through the gates and sat down admiring the chestnut-coloured, red-roofed house built back in the 1880s. Vegetable plots lined the front of the house with healthy, vibrant plants growing strongly. I took off my shoes and walked down a grassy slope to an outbuilding where a few hikers mingled, relaxing. Ken, Margaret, Flint, Thirsty and Bush Goggles all dribbled in as well as Lazagne, fresh from his two-day stopover in Bland sitting out the rain. Even Lord Horatio Fonsworth Belvidere Bentley Tiberius III,

Esq. turned up.

It was a beautiful setting, miles from anywhere and away from any noise intrusion. The atmosphere rubbed off on everyone and we soon relaxed. I showered, did my laundry by hand as there was no machine, read sitting on a log and even managed a game of chess with Lazagne on the hostel's own, real chess board.

We ate like kings and queens that evening, spoilt by a table groaning with home produce. The tradition at Woods Hole dictates that just prior to eating, all thru-hikers gather in a ring around the fire and, holding hands, introduce themselves and say a short piece. I was one of the first and as I watched the introductions filter down the line, I saw it was only a matter of time before Lord Horatio Fonsworth Belvidere Bentley Tiberius III, Esq. had to introduce himself.

I couldn't stop giggling. Before he had even started, just the thought of his eight-worded title was too much. After some tweaking, lengthening, shortening and playing around with, Lord Horatio Fonsworth Belvidere Bentley Tiberius III, Esq. was where he had settled.

I slept in the loft of the outbuilding, next to an open window where the breeze kept me cool and a little moonlight filtered through.

I was excited — Trail Days was imminent.

Chapter 8
Trail Days

May 17th to May 31st
Mile 620 to 800

The Plaza Motel in Pearisburg was quiet but the car rental businesses weren't. I made several calls in vain to try and secure transport for Lazagne and I back down to Damascus, just over 100 miles south. Eventually, tired of trying, we walked through town, placed our packs on the verge beside us and stuck out a thumb. The locals are used to hikers and putting the pack beside me when trying to get a lift is something I always did — it showed that I was not a rampant murderer. Butch Simpkins pulled over a mere five minutes later and took us an hour down the road to Wytheville, as far as he was going. We had barely raised another thumb before Steve and Annie Chambers waved us over from the petrol station and took us all the way to the main street in Damascus. It couldn't have been easier.

The hostel known as the Place, where we had stayed a few days before, was brimming. We were about to pitch in the grounds when Daffy came over and beckoned us to what is known as tent city at the other end of town. A field and the surrounding woods near the creek was packed with hundreds of tents, hammocks, and hikers. The police milled around conspicuously.

Food stalls plied their trade effortlessly as a steady queue of hikers kept them solvent. Equipment manufacturers extolled their latest products and after meeting Ron Bell, owner of Mountain Laurel Designs, he kindly struck me a great deal for one of his Spirit quilts. The advantage of the quilt was that it just lay over me, instead of getting into a sleeping bag which I had

133

always found restricting. I also chatted with the legend that is Tom Hennessy, owner of Hennessy Hammocks and I returned to the woods to sling my new hammock between two suitable trees under the guidance of Lazagne and Daffy. With both the quilt and the hammock, I was relishing the prospect of a good sleep every night.

One of the local churches offered free medical check-ups and after my blood pressure was deemed excellent, they cleaned up a wound on my leg, the result of some overzealous scratching of a mosquito bite in the middle of the night. They washed and massaged my feet and even threw in some cake and a cup of coffee, although I hasten to add not on my feet.

I was delighted to bump into some PCT hikers I had met in 2010 on my thru-hike. Detective Bubbles, Karma and Wiffle Chicken all came over to say hello and Stanimal surprised me in the diner when he walked in the door. Scott 'Squatch' Herriot, who had made a name for himself by producing several films on the PCT, was busy advertising his effort on the AT: 'Flip Flop Flippin', which he had filmed the year before. 'Flip Flop Flippin 2' was a work in progress and he was hiking up and down the AT to film. We parted with a promise to bump into each other at some point on the trail.

I awoke the following morning in the same position as I had gone to sleep; the hammock was that comfortable. At last, I hoped, my lack of sleep in tents was behind me. Walking back through town with Daffy and Lazagne, we dodged an onslaught from the traditional water fight and hiker parade before getting a ride back to Pearisburg with K2 and Tarp Water who had managed to hire a car. They dropped us at the Plaza Motel, I debated staying another night but the need for mileage got the better of me — although I did take up Earthling and Yodler's offer of a quick shower in their room. I left alone and made a quick five miles to camp.

The ensuing days were quiet. Hiker numbers had dwindled, partly due to some still working their way back from Damascus and also because, approaching the end of the second month on the AT, many had given up. The first month sees many hikers drop out of their thru-hike for various reasons: it was physically and psychologically harder than they had thought, finances weren't holding up, blisters were too much to handle or the experience just didn't suit them.

Daffy and Lazagne had travelled back from Pearisburg to take five days out with relatives so I was on my own for much of the time, albeit with some familiar faces cropping up. I didn't mind the solitude — in fact I bathed in it. I am met with surprised looks from people when I tell them about thru-hiking and even further amazement when they realise I go alone. On any thru-hike, there are many others going solo and I often spend the first couple of weeks socialising briefly with others, chatting and finding out about them. I quickly realise who I could spend more time with and subsequently I do hike with others, but equally relish the prospect of time alone. On the PCT I thrived over one section of the Sierra Nevada, where I saw no-one for five days.

On the AT there are literally thousands attempting a thru-hike each year, less on the PCT and under a hundred on the CDT, although the figures enjoy a steady upward curve. The option is always there for company if needed. Friendships are tested to their limits on thru-hikes, even if you go out with your best friend — suddenly spending twenty-four hours a day in their company stretches even the closets of alliances and it is something I have never done for that reason. I prefer to spend time with those that I meet and connect with but I can honestly say that I could have quite happily hiked the whole of the AT on my own, seeing no one.

I'm an introvert by nature. Shy as a kid, it is only the last ten years that I have come out of my shell and become more confident. During my twenties I suffered from long bouts of depression because of an inability to socialise in groups of more than four people. I hated being the centre of attention, struggled expressing myself and hid away at home, sometimes not venturing out for weeks except to work. I declined invitations to attend social events because I couldn't deal with them.

Introverts have always had a raw deal. Society has pushed the extrovert on us as the successful human being, the one we should all strive to become but I don't buy into that. Their confidence does indeed give them the ability to make a success of careers and their characters handle social situations easily. They thrive and gain energy from being amongst others.

Introverts prefer to stay in the background. We recharge through solitude and easily drain with too much social stimulation. This, you would think, may suggest that the extroverts make more successful people and although around 50 to 65% of the population are extroverts, bear in mind that Bill Gates is an introvert, as were Abraham Lincoln, Albert Einstein and Mahatma Gandhi. The extrovert may be the one at the helm of the board meeting, holding court and controlling the room but it's the quiet person sat at the back who is digesting the events, turning them over and coming up with the great ideas.

Being introverted is a great attribute for which I am grateful. I wouldn't change it. My best ideas come when I am alone and I feel energised through solitude, I live for it and I thrive through it. I will always escape to my local hills when I can, usually in the middle of the week when they are quieter — and within minutes, my escape from the madness of society makes me happy. I am able to think clearly on my own.

My ability to thrive away from people often reaches extremes. During my time on the AT not only did I revel in the occasional bout of solitude, as rare as it was, but often I escaped further. At the end of the day, I'd take a side trail, or even tramp through the undergrowth to get away. I'd spend a solitary evening there, and quite often the following morning as well, immersed in my own company and thoughts. If I heard hikers ahead of me I would take a break to let them move on. Conversely, if I knew people were behind me I'd increase my pace to escape.

At the far end of the solitude spectrum, where I could push the boundaries of this world no more, I dreamt up scenarios to please my isolation further. I fantasied about the apocalypse, the final days of humankind where I never saw another soul — a lone survivor drifting through a world of decaying cities and towns. Surveying a legacy rotting, crumbling and deteriorating, I was free to wander, a dromomaniac indulging their ultimate fantasy. As extreme and intense as it may sound, I know I would be happy there.

Thru-hiking is my escape. It is the only time that I am free to spend several months devoid of regulations and to live my life with minimal constraints. Or, to quote James Thurber:

"Two is company, four is a party, three is a crowd. One is a wanderer."

***

I crossed the VA-630 and walked over a footbridge, neglecting to collect water for the evening camp. The AT climbed 1300 feet to Bruisers Knob and I swallowed harshly as I reached the summit, my mouth dry and starved of moisture. I grabbed my water bottle from the side pocket of my pack and poured out a last, warm, pathetic dribble.

Shit, Fozzie. Why didn't you pick up water?

The trail emerged from the shade of the woods and an afternoon sun blazed. Sweat dripped down my face; my shirt was dark and sodden with perspiration. I sat down, wiped a hand across my forehead and looked at my palm as a mix of dirt, sweat, salt and sunscreen left an oily mess. My hair was oily, matted and smelt, as did I. My fingernails appeared like black crescent moons, dark with ingrained dirt and my legs were caked with a layer of dust and sweat, interspersed with red, swollen mosquito bites.

I checked the guidebook. Sarver Hollow shelter nestled, somewhat annoyingly, half a mile down a steep hill off the trail and the water source was even further down. It was the only water for five miles and my day was coming to an end. I didn't need the walk down — and more importantly back up again — and I didn't want to see anyone at the shelter. I wanted to be alone. Begrudgingly I sat up, hoisted my pack and trudged down. Faces I didn't recognise were setting up for the night in Sarver Hollow, but I nodded a greeting to Tinkerbell whom I had already met and carried on down to collect water. Slowly, in the sapping heat I walked back up to the ridge.

The views either side opened out majestically as I made my way along the ridge towards Sinking Creek Mountain. Ominous clouds piled up the east side and rain shadows darkened the lowlands. I glanced to the west, felt a strong wind coming straight at me with more threatening clouds getting closer. The heavens opened in a matter of minutes so I ducked into the woods and searched for a suitable camp spot. The ground sloped sharply down the west side of the ridge which didn't bother me because I now had the hammock which could pitch over any uneven ground. I took it out and searched for the two support slings which wrapped around the trees at either end. I couldn't find them.

Wind started to tear through the woods. I looked up as trees creaked overhead and gales tore at the leaves. I was a little exposed but the woods offered some shelter and it wasn't cold; at worst I would get wet. I retrieved the waterproof flysheet and fashioned two, weak anchor points between the trees, low to the ground. I had sent my air pad back because it wasn't used in the hammock and instead, piled up leaves for insulation and a modicum of comfort. For a little more insulation, I lay my groundsheet and pack down. The fly was perfect for the hammock but, not designed for use low to the ground, it was a little narrow and as I cooked my meal, the sides lifted in the gusts and rain worked underneath.

I spent an uncomfortable night with little sleep. Although I stayed relatively dry, stones protruded from the uneven ground and I had to adjust my position constantly. As I lifted my pack to clear away, the two, lost hammock slings peered at me mockingly.

Clouds had congregated in the valley appearing like a vast ocean below me. Distant ridges appeared briefly through the cloud before disappearing like huge serpents. I descended down to Craig Creek road, passing Juggles and Rainbow Eyes collecting water just before the Niday shelter. I had met Juggles briefly and we chatted. He had also heard that PJ's stress fracture was confirmed and he was taking a month off trail to recuperate.

I struggled up Cove Mountain and onto the jagged, fluctuating ups-and-downs of a section appropriately known as the Dragon's Tooth which tired me quickly. I wasn't progressing well, my speed was slow, albeit hampered by a difficult section; but I felt lethargic, as though only firing on three cylinders. I put it down to my lack of sleep the previous night.

It was warm, each week the temperature seemed to be increasing and the humidity was creeping up as well. I don't mind walking in a dry heat; on the PCT it often went over 100 F in the Californian desert but there was no humidity so I coped well. However, as soon as it became muggy I struggled, along with everyone else.

The water sources were, thankfully, still flowing and up in the mountains it ran clear and cold. Very often, where we passed these sources, be it usually a creek or spring, we were near the top of the Appalachian hills where the water drained off the summits so the quality was excellent. I filtered everything I drank, even the spring water. My filter unit required no pumping; I just filled up the bottle and screwed the unit on top, then sucked the water through the filter so water stops were quick. I pulled my bottle from a side pocket, dipped it in a creek, screwed the filter back on and I was off, the whole process often taking as little as fifteen seconds.

But as the summer became hotter, the smaller water sources

lower down were drying up or reducing to pathetic dribbles so I couldn't dip my bottle in — they were becoming too shallow. To solve the problem, most hikers would take a leaf, fresh from a nearby bush, and wedge it into the dribble, weighed down with the help of a stone. Often, the water sources would still have these leaves there, thoughtfully left by someone else. The leaf funnelled the water down to its tip where we could hold our bottles underneath.

***

I smiled as I finally reached the top of the hill and saw McAfee Knob. This famous rock outcrop, appearing to protrude like a diving board, is thought to be the most photographed spot on the entire trail. Pick up any AT calendar, or search the internet for Appalachian Trail and sure enough, McAfee Knob will appear somewhere with a hiker sitting on the edge, legs dangling over the precipice.

Unfortunately it was bustling with day trippers when I arrived so I decided to keep going and a good idea it turned out to be. Seven miles further on was the delightfully named Tinker Cliffs, a half-mile section where the trail skirts along the edge of the same precipice, weaving up to and away from the drop. I wondered why this section wasn't more popular. The view was easily on par, if not better and it wasn't centred on one spot, but more of a ten-minute travelling delight. It was also quiet, away from the tourists so only the occasional thru-hiker passed by. Taking full advantage of my loose planning approach, even though it was only 10 a.m., I smiled, dropped my pack and slung up the hammock twenty feet from the edge to indulge in a little randomness.

A cooling breeze lifted up from the valley and swept over me. There I lay, sometimes taking my trekking pole and pushing the ground to sway the hammock. If anyone passed by I occasionally received a greeting which I either ignored, offering a fake snore so I didn't appear rude, or just waved a casual arm in lazy recognition. After days of pushing out miles, it was a wonderful tonic to just stay in one place and experience a small section of the trail for a day instead of a flashing glimpse.

As the sun lowered, a receding light chased it, fighting a losing battle with skies above becoming an inky canvas. Reds joined the celebration brushed with oranges, caressed with yellows and flicked by casual violets. Slowly, my surroundings darkened and I waved my hand, pretending to orchestrate the playing of the stars. They obliged willingly, each one joining in the symphony, visual musical instruments sharing the ensemble.

The moon appeared shyly, peeking over distant mountains and slowly bathed my world in silvers and greys. As it rose, becoming more confident like a child making friends at nursery, its initial coyness fading as it climbed higher to take command of the sky.

I was alone, a solitary hiker, making a small section of the Appalachian Trail my own. This was my home, at least for the night and it welcomed me. There were no noise interruptions save a few leaves rustling. I heard no cars, no planes, nothing except what nature offered me.

Daleville, by stark contrast, was completely the opposite. Situated just off the US-81, it epitomised everything I loathed about some US towns. The VA-220 carved a straight line straight through the middle of a collection of fast food restaurants, garages and motels. It did have everything a thru-hiker could hope for, just lacked character and presentation. I checked into the Howard Johnson Motel, a short walk from where the trail popped out of the woods. Juggles arrived in the afternoon as we had agreed to share a room.

It had been five days since my last wash, which was about normal. Salt stains streaked my shirt, my shorts were blotched with dust and dirt and I picked out debris from the wool entwines of my socks. A clear line of dirt around my ankles contrasted with the white skin of the sock line and my wrinkled feet sported ingrained dirt around the toes and nails.

The problem with laundry day was that everything needed washing, which in turn meant I had nothing to wear. You can always spot a thru-hiker in the laundry because they will either be sitting there sweating in Gore-Tex, the only item of clothing available, or with a meagre towel wrapped around them as they sit tightly crossed legged. I usually did my laundry first because I hated taking a shower to get into dirty clothes. All I had was my poncho so there I sat, in the Howard Johnson laundry room, with a silver section of cuben fibre wrapped around me, scanning the singles ads in some obscure local magazine.

I watched dark brown trickles of water slide off me in the shower and helped myself to a generous portion of shampoo which failed to lather and eventually, after two washes, the drainage ran clear. A sweat rash circled both ankles caused by my socks and a speckled fungus wove in and around my toes as I dusted them with foot powder.

Being filthy on a thru-hike is hard to accept at first but, once resigned to the fact that there is little that can be done, a thru-hiker becomes used to it. Just a day's walk in summer is enough to make most people smell somewhat undesirable, but after five or more days without washing or laundry the aroma reaches a stage where it's borderline dangerous. We don't notice it, as someone may forget they are wearing perfume, and the nose becomes immune after a while.

However, having reached town, if food is first priority (which it often is), once in the air-conditioned environment of a restaurant the smell of our bodies suddenly reaches our noses and we grimace. Arms are raised and arm pits smelt, invitations to smell each other are accepted and waiting staff casually point fans in our direction.

"There you go," a waitress may say, coyly standing as close as she dare. "You'll be more comfortable in this cooler air. Or perhaps you'd like a table outside?"

***

Chris 'Juggles' Chiappini was patching up and repairing some war wounds to his gear when I got back to the room. He came from Midland Park on the outskirts of New York City. As his trail name suggested, he was a professional juggler. Having learnt his craft from a young age, and encouraged by his father, he worked for agencies who found him work. Albeit a niche trade, there isn't exactly an abundance of jugglers out there so he found gigs fairly regularly.

He also wanted to be a stand-up comedian which may paint a picture of a guy that runs off a series of jokes every time you see him. Not so, but it wasn't his lack of material that I found funny, it was his delivery. Even during conversation, I would often ask him a question and he would pause, raise his hand with one finger extended, and look somewhat confused with his mouth slightly ajar, suggesting he was going to answer. But he didn't — for a few seconds, he would ponder the question, occasionally make a false start to respond, and eventually he'd answer. Why I found this funny I don't know, but it just made me laugh.

Bush Goggles appeared in the evening, then Thirsty, and we all spent the evening chatting in the room.

I was glad to get out of Daleville; not an unpleasant place, just lacking identity. I disappeared off into the woods and despite a climb up to the Fullhardt shelter, the hiking was easy. With no big elevation changes, the trail floated along between 2000 to 3000 feet in a series of short, non-taxing ups-and-downs. I stopped briefly to chat to Kaleidoscope and Not Worthy at the Wilson Creek shelter before bouncing up and down the trail further.

Strange insects called from the woods and the mosquitos were out in force. I don't know why I attract mosquitos, or mozzies as I call them. The accepted theory is based on their ability to detect carbon dioxide which all humans emit. Others speculate that increased body temperature and metabolism, blood type and the colour of clothing all have an impact. I don't know what it is I have but if I'm in the vicinity of mozzies, which at that point of my thru-hike was basically everywhere, then I got mauled.

They weren't so prevalent during the hotter daytime temperatures, but came out for feeding when it cooled in the late afternoon and early evening. I prayed for wind, or even a breeze as they couldn't fly well in those conditions and, after a while, I learnt to seek out the ridges at the edge of the tree line where I could count on some airflow. That was the only weapon in my armoury I could rely on.

During the still evenings, as soon as I stopped for camp, I was pounced on. I might have been sitting down eating my dinner when a familiar droning circled around my ear. In between mouthfuls I would swipe the air erratically and slap myself, becoming more frustrated. As their numbers increased, so did my temper. After perhaps thirty minutes of trying to stay calm, I'd eventually just flip out and lose it, much to the amusement of anyone in the vicinity.

"Fuck off will yer?!" I'd yell, jumping around camp smacking the living daylights out of my exposed skin. "Just fuck the fuck off! Seriously! FUCK OFF!"

Deet never worked and I hated using it anyway. The only effective method I'd employed in the past was to don my waterproofs, which they struggled to bite through. Apart from the fact that I'd just sit there with my Gore-Tex slowly filling up with sweat, I hadn't brought them anyway as I used just the poncho. Often I'd retreat into my hammock which, unless one of them stole in before I could zip up the netting, was the only effective method. But, once inside I was restricted to staying there except for mad dash pee breaks.

Thirsty and I had discussed the dilemma and agreed to trial a little known method which we had both read about and agreed made sense. Eating garlic is not the first deterrent that springs to mind for most people but it does, apparently, work. Garlic gets quickly into the blood stream and judging by the smell of most garlic lovers, is also emitted from the pores. Mozzies don't like the smell, or indeed the taste.

Thirsty claimed that it took a week to kick in so I stocked up in town and started throwing two fat cloves into my dinner every evening. Breakfast, however, was proving a problem. Garlic does compliment a lot of food but granola isn't one of them. Believe me, I tried it — it's not good. I love garlic and I really don't care who smells it, on or off trail. However, a raw, fat, garlic clove first thing in the morning on an empty stomach was too much even for my digestive system.

I had managed to chew and swallow some for two mornings but on the third, as I sat there with coffee in hand, staring at a worryingly obese clove, it proved a bad idea. I weighed up the option of either drinking my coffee with a bowl of granola first to line the stomach, or starting with the garlic to get it out of the way and letting the food and drink take the strong taste away. I chose the latter. Garlic is great chopped up into slices and spread around a meal but raw and all at once wasn't a good idea.

I started chewing. The heat hit me first and I started to sweat. Then my sinuses flooded with onion and my eyes watered. Valiant to the last I forced it down, wincing, convinced I was a small way further down the road of insect immunity. My stomach, however, had other plans and immediately ordered an emergency evacuation.

I vomited a mix of brown masticated dinner from the previous night and dark roast Italian coffee. My body immediately felt better but I bemoaned the waste of a decent mug of coffee. After that incident, I stuck to two or three cloves mixed in with my evening meal.

The rhododendrons were now in full bloom and I entered shaded tunnels awash with pink flowers and sweet scent. It was hot and sticky, even up in the mountains, albeit slightly more bearable at higher altitude. The land was green, all the plants were growing quickly and the trees, now sporting a coat of foliage, sheltered me from the sun. I remembered a conversation with Daffy some weeks earlier when I commented on the stark landscape of post winter. "Don't worry Fozzie," he said, "Give it a few weeks and it'll be a God damn jungle out there."

He was right. Whilst the peaks were just changing from browns, the lower elevations were awash with a thousand shades of green. Plants encroached onto the trail, their moisture wetting my clothing and slowly the paths had narrowed as the season wore on. I dodged around poison ivy, ducked under branches and squeezed through overgrown sections.

I loved life in the woods. Many found the confined world amongst the trees too much, some even quitting for that reason, but I was revelling in it. I adored both the open spaces and the trees when I walked anywhere and England offered a varied mix of both. The AT reminded me of home.

I lived in the woods, respected them and in return they looked after me. They shaded me from the fierce sun and shielded me from strong winds. During light showers the canopy above dealt with most of the rain before it even reached me. Streams offered water to drink and at times wild food was found. Occasionally a pool or creek would offer itself up so I could wash and every single night, two stout trees held me aloft as I slept in my hammock. The woods provided firewood for the colder nights and during the warmer nights the smoke chased away some of the mosquitos. I was given logs to sit on or trunks to rest my back against. Sand from the creek beds washed my mug, spoon and even cleaned the grime off my hands.

Take a look at a map of east America and you'll see a broad swathe of green stretching from Georgia all the way up to Maine. The Appalachian Mountains were now my home and the best was still to come. When society collapses, for whatever reason, I will pack my rucksack and run for the woods. I know I can survive there and I know they will help me. I bow to the woods.

***

It was May 28th. I had been on trail for 59 days and covered 745 miles. This was slow progress but expected after my successful anti-blister plan, and it was the first hike I had ever done without suffering from them. My careful start and low-mileage days had worked. The soles of my feet had formed the usual hard covering of skin, the body's method of dealing with constant wear and tear. Two, small ridges ran along the underside of my little toes which always happened on thru-hikes and the pads below my big toes were hard and calloused.

Now on full throttle and fighting fit, I slowly started making inroads into the mileage deficit. My mileage was hovering around twenty-five each day and I'd even thrown in a couple of thirties.

I passed under the guillotine, a gap between two vertical slabs of rock with a round boulder wedged above, and then I plummeted down 3412 feet over fifteen miles to arrive at the James River footbridge, the longest pedestrian-only bridge on the AT, some 650 feet long.

Crossing the VA-130 the 2700-foot climb up to Bluff Mountain wasn't as severe as I had anticipated. I passed Day-Glo, Slim and Sun on the way up and by the time I'd reached the top I was sweating already as the heat of the day intensified. A clear cut provided a great view as power lines stretched over me and I admired the landscape to both sides as the mountain dropped away to the lowlands, dotted with rivers and towns.

I leaned back against a rock and glanced to my right; something had caught my eye. It was a hiker, his small pack suggested he was out for the day.

"Hey, how's it going?" I asked.

He glanced in my direction but said nothing.

"Hey," I repeated, "You doing OK?"

Again there was no response. He was wiping his brow and walking unsteadily. I figured he just didn't hear me so ate a quick snack and thought I would ask again as I passed him. Instead, he came over a couple of minutes later, still looking slightly disorientated.

"Hey," he said. "I'm sorry, I heard you but ..." he trailed off.

"Mate, are you OK? Is everything all right?" I stood up.

"I ... I ... don't know."

I noticed he had grazes to his face, his lip was swollen and he had cuts to his legs.

"I think I fell, I ... I, don't remember. Where am I?"

He looked beaten up. As well as his injuries he was shaking, sweating and his face was pale.

"Mate, sit down. Here." I offered my shaded perch against the rock as he dabbed blood from his lip. "You have any water?" I asked.

"Yes." He took his bottle but fumbled aimlessly with the cap. I took it, unscrewed the lid and handed it back.

"Drink some water," I said. "Rest, take some deep breaths, move into the shade here and just take a few minutes. I ain't going anywhere."

"Thanks."

He gulped down his water and took big, heavy breaths, his chest rising and falling.

"Do you have any electrolytes, sugar maybe? A salty snack, something like that?"

"No."

I handed him a sachet of electrolyte mix and some peanuts. "Take it easy on the nuts but drink that. Do you have more water?"

"Yes. No. I don't think so."

I filled his bottle with some of mine and slowly his pale complexion coloured.

"I fell," he confirmed. "I did fall. I felt terrible, nauseous, weak, shaky. I did fall."

His injuries were minor but his condition worried me. He was slowly coming back to normal but a long way off being capable of hiking. The heat was unbearable and he was eleven miles from the road.

"Do you have any medical issues? Do you take any medication?"

"Just blood pressure pills."

"Look mate, I think you've probably just pushed yourself a little hard. It's hot, and you look dehydrated. The electrolytes will kick in but keep drinking and rest for thirty minutes OK?"

"OK, thanks."

I stayed with him for an hour, still concerned for his condition.

He eventually got up, took a deep breath and smiled.

"I'm OK, I'm good, really."

"You sure?"

"Yup."

"Where you heading?"

"Down to the James River."

"Do you want me to walk down with you?"

"No, I'm fine, really."

"Listen mate, I've just climbed eleven miles to get up here. Believe me, the last thing I want to do is go all the way back down again and then come back up. But, BUT, if you're not up to getting down there, you need to tell me. I will come back down with you."

I looked him in the eye and he returned the gaze, solidly.

"I will come back with you if I don't think you're OK, or you want me to," I added.

"I'm fine, thank you, really, I'm good to go."

"This is my cell number." I wrote it on a scrap of paper. "Please message me when you get down so I know you're OK. There are other hikers behind me — stop them if you need to, they'll help you out."

I gave him the last of my water as I knew there was more a further mile away at the Punchbowl shelter, and another sachet of electrolytes. He shook my hand and set off back down the hill.

I downed a litre of water at the Punchbowl shelter spring and took another litre with me. Rounding a switchback I came face to face with a fawn. We stopped just six feet apart and for a few fleeting seconds just stared at each other. I saw the colour of its eyes and the sun shining through its fur. It was beautiful. It stood motionless looking at me, and its eyes showed no fear. It didn't seem startled — more curious. Suddenly my phone beeped and it darted quickly to one side, bounding through the undergrowth but turned, head over its shoulder and took one last look. Then it was gone.

I checked my phone: 'Got down. I'm all good, thank you so much for your help, Dave.'

I smiled; it was good to know he'd made it.

I was keen to get to Brown Mountain shelter, or at least near it. I was later than usual, partly due to taking time to help Dave and I was also tired.

Deep, Bush Goggles, Turbo Toes, Dayglo and Sun had made camp by a sweet little flat area bordering the creek. I slung the hammock between two trees that could almost have been put there for me. A small fire illuminated our surroundings as the day came to an end and Brown Mountain Creek slid quietly past.

Talk was of the Shenandoahs. The Shenandoah National Park is held in high esteem by hikers. The terrain is easier and there are numerous places to stop and eat along Skyline Drive which caters to the many motorists enjoying the scenic stretch of road, which the trail crosses several times. Gabriele had arranged to come out for a week with her son Max, and the area seemed like the ideal place for them to experience a little bit of the AT.

However, as always when friends joined me for a portion of a thru-hike, things never went quite as planned.

Chapter 9
Half Way Done

June 1st to June 16th
Mile 800 to 1089

I tended to score the towns I stayed in according to various criteria. Amenities, appearance, compactness, quality of the restaurants, cafés and suchlike. I compared everything else against Hot Springs after my excellent stay there. It had been relaxing — a smattering of old, red brick buildings reminded me somewhat of home, a great café tended to my coffee needs and all the conveniences were close to hand. Damascus was also wonderful and I was to experience more great trail towns as I travelled further north.

On initial inspection, Waynesboro wasn't one of them. Although historic, it wasn't visually stimulating. Most of the buildings were fairly new and uninspiring. It wasn't a huge place but neither was it small, which meant walking about to shop, to do laundry and to eat. It's ironic how a thru-hiker can negotiate several thousand miles without grumbling but ask them to walk around town on a rest day and they'd look at you as if you're insane.

The Comfort Inn provided accommodation and Juggles, Goggles, Thirsty and I shared a room. Walking to the laundrette with Bush Goggles we realised we had no spare clothing to wear, as usual, because we had to wash everything. So we sat watching the clothes go round whilst wearing a couple of dangerously small discarded towels around our waists, much to the amusement of the locals.

Relaxing over a beer back in the room, I became curious about Juggles. He had written his email address down for me, which was associated with his website, so I took a look.

"Holy Shit!" I cried out.

Bush Goggles looked up from his ice cream, spoon still in his mouth.

"Wasup?!" he spluttered.

"Juggles was a World Champion!" I exclaimed.

"No shit?"

"Straight up, mate. He won the title in 2000! We're walking with a World Champion! I don't know about you, but if you're going to be World Champion at something, juggling has to be right up there for originality!"

Gabriele had travelled up to Waynesboro from Florida with her son Max for their week's taster on the trail. I experience confusing feelings when friends join me for a few days. It's great to see people I know, they invariably bring luxuries like dark chocolate and to have different faces around is wonderful. Conversely, the main problem is one of fitness. Two months into any trail and most hikers are in great shape, approaching the top of their game. The muscles are strong, lungs are working efficiently and the feet are hardened. Suddenly, when eager eyed and keen individuals join the fray, it invariably all goes wrong.

Mileage plummets, breaks are frequent, pace drops off and your opinion, help and knowledge are sought frequently. Despite this, I was keen to see them both and compromise was inevitable.

Gabriele arrived in my life at a time when I was beginning to figure out what I actually wanted out of it. Her farm back in Homestead had advertised for seasonal help in exchange for food and board. I had just returned from walking El Camino de Santiago in Spain. England was cold and damp, and I was eager to seek out warmer climes for a few months at minimal expense, so when she replied positively to my emailed plea, I jumped on the next available plane.

She was a very spiritual person, living healthily and had transitioned from a vegetarian diet to eating completely raw food. Always viewing the world positively, she had made a success of her farm from difficult beginnings. I had great memories from the three months I spent there and left feeling rejuvenated after a diet change, good hard work and plenty of opportunity to reflect and plan for the future.

Under his mother's guidance and direction, Max was destined to turn out good and he had. He was only twelve when I first met him on the farm and it was hard to believe this twenty-two-year-old man was the same person. He was studying hard and doing well. Softly spoken and with a gentle demeanour, he was easy to get on with.

They were both eager to spend time in the woods and taste this classic trail for a week. I had deliberately chosen a section in Virginia as the terrain was relatively easy and, just into June, the weather warm. After a few chores around town we hit the trail late, managing only seven miles before pulling up at the Calf Mountain Shelter. Gabriele had hiked well, never out of eyesight but Max was already struggling. They had hit the ground running but realised quickly that most of it was uphill.

Calf Mountain Shelter sat on top of a 3000-foot peak, but tucked away in the woods it felt more like a dark hollow. Wise Guy, Socks, Atlas and several others were milling in and around the full shelter. Gabriele and Max needed little guidance, having quickly set up their tent. Food as always was next on the agenda and they sat down to cook, making friends quickly with the others. A few raindrops found a way through the canopy but not enough for anyone to take evasive action as we congregated around the fire, our bodies flickering silhouettes around the woods.

I had faith in both of my new companions' abilities. They had researched their gear well and had even done a reasonable amount of training in preparation for their little outdoor foray. However, a couple of hours into day two and plans were not going well. I had slowed my pace to take their abilities into account and, although Gabriele was progressing well, Max very clearly was having problems. I took regular breaks, feeling obliged to act as their guide and look after them — although I was of course glad to do so. Gabriele always rolled in within a couple of minutes and was still either visible behind me, or walking with me. Max, however, was dropping further and further behind.

A mere three miles into the day, I reached the Turk Mountain Trail junction with Gabriele. We stopped to wait. The weather had turned for the worse, alternating between drizzle and heavy rain. The temperature had also plummeted; it felt more like October, not the start of summer. As we kept peering down a tunnel of trees behind us, eventually a lone, sodden figure emerged through the mist with a pronounced hobble.

"Max, you all right?" I enquired, fully aware he wasn't.

"No. My legs hurt, and I'm tired."

He put on a brave face, forcing down some energy snacks as Gabriele delved into her bag of natural remedies and wonder fixes. I tried to persuade them to push through to the Blackrock Hut, a further ten miles down the trail, making a potential thirteen mile total for the day but after a quick discussion, it was clear Max wasn't up to par. They stood by a road that intersected the AT many times in that section, and attempted to get a lift as I carried on to the Blackrock Hut. The understanding was that a decent meal, some rest, and maybe a shower would revitalise Max. We agreed to meet later that evening at the hut.

Despite seeing Max struggle, and the constant rain and chill, back on my own I felt like an unstoppable powerhouse. My legs in particular had never felt stronger and I began to toy with their limits, dipping in and out of my lactic thresholds. I approached hills and momentarily eyed them up as a boxer would an opponent. At times I ignored the elevation statistics in my data book, purely to revel in ignorance. Without breaking pace or stride, my eyes narrowed as each ascent came into view and I sized them up. Steepness, camber, length, surface, obstacles. My head buzzed in excitement, calculating the optimal form of attack. Hit them hard and quick or go in slower, conserving energy?

In the end I attacked them with no mercy and ascended higher, laughing at my ability to dip in and out of my pain barrier. Planting one foot precisely at the intended point, trusting in the decision that it would hold there whilst scanning the next landing option. On the rock? Land on the tree roots? Maybe not, they look slippery. Risk the wet dirt? Was the camber too much to hold my foot? Making the decisions, trusting them, I stormed on and repeated the process over and over again. Bam! Bam! Bam!

Reaching the limit, legs screaming, I held it there, dealing with the pain, toying with my bounds and discovering what I was truly capable of.

For a few minutes at the top of my game, there was always a sweet moment every day when it all came together. All the judgements, speed, and concentration merged into moments of hiking epiphany. Like a trance, a meditation, the outside world was a memory. My world centred onto a few feet of one of the world's classic hiking trails, in my small bubble where nothing else existed, mattered, or affected me.

I loved cracking along the trail at speed. The focus and judgement was almost euphoric. I demanded complete commitment in my decisions for each step over difficult terrain, focusing on the trail in front ready for each foot placement, the speed of it all, and trusting in my decisions. It was like a meditation. When everything came together and I reached that sweet spot, nothing else mattered because I felt I was in a different world.

I passed three women whom I remembered from earlier in the day. Peeking from under my umbrella I nodded a greeting.

"Didn't you pass us in that downpour earlier?" one of them asked.

"Yes, I did," I replied.

"And you're still smiling?"

I felt no need to reply. I just gave them another smile but it did make me think. I always tried to smile and acknowledge anyone I met on the trail, out of courtesy and because it made me feel good when I was on the receiving end. However, it suddenly made me realise that, despite the rain and cold, I *was* having a great time. Rarely did I feel that content in my everyday life. In fact, one of the few times I did feel happy back home was when I was either out walking for the day, or even better, counting down the days before I left on a thru-hike.

Once out there in the wilds, I always felt as though I belonged, as if it were my home. A friend once collected me from the airport after three months hiking and in the car he asked what my plans were now I was home.

"I'm not home," I replied. "Home is back where the trail is, and I've just left it."

I think my happiness on trail stemmed from the freedom, or being as close to freedom as I could ever hope to be. Although the AT and the terrain it passed through was still part of US society, and its rules and regulations, escaping to the wilds offered me a barrier between what I considered to be two very different worlds. Yes, anyone on trail for a few months is governed by the same restrictions as they were back in the city. But, on the other side of this barrier, out there in the woods, it was easy, thankfully, to forget that they ever existed.

There were virtually no buildings, no one in authority, no signs stating orders, no man-made noise, and there was no need to be in a certain place at a certain time. We were free to escape, to live our lives how we always used to live them, and I believe making this connection with nature reminds our bodies and minds of a time long ago when we were truly free. We all came from the wilds. The history, although long gone and forgotten for all of us, still occupies a small space in the back of our minds. Somewhere, subconsciously, our minds remember the woods where we spent our infancy; and spending time there rekindles those distant times in the past.

It *was* home.

***

The Blackrock Hut nestled in a small clearing a couple of minutes off trail. It slept just six and, being one of the first to arrive, I grabbed one of the bottom bunks in case the rain, which had finally stopped, decided to return.

Gabriele and Max were nowhere to be seen. I checked my phone for a signal but it didn't oblige. I was slightly worried that they may be in trouble, but knew they would be in town as I had last left them trying to get a lift.

I took half an hour to wind down and I stood, smoking, by the side of the shelter. A twig cracked in the woods. As I looked out of instinct, a bear paused perhaps fifty feet away, appearing to berate its mistake. It looked straight at me and carried on. Curious, I followed it, keeping my distance until it sloped off amongst the trees.

A new face had arrived at the shelter when I returned.

"Did you see that bear? Hey, I'm Hotshot!" We shook hands.

"Yes," I confirmed. "I followed it for a short while. I was a little concerned that it was heading in the direction of the trail but I think it's veered off somewhat."

"Ya'll not from around here are you? Where ya'll from? British?"

Oh crikey, not again.

"I'm English, name's Fozzie. Nice to meet you."

Hotshot thankfully didn't pursue the nationality subject but he told me about an incident with another bear earlier that day. He had been on the receiving end of a bluff charge, which is where a bear will run at someone threatening to attack and then, usually, call off the manoeuvre. I generally viewed a bluff charge as a test, for a bear to see if someone would run off and therefore appear weaker. If the hiker stood their ground — which is what we are advised to do — then generally a bear took the argument no further. Hotshot had stood his ground but he described it as one of the scariest moments of his life, comparing it to standing on a railway line when a train is hurtling towards you, hoping it would stop in time.

Frankly, the bear wasn't worrying me. The huge spider that had appeared inside the shelter concerned me more. A hiker called Boots had arrived and was occupying the top bunk, just below what he had identified as a wolf spider. He didn't seem to mind its presence and, in fact, commented that it was looking after him. We don't have big spiders back in the UK, and not being used to such large specimens, I kept a close eye on its location, sleeping fitfully.

***

I didn't listen to music very often on trail, preferring the sounds around me. On this occasion, however, I was keen to carry on reeling in the miles so I selected The Stranglers playlist on my phone. As 'Mercy' wafted through my earphones, my stride matched the rhythm.

The trail skirted around Blackrock summit, smoothing a path through a crazy mixture of huge boulders and slabs.

"Fozzie!"

I turned to see Juggles approaching from behind.

"Message from Gabriele," he continued. "They're bailing out."

"They are? Where did you see them?"

"At the Black Rock parking area."

I was surprised but part of me had expected it. It was sad to see them go after such a short while, but now I was free to carry on at my own pace.

Bush Goggles also showed and the three of us teamed up, stopping at Loft Mountain Wayside to enjoy a sorely needed burger and fries, nicely washed down with one of their speciality blackberry shakes.

Bush Goggles was complaining about a lack of sleep in the shelters due to what he referred to as the 'snorechestra'. I sympathised; a couple of hikers always kept the others awake with not just any old snoring, but often synchronised playlists reverberating off the wooden walls. I was still following my principle of sleeping in the tent unless there was a particularly bad storm forecast but the snorechestra wasn't my only problem.

The shelters weren't exactly renowned for their spacious interiors and often we slept on platforms, raised off the ground. The roofs generally sloped down to meet these platforms and I had hit my head on several occasions, forgetting that there was such a small gap between the two. A bruised head was becoming such a regular occurrence that I had now started referring to the shelters as 'headaches' instead.

Skyline Drive made regular appearances during that section of trail. Running a distance of 105 miles from Front Royal to Rockfish Gap through the Shenandoah National Park. Intersecting the AT many times and being described as one of the most scenic drives in America, it was popular with cyclists and motorists. Subsequently, to our delight, Skyline was dotted with places to eat, known as 'waysides'. We enjoyed regular calorie top ups, and were also able to carry less food. With our packs being lighter, and the terrain in the Shenandoah National Park being kinder, not only were we crushing good mileage, but stomachs were full and our fatigue subsided.

The Shenandoahs enjoy a great reputation amongst AT hikers. The elevation loss and gain was minimal compared to what we had become used to. It was also stunning to look at. Spoilt with many wide-open meadows commanding fine views over Virginia, it was home to a variety of wildlife such as deer, black bear, bobcat, raccoon, skunk, fox and rabbit.

As we hightailed it up Weaver Mountain, Bush Goggles, Juggles and I bumped into Squatch coming down. We stopped, and he took some video footage for Flip Flop Flippin' 2, whilst Juggles plied his trade in the background, thankfully with no drops.

Spending that night in the Hightop Headache, sorry Shelter, discussion was rife between the three of us that we push ourselves, get an early start and pull in a day with some decent mileage.

We hit the trail at 7 a.m., full of energy. The weather was stunning, the trail smooth and we flew along, albeit aided by some ibuprofen and Five Hour Energy drinks. By 8 p.m. we pulled up to camp having hiked thirty miles and bringing our tally on the AT to 928 miles. After sixty-nine days we were approaching half way and Harpers Ferry was just a few days away.

The mornings, in particular, were proving an exquisite time of day to walk. The cool air and quiet trail before the day trippers appeared was welcome. Early morning moisture dampened the trail to a dark brown, lightening as the day progressed and the sun dried it out. Rhododendron leaves speckled the ground, their red and yellow coats crunching underfoot. There were few sounds; birds chirped, rabbits scampered and rustled through the leaves as an occasional breeze murmured through the tree canopy. Occasional clouds drifted through my world like lost ghosts and my surroundings consisted of three colours: blue sky, green woods and brown ground.

Although I joined Bush Goggles and Juggles for most of the day, we also enjoyed time on our own as well. We had gelled, enjoying each other's company but relishing some solitude as well. With each of us pushing the miles, we had agreed to reach Harpers Ferry on June 11th. This entailed increasing our distances each day and I felt my mileage deficit from the start was gradually being eaten into. Over three days I had covered ninety miles.

I bumped along through the Shenandoahs, cresting regular peaks such as the Pinnacle, Pass Mountain and South Marshall Mountain before falling down from Compton Peak to intersect the US-522.

I was keen to keep up the mileage. Until, that is, I passed the Jim and Molly Denton Headache, sorry Shelter, a few yards off trail. With a large veranda to the front, including tables and chairs, I was tempted to lay up for the night. I managed to resist, just, although I did succumb to a shower and a quick laundry session under the solar-powered shower.

This could catch on. Nip into town, fill your stomach, do a quick resupply, grab a shower and wash your clothes at the same time. Long stops could be history.

A quick energy drink now known as 'rocket fuel', and two ibuprofen to argue it out with a sore shin, I sped off in the direction of the Rod Hollow Shelter, eager to pull in another thirty-mile day. It proved a big mistake.

Leaving at 1.30 p.m., there were eighteen miles to reach my destination. The first four and a half miles took me just an hour. I enjoyed a good rhythm over easy terrain, my trekking poles synchronised with my stride, breathing perfect, focus concentrated. In two hours I had covered nine miles, half the distance. When fully warmed up I felt little need to rest but revelled in my ability to cover distance quickly. I was sweating profusely; I wiped my shirt over my face and dried my trekking pole handles against my shorts. My shin started to ache but I ignored it and the trail continued to flash under my shoes until, finally, the turn off for the shelter signalled day's end. I was buzzing, on a high and soaked in the excitement of the afternoon. I had hiked eighteen miles fully loaded in a little over four hours.

The shelter was quiet; just two other hikers occupied the table outside. I did a double take and recognised one of them.

"Fozzie! Wassup!"

Pausing briefly, I struggled to remember his name.

"Onespeed! Hey! I'm good, how the hell are you?"

"Doing great."

I had last seen him in Irwin where we shared a motel room.

"This is Medic," he added, motioning to the woman sitting next to him.

I introduced myself and we shook hands.

"I'm going to get the hammock set up and I'll be back," I said.

After sitting for just ten minutes, my body had already cooled. I rose to reach for the jacket in my rucksack and pain shot through my shin. Wincing, I ran my hand over it. It was tender and swollen.

"You OK?" enquired Medic.

"Not sure. Does your trail name hold any relevance to your profession by any chance?"

She laughed.

"Yes. Here, let me take a look."

I gingerly raised my leg and rested it on the picnic table seat beside her.

"Any problems with your shin before?" she asked, gently running her hand over the area.

"No, never," I replied.

"How was your day? Have you been taking it easy? Did you fall? Were you pushing yourself?"

"Er, great day, I didn't fall and yes, I was pushing hard."

"This is not my specialised area but being a hiker, and a runner, I know a little about sport injuries. I'm pretty sure this is a shin splint."

I was aware of shin splints although they hadn't affected me in the past. I did know that in the worst cases it meant stopping all exercise and resting. I cursed myself for pushing too hard. Damage to the connective layer of tissue which covers the shin bone, or periosteum, causes inflammation. It can be caused by several factors; a rolling of the feet known as over-pronation during hiking or running is one, but usually it is caused by periods of intense exercise when you ask too much of your body. Even at the peak of physical fitness, we can still push too hard, and pushing too hard was exactly what I had been guilty of.

I faced the prospect of a two-week rest period. Medic saw my disappointment and tried to placate it.

"Don't worry," she said. "It's probably not as bad as you think. Try and be positive. There's an ice-cold spring over there, sit down, hold your shin under the running water for at least ten minutes and take ibuprofen. Both of these will reduce the swelling and help the healing process. Stretch it out when you can and new shoes may help. Yes, you may need rest but I've seen people in exactly this situation and the following morning they've hiked off with no problem at all. Hold it under the water whenever you can. Finally, if it is OK in the morning then carry on. Gently!"

I hobbled off to the spring and sat there for fifteen minutes, letting the water tumble over my shin and swallowed a couple of ibuprofen. The pain subsided somewhat. I ate heartily and slid into my hammock for a decent nights rest.

***

The Roller Coaster is a thirteen-mile section of trail, sixteen miles prior to Harpers Ferry. Its name pretty much describes better than I can what it involves and, whilst the series of ascents and descents aren't particularly high, nor at any great altitude, there are lots of them. Halfway through and I was knackered. The swelling on my shin, amazingly, had gone down and it didn't hurt. Nevertheless, I took the Roller Coaster easy, dropped my pace and continued to hold my shin under water a few times during the day.

Bush Goggles joined me for the afternoon. Whilst we rested, taking in the view from Raven Rocks, a new face going by the name of Dr Attractive sat with us. Bush Goggle's eyes lit up when he saw her and, leaving me to rest, he took off in hot pursuit.

I've explained that 'blue blazing' is the term coined for taking a side trail. Another is 'yellow blazing' whereby a hiker may take the road to cut off a section of trail and this stems from following the yellow lines on a road. Well, Bush Goggles was indulging in what we refer to on the trail as 'pink blazing', when a male deliberately follows a female in the hope of some reciprocal interest. I didn't see him for the rest of the day but eventually caught him just after the Virginia and West Virginia border, perfectly placed exactly on the thousand-mile mark.

Being late evening, the glimmering lights of Torlone's Pizza and Bar winked at us just down the road. With an absence of bars to that point, we promptly went in, ordered a Jack Daniel's and Coke each, and slumped in one corner with instructions to the waitress to keep a watchful eye on our drinks.

"Less than quarter full and feel free to replenish them," I advised, smiling.

We ate, then ate some more and finally, just after dusk, left Torlone's with more than a slight stagger to pitch camp a short way into the woods.

We had a mere five miles left to Harpers Ferry in the morning. The mercury was tickling ninety degrees and humidity was on the increase. The AT cut straight through Harpers Ferry and first stop was the Appalachian Trail Conservancy on Washington Street. Most hikers stopped there to say hello and the staff always insisted on taking everyone's photo out front for a visual, yearly record. It also acted as a great reference to see who was ahead, behind, and at what time they had passed through.

I had high expectations of Harpers Ferry. When I first became aware of the AT some twelve years earlier, the town regularly cropped up during my research. Perhaps the most famous place on the trail, it was considered to be the halfway mark although that actual point was around seventy-two miles further.

My expectations were met. The town nestled beautifully between the confluence of the Potomac and Shenandoah rivers. Crossing the Byron Memorial Footbridge over the Potomac I left West Virginia and entered Maryland, the sixth state of the AT.

Harpers Ferry is bathed in history and named after Robert Harper, who first settled there in 1747. In 1761 he established a ferry service across the Potomac, drawing settlers wishing to head further west into the Shenandoah Valley. Thomas Jefferson visited the town in 1783, referring to it as 'Perhaps one of the most stupendous scenes in nature'.

Thirsty, Juggles, Goggles and I were a little way from the centre of town, which entailed a lot of walking to reach the amenities but it proved a pleasure. The streets tumbled up and down, bordered by old, rickety wood and red-brick-fronted houses, their front gardens speckled with summer flowers. The restaurants, bars and shops were independent and all around me the surrounding hills kept sentinel. Harpers Ferry surpassed all of my expectations.

We spent our time, as usual, resupplying with food for the next stage as well as filling our stomachs with three good meals. My shoes, having lasted well from the start, now had 1000 miles on them and were finished. I had purchased a new pair back in Waynesboro and mailed them up to the post office. My new shoes were light trail runners — and although I had doubts about their durability, I was looking forward to the comfort they promised.

The guys were in good spirits. Our room quickly became swamped with piles of dirty laundry, opened packages from the post office, beer bottles and food containers. Every available anchor point was utilised to hang damp gear to dry. It smelt fine when we were in there, but after trips to town we returned to hold our noses at the aroma of sweat, week-old socks and damp gear. The cleaners, bless them, never batted an eyelid.

The four of us left late the following morning, clearing up the last of our chores and enjoying a late breakfast at the Town Inn. Most of us sported new shoes and T-shirts and with everything washed, including rucksacks, we could have passed for day hikers, our beards perhaps the only giveaways. We were always excited to arrive in town, especially one as notable as Harpers Ferry, but the feeling never quite lived up to the excitement of returning to the woods.

The trail ran parallel to Shenandoah Street as we passed Jefferson Rock, John Brown's Fort and over the Potomac River by way of the bridge and railway line. A flat, dead-straight path hugged the C&O Canal for two and a half miles and soon the sounds of town faded.

Juggles dropped back but Thirsty, Bush Goggles and I carried on, passing the Ed Garvey, Crampton Gap, Rocky Run and Pine Knob shelters. We enjoyed a delightfully flat trail before pulling over after twenty-five miles to camp near Annapolis Rocks.

The trail was becoming rockier. The AT through Maryland was just forty miles long before entering the next state of Pennsylvania, famed for its hard-going, rocky trail. I figured the section near Annapolis Rocks was a precursor to this.

The day after a town stop I was constantly hungry. With the amount of food I used to eat when in town, my stomach figured I must have been back in civilisation and therefore expected further gratification. After sixteen miles we reached Pen Mar Park. Noticing some sort of military retirement party, or more importantly, the surrounding tables groaning under copious piles of food, Thirsty made plans.

Looking hungry, he headed off to make some polite conversation. The ultimate aim was to procure some form of sustenance for Bush Goggles and me. He returned a few minutes later looking dejected and empty-handed. If civilisation couldn't help us, the woods certainly did. The summer berries were just starting to ripen and we stopped regularly to feast on blackberries and raspberries. Wild strawberries were also nearly ready and we had little inkling of the feasts that lurked further north, including blueberries. A lack of fruit from that point in the trail was never a problem again.

Having left Maryland that morning, we eventually pulled off trail in Pennsylvania at the Tumbling Run shelters. Curious as to why there were two of them, I presumed it was purely to meet demand until I noticed a sign on each one. One read 'snorers', the other 'non-snorers'. Juggles eventually caught up with us, pitching his home-made tarp and inner mosquito net near to Bush Goggles' tent, whilst Thirsty and I strung up our respective hammocks. Juggles loved his camp setup, it had cost him very little as he had made most of it with the aid of his sewing machine back home.

"That's not my best piece of gear though, Fozzie," he announced. "Take a look at this!"

He delved into this backpack and pulled out his sleeping mat. Thru-hikers often utilised various items of gear for use when trying to get a ride into town at road junctions. 'Hiker to Town' was commonly inked onto anything large enough to be spotted by speeding vehicles and Juggles had used his sleeping mat to good effect.

"There's more," he continued, giggling.

He turned it over. We collapsed laughing after reading what he had written on the other side, for use purely as amusement, and to see the reaction from motorists.

'Psycho Killer!'

We commandeered the picnic table nestled between the two shelters and each of us ate like wolves, desperately trying to placate our respective appetites. We had the place to ourselves and the table quickly disappeared under a pile of food. Stoves were lit and there we stayed for the rest of the evening, occasionally topping up our calorie intake with nibbling and drinking.

When I read the shelter register I saw an entry from a hiker whose name wasn't legible but it said that Nito, who I had last seen near Damascus, had left the trail. He had succumbed to a case of tendonitis, which even after five days rest hadn't healed. There was also a message from Pink Bits — sorry, Lady Forward — dated four days earlier. I was still carrying the gauntlet and eager to return it to her.

Although we had yet to hit any major rocky sections in Pennsylvania, we knew they were coming and, even though the state was relatively flat compared to most, efforts were being made to continue with the high mileage to counteract any possible difficult days. Since Harpers Ferry we had covered eighty-five miles in three days. The trail was indeed easy, lacking any serious climbs and descents and we happily floated along between one and two thousand feet enjoying fine weather.

***

As far as thru-hikes go, Saturday 16th June was always going to be notable. We were all up at 5 a.m. and away by 6 a.m, although I walked with Juggles for the day, losing Bush Goggles and Thirsty during the morning. At mile 1069, both of us downed our packs, shook hands and had a hug before taking a few minutes to rest by a sign that most AT thru-hikers remember.

Appalachian Trail – Maine to Georgia
1069 Springer Mt S
1069 Mt Katahdin N

We were halfway. I felt elated, and surprised. It seemed to have arrived too quickly, and that it was only recently that I had stood on top of Springer Mountain. For a brief moment I felt sad, for I knew that it was only a matter of a few more weeks before, hopefully, I would stand on top of Mt Katahdin and my journey would be finished.

Until that time, I was determined to approach the second half of the AT with the same excitement as I had on the first half.

Chapter 10
Awesomely Nasty

June 17th to June 28th
Mile 1089 to 1300

A small town known as Pine Grove was on the guys' radars. I wasn't too bothered about their reasons why but, just after the halfway point, those few scattered houses were a renowned stop on the AT. The Pine Grove Furnace General Store was famous for a tradition known as the Half Gallon Challenge.

Instead of a hiker's usual preference for beer at reaching halfway, the Half Gallon Challenge of ice cream, or nearly two litres if that's your unit preference, was the accepted method of celebration. But I didn't have a sweet tooth, and besides, the prospect of eating that much ice cream didn't appeal to me. Besides, they didn't stock Mint Choc Chip and Raspberry Ripple just drew blank looks.

Juggles also chose not to participate but Thirsty and Bush Goggles were all over it. They were both successful and Bush Goggles, having had his dessert first and missed out on the first course, resolved that minor dilemma by finishing off a couple of burgers as well.

A few minutes further up trail, Fuller Lake in Pine Grove Furnace State Park also sported a shower block and we all took the chance to clean up. Juggles arrived just as I was leaving, complaining of soreness around his groin, or the 'sac' as the Americans like to call it, and judging by his facial expressions it wasn't too pleasant. I left him with a cotton wool ball and some rubbing alcohol, which I used for pretty much any medical problem. For sore skin, rashes, fungal issues and a decent disinfectant it was very effective. The only downside was it stung like I can't begin to describe, particularly when used for a sore sac. I kid you not when I say I have seen rubbing alcohol reduce a hiker to their knees. Juggles, I think, was also aware of its potency and I left him holding a plastic bottle of alcohol in one hand, cotton wool in the other, pondering whether to start juggling with them or contemplate his fate. Little did I know how those early signs of sore sac syndrome were to affect us.

We settled in a corner of the sports field for the night and I dreamt of being chased by giant cotton wool balls. Not concentrating in the morning, I lost a mile on the approach to the town of Boiling Springs when I inadvertently took a side trail for half a mile, and then had to return when I realised. Thirsty trusted my often dubious navigational skills, and despite an abundance of signs, followed me until I realised my error.

Boiling Springs did not, as you might imagine, refer to any thermal activity. Springs, yes, but the bubbling aspect referred to the pressure at which the water emerged from several artesian wells dotted around the town.

The AT ran straight through the middle and was therefore a popular place to grab some food and use the post office as an easily accessible destination for mail drops, as the trail passed right outside.

Although undeniably pretty, Hot Springs was a little twee for me. Prices were inflated from tourism and the gardeners appeared to have gone a little too far. Verges were neatly trimmed and often bordered with symmetrical rocks, regimental flowers stood guard, the grass was aggressively mown and artificial landscaping was prevalent. I grabbed some lunch at the Caffe 101 with Bush Goggles and Thirsty before they headed off, agreeing to meet me in Duncannon, twenty-six miles up trail. I had a parcel to collect but as usual timed my arrival to perfection on a Sunday, when it was closed, so I had to hang around until Monday morning.

The Allenberry Resort Inn and Playhouse, about half a mile out of town, offered reasonable rates so, unable to hike any further that day, I took care of some chores such as laundry and a small food resupply. I figured my shin, although not causing many problems, would benefit from some rest, just in case.

The weather forecast for the week was excellent and I had considered myself lucky up until that point. The AT's reputation for wet conditions, so far, hadn't come to fruition. The evenings were also cool so mosquitos were rare, and the famous

Pennsylvanian rocks had still yet to say hello. It was proving ideal hiking and I wondered if, in the future, 2012 would be regarded as one of the few dry years to hike the AT.

I collected my parcel in the morning and started to make inroads into the twenty six miles to Duncannon where the guys were holing up for the night.

The trail was below 1000 feet for much of the way and gloriously flat, so progress was rapid. The woods thinned, I passed over bridges, crossed through fields and wandered through an agricultural landscape. I admit to actually skipping for a couple of minutes when no one was about.

"Hey! Ya'll hiking the trail huh?"

A man out walking his dog forced me to stop by taking up a stationary position in the middle of the track. His opening question was standard fare and I disguised a groan, knowing he would probably ask a load more. Everyone I met on trail was polite, the locals usually interested despite several thousand hikers passing through each year. However, I did tire of the same questions.

'Ya'll hiking the trail?' was invariably followed by 'where did ya'll start?' 'where ya'll heading?' 'how far do ya'll walk each day?' 'when do ya'll think ya'll finish?' 'how much does ya'll pack weigh?' and so on.

After replying to everything he threw at me, I bode him farewell and spent the rest of the afternoon pondering those questions and inventing scenarios to flip everything around. My favourite was imagining entering a restaurant and cornering an unsuspecting diner. My questions of choice included — "Hey! You're sitting in a restaurant huh? What you eating there? Burger huh? How's it going so far? When did you start? When do you think you'll finish? That's a big burger! What sort of weight we talking? Must be a pound at least!"

A short but steep hill shook me from my daydreams and I rested in the empty Darlington Shelter at the top, taking a quick lunch including some wild strawberries I had collected. Pink Bits, sorry, Lady Forward, had left a progress note in the shelter register and I discovered I had gained ground on her. She was four days ahead and I was looking forward to relinquishing the gauntlet.

"Starting to get rocky!" I said to Easy Rider, a hiker I'd not met before, as he rested on a slab of rock overlooking the approach to Duncannon later that day. The descent to town was one of few rocky sections I had walked through but gave me some idea of what was coming.

"Sure is!" he replied. "Gets worse as well."

Duncannon sported some wonderful architecture. The AT followed the High Street, which, along with the surrounding streets, provided some visual clues to its age. The Doyle Hotel was one of them, being a favourite stop for thru-hikers because of its cheap prices. A balcony ringed the first floor of this red brick building and one rounded front corner looked like a castle turret. Unfortunately the Doyle, and apparently most of Duncannon itself, seemed to be lacking in local funding: faded paint flaked here and there, repairs long overdue. It definitely had charm, perhaps just in need of a little polish to allow it to shine.

I had heard mixed reports about the Doyle on Market Street, ranging from being 'worse than an overflowing privy' to 'an absolute must stop' and even 'awesomely nasty'.

When I swung open the front door my eyes momentarily adjusted to the lower light level. Bush Goggles and Thirsty glanced round and each raised a beer bottle in unison, complete with a suggestive 'come drink' expression. Some unfamiliar faces peered from the corners and baskets of chicken and chips dotted the tables.

Pat and Vicky Kelly, the owners, bought the hotel in 2001. It was originally constructed in the 1770s but burnt down. The current incarnation was built in 1903. The Ritz it wasn't, but with the majority of the clientele sporting beards, rucksacks, appearing in sore need of a shower and muttering 'food', or 'beer', it didn't need to be. The Doyle unashamedly catered for thru-hikers, which was reflected in the $25 room price, even less if shared.

The rumours had made me slightly wary but I immediately loved the place. The bar was the Doyle's focal point, acting as the feeding, drinking, Internet-checking, social and general hanging out point. Tables and chairs made from dark wood skidded and screeched around on a tiled floor. Wood panelling adorned the lower half of the walls, rising to tobacco-stained uppers occasionally interrupted by lighter, rectangular spaces from missing, long-forgotten pictures. A deep polished wood ceiling stared down on hikers catching up with the news.

I stayed for one night but left early with Bush Goggles, eager to return to the trail and preserve my hiking budget after two consecutive nights in a hotel. We followed the High Street as, gradually, Duncannon started showing signs of life. Car exhausts released a slow rise of smoke, drifting to meet a low mist. Front doors slammed, and cries of 'see ya later!' echoed as the locals began their commute.

We crossed the railway line and walked over a short bridge spanning the River Juniata which fell to a narrow strip of land before the Clarks Ferry Bridge, which stretched out and carried us both over the Susquehanna River.

From 400 feet the trail rose sharply to around 1242 feet. Bush Goggles pulled away; having no desire to push my shin, I fell back, spending the rest of the day on my own. It was hot, and as I stopped briefly to chat with Chez 11, he informed me it was 100°F with humidity off the scale.

Finally, Pennsylvania had delivered on its rocks — often moist from early morning dew, making them slippery. Several different routes wove through rock sections, around and beside them; clear, worn trails where past hikers had picked out the line of least resistance. Most days there was little wind and mosquitos droned annoyingly as cobwebs constantly wrapped round my face, arms and legs followed by a frantic slapping of my cheeks, praying that the actual spider wasn't also attached. Often, perhaps an hour into the day, hikers would meet coming from opposite directions and relief was palpable from both parties, aware that the other had cleared the trail.

"Oh, thank God!" One sobo exclaimed, wiping her face as we surprised each other. "No more cobwebs!"

There was no getting away from cobwebs. The short-term solution I used was holding one trekking pole in front to clear them; but there was only one, sure-fire winner and that was to walk behind someone else.

Pennsylvania's rock came in all manner of different forms and I soon learnt how to deal with its whims. Often I was confronted by a crazy mess of loose blocks, like a stone wall that had been knocked down and abandoned. A fine balancing act ensued and, as I educated myself to this new obstacle, it became second nature to stick to the high points and 'float' over the surface. Getting bogged down in the indentations, hollows and low points left a hiker plodding through and lifting their legs each time to make any progress. Picking out the pointed, raised rocks, my eyes flicked from one landing point to the next in quick succession. When I became complacent, I had to force myself to lay off the speed a little for fear of making a mistake. Many a thru-hike of the Appalachian Trail has ended unceremoniously in Pennsylvania.

Raised lines of stone, which we referred to as 'shark's fins' or 'ankle breakers', bisected other sections. Hopping from one to the next, I teetered, and flapped my arms ungracefully in a balancing act before regaining my composure. They often came into view only as I climbed higher and scanned the trail ahead for a familiar white blaze. It's not unusual for hikers to inadvertently end up on side trails in Pennsylvania as the need to focus so much on the terrain, with head down, meant they kept missing the white blazes.

I lost time and distance through those sections, but the flat, smooth, dirt trails in between more than made up for it. The relief of hitting soil after an hour negotiating a rock field was almost exciting.

I reached the 501 Shelter, named after the 501 road it stood near. It was a welcome change, boasting four walls, plenty of internal space and a clear, plastic dome on the roof where sunlight poured in. It was June 21st, eighty-three days into my hike and I smiled as I wrote in my diary that evening, having checked the data book, for there were less than 1000 miles to the finish.

I sat outside swatting mosquitos with Bush Goggles, Thirsty and Juggles. The talk turned to the problem of soreness around the groin area. Juggles's condition had deteriorated, whilst the rest of us were rapidly descending also into what most referred to as 'crotch rot'.

The result of walking for hours every day, in high temperatures and humidity, with shorts rubbing was that the area concerned was constantly damp, dirty and chafed, resulting in an incredibly sore and painful rash which became infected. Several days between showers and neglecting our personal hygiene weren't helping matters either. It wasn't as if we had access to a shower every day so little could be done.

"Mate, you could try losing the shorts," I said to Juggles. He had been wearing tight-fitting, Lycra cycling models. "They're black so they heat up and your boys need some air down there. Let them breathe!"

There were mutterings of agreement from the collective but Juggles was very fond of his shorts. However, as he constantly shifted around on his seat, he was clearly not comfortable. Bush

Goggles and Thirsty were also suffering from early symptoms. As usual at the shelters in the evening, many minds strived to reach solutions and others also appeared to have fallen foul of crotch rot. With so many casualties, the advice was generous.

Some advocated cleaning the area with a damp cloth, usually a bandana with a little soap, although I hasten to add it was not then used for headwear as well. Before long, wise words and suggestions were aired.

"Drop your shorts and offer your arse to the wind for five minutes every day," floated out from the shelter.

"Cut the lining out of your shorts. Never had a problem, but be careful sitting during rest breaks when talking to the ladies," drifted over from the direction of the privy.

Daily swabs with baby wipes, antiseptic cream, a medicated foot powder known as Gold Bond and rubbing alcohol were also firm favourites. I used a mixture of alcohol and powder and, although sore, it wasn't bothering me as much as some. I dusted twice a day and if things got really sore then out came the rubbing alcohol. 'Rubbing' is not the technique I'd recommend for applying the demon fluid. The upmost respect had to be exercised and, although the actual application took just a few seconds, my personal routine stretched out to at least five minutes as I needed that length of time to summon up enough courage to do it in the first place.

I usually swabbed myself in the evening, retiring to the privy with my cotton wool bud in hand. After a short, but intense period of meditation and deep breathing I looked skyward and prayed to the hiking gods. The sooner the finish, the sooner the stinging subsided — but the initial few seconds, when I hesitantly dabbed and wiped my undercarriage, and subsequent minute's worth of pain brought me to my knees stifling a scream. As I gritted my teeth and rocked back and forth on the toilet, my breathing rate and volume approached that of a woman giving birth during a particularly bad labour. However, in the following days my boys often returned to something approaching normality.

In the morning I rounded a bend in the trail to see Bush Goggles, or 'Goggles' as his trail name had shortened to, standing in the middle of the trail, peering down into the recesses of his shorts and one hand rubbing lotion down there. Seeing me, he looked up smirking with a knowing glint in his eye and just said,

"Pro-active sac day."

* * *

Several times a day throughout a thru-hike, my head took time to calculate progress. Occasionally in the evenings I would scribble down a few numbers just to keep check on the mileage I had covered, and the distance left. Even checking my diaries now, as I write this, the margins are dotted with scribbles, figures and plans.

I had indulged in this process so many times that embedded in my memory were a series of predictions enabling me to reach certain points at certain times, and every day I repeated the process.

OK, twenty miles each day is 120 miles per week, taking one day as rest. Up that to twenty-five, Fozzie, and you can cover 150 miles in the coming week. If you make a quick town stop then maybe it's a 170. Let's be cautious and call it twenty-five; this time next month you'll be 600 miles further. You've got another fifty-six to Delaware Water Gap, that's two days — maybe two days and a couple of hours. Get there, get cleaned up quickly and you can avoid an overnight stay. If you can pull in twenty to twenty-five each day, you'll hit Katahdin at the end of August with a sub-five-month trip.

I had worked that out prior to the halfway point. my average daily distance was thirteen miles including days resting, or sixteen miles per day actually walking. The plan to cut into the mileage deficit during the second half was progressing well and I had averaged nineteen miles per day including rest days, or a pleasing twenty-five each day actually walking. During one fourteen-day stretch I had averaged 26.1 miles per day. The guys were covering similar distances. We were all warmed up and in fine fettle, considering twenty-five milers as a minimum goal, and often we pulled in thirties.

Respectable mileage wasn't intended as an ego boost, and we weren't rushing — although thirty-mile days may seem like we were. On my Pacific Crest thru-hike two years earlier, I hadn't paid enough attention to distance targets and took far too many rest days. Most hikers looked to finish the PCT at some point in September, or early October at the very latest, taking on average six months for the entire trail. We never had a choice, really; as with most south to north thru-hikes, the onset of winter and the first snow meant September was the optimal target.

On the PCT I became lax keeping to those targets, and I realised during the latter stages that my hike was in serious jeopardy of failing. I became depressed, and made matters worse by taking even more rest days to swim in my own disappointment because I really didn't think I would make it. I had invested a lot of time and money to complete that dream and, having realised that failure was very possible, I picked myself up, set a demanding target to finish and kept to it. In the middle of November, a good two months over what was generally accepted, I finally reached the end having fought my way through several weeks of snow and cold weather.

I had made mistakes but I never saw mistakes as a bad thing. I always learnt from them and there was no better way to learn on a thru-hike than to nearly fail. I had witnessed others failing, and keeping an eye on my progress was now firmly embedded.

The northern states, especially Vermont, New Hampshire and Maine, were considered the hardest. Steep climbs and descents were the norm, often over rock slabs, slippery and damp from the wetter climes. The weather was sure to be colder and wetter further up.

"Fozzie!" Juggles made me jump as he appeared from behind. "Did you hear the one about the hikers, the soup and a fly?"

I smiled. Juggles harboured dreams of becoming a stand-up comedian and occasionally practiced his repertoire. We had been discussing how little food a thru-hiker wasted the previous day so his gag followed on from that.

"No mate, but go on."

"Well, there's a day hiker, section hiker, and a thru-hiker in a restaurant. They all order the soup. The day hiker notices a fly in the soup, rejects it and asks the waiter for a fresh bowl. The section hiker also has a fly in his, but picks it out, then proceeds to finish the soup."

"Yes, go on," I said.

"The thru-hiker picks up the fly gently, holds it at eye level and says 'Now you spit that back out!'"

I got the impression that Juggles enjoyed his solitude as well as me. Although Goggles, Thirsty and I had now reached the point where we pretty much hiked, camped and shared motels together, Juggles spent a lot of time with us but also drifted in and out. We all did that to a certain extent. Perhaps I wouldn't see Goggles for half a day, Thirsty camped on his own occasionally and sometimes I took a day out in solitude. Juggles regularly disappeared, re-appeared, took breaks on his own or with us but we all considered him to be part of our group.

I had formed a strong bond with Thirsty, Goggles and Juggles. I hoped Lazagne and Daffy somehow caught us up because I had a good feeling they would fit in well. I had heard from PJ that he had got back on trail on June 26th. He was well behind us now, at least a month, so it was highly unlikely that we would see him again. I sent him a good luck message, knowing he would pull through.

We were aware of each other's behaviour, preferences, speed and habits. Juggles, as I have said, drifted in and out but we all found his sense of humour, juggling antics and overall light-hearted outlook on life amusing. Thirsty was dependable; if he said he would be at a certain campsite at a particular time then I could count on it. He dipped in and out of his limits, sometimes flying along and covering distance at unbelievable rates, but more often than not his hiking style was solid although relaxed and he appeared in no hurry. Goggles was a physical firework. He was young, enjoyed the challenge of pushing miles at high speed, and constantly had his eye on breaking a forty-mile day (or even further). Somehow, we all worked.

Since shortening Bush Goggles to just Goggles, I kept getting his name confused with Juggles — so much so that, on occasion, I referred to one as Guggles, and the other as Joggles. I couldn't get my tongue around it and many times one of them had to correct me, despite my pleas of ignorance.

Goggles was following me after we had taken a break at the Eckville Shelter, and there was a short climb to a hill known as Dan's Pulpit. He was right on my tail; I could hear his footfall just a few feet behind and I sensed he was enjoying the pace I was setting, without feeling the need to overtake me. I was capable of keeping up with him, but being around twenty years younger than me he had the advantages of youth and stamina. Often, begrudgingly, I had to let him go.

On that climb, I thought I'd dip into my reserves and show him that, despite the age difference, I could, hopefully, still show most hikers a clean pair of heels. Gradually, as we made inroads into the climb, I warmed and started to push harder. Every half a minute I increased the pace slightly and took tight lines through the switchbacks to gain a couple of feet. Reaching forward with my trekking poles, I hauled myself up, jumping from one boulder to the next, planted a foot on damp soil and forcing my weight on it to gain purchase.

I glanced back occasionally when I thought he wasn't looking. One aspect of Goggles we all knew well was that when he pushed hard he sweated, particularly his face. His forehead glistened with shiny beads and his T-shirt was damp, as was mine. His expression was one of concentration, tinged with a little hurt. I upped the pace further, trying not to giggle at the game we were involved in.

We were both gulping in lungfuls of air, and my legs started to scream, so for a couple of seconds I backed off slightly to bring them back, then pushed hard once more. I pulled over at a gap in the trees revealing a sun-bathed rock slab with a fine view.

We were exhausted, covered in sweat, our legs burning and capable of nothing more.

"Man! I was digging deep just to stay with you!" he cried, sparing a few seconds of oxygen intake to laugh.

Supported by our trekking poles, we bent over and fought to control our breathing before eventually collapsing on the warm rock. I just smiled at him. It was reassuring to know that I was still capable of pushing others to their limits.

I can't remember whether I lost Goggles in the afternoon, or, more probably, he lost me. The interestingly named Bake Oven Knob Shelter was my planned overnight point, although I now rarely stayed in the shelters, preferring the relative comfort and seclusion of my hammock.

Pennsylvania was still offering flatter terrain and I made quick progress over Blue Mountain, the Knife Edge and Bear Rocks before huge slabs of sloping rock rose up and hindered my way. A recent white blaze confirmed I was on the right track but I took some convincing before realising that the slabs needed to be negotiated. Protruding from the ridge, they commanded fine views north and south to the lowlands but I had little chance to admire them. It took all my concentration and a fine balancing act to manoeuvre through.

I tried to pick the best route and teetered, arms flapping, trying to regain composure. Summoning up courage, I leapt from one rock to the next and inched cautiously down whilst praying my shoes would grip the surface and not whip out from beneath me. Then I moved slowly up the next section, my hands scrabbling for any protrusions to grab. The rocks straddled the ridge itself about thirty feet below so a slip would be high enough to cause injury, but wouldn't result in a 1000-foot fall down the mountainside to the Lehigh Valley below.

At the tail end I came up behind more hikers, each tentatively finishing off the last rock slab before returning to a dirt trail, and the turn off for the Bake Oven Knob Shelter. Its capacity of six was already accounted for but I had already seen a flat area where one other hiker had set up camp. On closer inspection my companion for the night turned out to be the Kindle Ninja, whom I hadn't seen since the Blue Mountain Shelter back at the start. It was some coincidence that we had just passed over another peak called Blue Mountain. It was great to see he had taken to the trail name I had given him. I strung up the hammock and we chatted the hours away idly. Juggles and Goggles were a no show but Thirsty announced his presence with an ominous thud just after sunset, which reverberated around most of northern Pennsylvania.

"Shit. Fozzie, I fell out of my hammock!"

Eight miles from Bake Oven Knob the following day, Thirsty and I caught up with Juggles and Goggles as we crossed a bridge over the Lehigh River and met the PA-248. We needed a ride to Palmerton, situated a mile and a half down the road. The traffic was moving quickly downhill and there was no verge for them to pull over so we moved uphill a short way to take advantage of motorists waiting by the traffic lights.

We waited for thirty minutes, doing our upmost to make eye contact with the vehicle occupants to make them feel guilty for not offering us a lift. Goggles only put in any effort when the drivers were good-looking members of the opposite sex, but eventually Tom waved us over and we sped off towards town. He subsequently missed the turn off and drove for ages before stopping, taking us pretty much back to square one. It was a first for me; I'd never managed to catch a ride to town and then been left farther away from where I had originally started.

The first aspect that struck me about Palmerton was the open space. The roads were laid out parallel to each other in grid fashion. Avenues and streets were wide and generous, trees dotted the pavements and the locals milled around the park in the centre walking their dogs. No one seemed in a hurry, cars glided past slowly and I wondered whether it was some sort of public holiday.

Goggles and I sorted out a laundry run for everyone and, as I caught up with news on my phone, he snoozed precariously in a chair whilst leaning against a pillar. Somehow, even during sleep, the guy still had a smirk on his face as if he knew something that no one else did. The Jail House Hostel, conveniently situated across the road from the launderette, provided accommodation for the night.

***

Lehigh Gap was a climb that I had seen in countless photos during my AT research. Most of them were taken looking down on hikers ascending, with the road and the Lehigh River just tiny strips some 1000 feet below. We reeled in thousand-footers easily now but the further north we ventured many were becoming far steeper, particularly after Pennsylvania. Lehigh was no exception; the 1000-foot climb was just under a mile in length. Under a mile for a 1000 feet ascent was usually our guide. From one mile to a mile and a half we expected to be hard going but anything under this distance was regarded as steep. It did prove exactly that, but another obstacle on our path to Katahdin was conquered.

Once Lehigh had levelled out onto the flat ridge of yet another Blue Mountain, we were greeted with extensive views north down to Palmerton and the valley it nestled in, before hills rose back up on the distant horizon.

We gorged on blueberries, blackberries and raspberries, our progress impeded by the regular stops but we were thankful that our vitamin C levels had been topped up. An occasional quiet road intersected our path. Passing the Leroy A. Smith Shelter, we ventured further to eventually break camp at Hahns Overlook.

I didn't sleep well, and neither did Thirsty. The temperature had cooled overnight and our first problem with the hammocks had become apparent. If conditions were too cold, we felt the effects under our shelters. With only a thin area of nylon to lie on, we had no insulation below us. Warm on top under our sleeping bags, and being the height of summer, it was an area we had both neglected. The usual solution is to suspend what is known as an insulating quilt below, keeping the warm air of our bodies from escaping beneath. We hoped the overnight temperature would increase until we managed to get hold of some insulation.

There were no plans to stop in Delaware Water Gap, just sixteen miles on from Hahns Overlook. However, both Thirsty and I had to wait for the Post Office to open. Coupled with our usual thinking of grabbing hot food when it was available, before long it was late afternoon. Goggles joined us to share a room in the Pocono Inn which was cheap, especially as the three of us shared, but well past its sell-by date. Juggles left town to link up with a side trail and hike the ninety miles to pop out of the woods not far from where he lived. He wanted to chill at home and we gladly agreed to call him when we reached the Arden Valley Road, where he had agreed to pick us up, share some down time with him and a possible trip for breakfast to The Big Apple. I was humming *Breakfast in America* by Supertramp for most of the evening.

We left weighed down after agreeing to a cook up in camp that evening. Walmart, the American chain supermarket, exchanged our dollars for a kilo of minced pork, several potatoes, peppers, onions and spices. We crossed the Delaware River Bridge and left Pennsylvania, entering the eighth state of New Jersey. I had enjoyed my time in Pennsylvania but, hopefully, our rocky excursion was now over.

The traffic noise slowly faded as we climbed back up into the hills. After five miles enjoying a gentle ascent we crested to the idyllic sight of Sunfish Pond, a glacial lake. Its crystal-clear, calm waters glinted in the mid-day sun as the surrounding low-lying hills circled us, cloaked in the vivid greens of summer. Glorious ivory clouds drifted across our delightful sanctuary, and submerged rocks basked in the sunshine before plunging further down to the depths. No words were needed. We put down our packs by the northern edge and spent a relaxing afternoon in the sun, swimming and listening to music.

We barely spoke for three hours. Goggles caught up with his sleep, Thirsty took regular dips in the cold water in between sitting on the warm rocks, and I split my time doing all three.

I felt a tickling on my arm and slowly opened my eyes to see a dragonfly. A black thorax merged into its abdomen where fine white hairs caught the light. Four transparent wings were divided into small sections by a web of crazed lines and there it rested for two minutes, where I studied it happily. Occasionally, a weak wind passed. Caught by the change, my little friend lowered its body parallel to my arm and I felt the tiny, delicate claws on the end of each leg subtly digging into my skin to ride out the unexpected breeze. Its body pulsated like a heartbeat and, once in a while, eyes flicked up to meet my gaze, as if reciprocating my studies.

We met Hal Evans that evening, a ridge runner who informed us that swimming was prohibited in Sunfish Pond. Ridge runners worked with the public, trail community and officials along the length of the AT, keeping log books and offering assistance if required. When I enquired why no swimming was allowed, he explained that it encouraged erosion.

I have mixed views on erosion. I understand it is a problem for many outdoor areas with high traffic but it seemed just a little ironic that all trails, including the AT, are in fact erosion in their own right because of building them in the first place.

On the Pacific Crest Trail, a parking lot sits at the trailhead of the Cotton Wood Trail not far from Mt Whitney in the High Sierra. A blazing scar of bitumen carved into the side of the hills stretches several miles down to link up with the road system. In the parking lot, signs state not to pick up wood for fires, based on the 'leave no trace' theory. I still find it hypocritical that the authorities erected such signs, and implemented these regulations, after destroying several miles of pristine wilderness by scraping a road up there in the first place.

That memory lurked as I digested Hal's words. Although trails are, in fact, erosion, I don't see them as that. They are a means to provide access to the great outdoors, necessary erosion if you like, but I still struggle to understand how we can then be told not to take part in an activity because it causes damage.

We pulled in at the uninvitingly named Rattlesnake Campground and made camp quickly, excited at the prospect of a huge feast. A camp fire was built and, after letting it settle down to a mesmerising flickering of reds and oranges, the mound of pork began spitting whilst onions, peppers and potatoes sizzled. With a generous dash of spices there was ample food for the three of us. I spent the rest of the evening digesting, and keeping a keen eye out for snakes.

**

Thirsty was rubbing a plant on his leg as the sun rose. I glanced over whilst breaking camp and eventually, out of curiosity, went over and enquired what he was doing.

"It's a plant called Jewel Weed, Fozzie. Apparently it's good for mosquito bites."

Further research on our phones confirmed just that. After rain, water beaded up on the velvety leaves, creating little sparkles of moisture which is how the name came about. It was another weapon in our armoury against bites — and although the mozzies weren't as prevalent as I had feared, they were due to get much worse. The garlic plan was still in force and I always had a few cloves tucked away somewhere to supplement my evening meal. I was also resisting the urge to scratch bites and discovered that if I kept to this plan, the irritation was minor. Jewel Weed, however, became a much-needed alleviant.

New Jersey was spoiling us. Although the AT weaved a meagre seventy-two miles through the state, it took those miles and made the most of them. For much of the day we surfed along a ridge, dipping down into the woods and then returning to the rocky heights, like swimming underwater and occasionally, gladly, coming up for air. Blueberry bushes encroached onto the trail edges and, although we tried to avoid treading on them, the occasional crunch acted like rumble strips at the edge of a motorway, nudging us back to the middle of the trail. Views from the summits revealed a valley either side of us, each cradling a long, narrow lake.

It was windy. Gusts ripped randomly around us bringing our surroundings to life as the woods rustled in reply. The trees were alive, lifting as the torrents struck, then bowing back down when it subsided.

We saw few others that day; New Jersey appeared deserted. Unable to hold a conversation in the wind, we were lost in our thoughts. Occasionally, whoever was out front glanced back to check on the others and a knowing smile confirmed what we all felt — the woods were truly alive and it was an atmospheric day to experience it.

After meeting Hal again we all took some lunch by Stony Brook, enjoying the sunshine. He shared his knowledge of the trail and told us about the White Mountains, where he had hiked regularly. The Whites were a difficult stretch in New Hampshire, and dotted through the park were mountain huts. Not used very often by thru-hikers due to the costs, some did offer work in exchange for stay — if, indeed, there were any places available. Hal explained he had stayed at one once.

"I spent an hour turning over waste from the privy," he explained. "And my wife's job was to empty the fridge of out-of-date food and then clean it."

"Bearing in mind the raging hunger of most thru-hikers," I said, "I don't think asking them to clean out a fridge would be conducive to any business."

Thirsty and Goggles munched and nodded their heads in agreement.

The Whites, still 440 miles up trail, gave us some indication that the second half of the AT may be harder than the first. We were looking forward to the Whites and everything else the trail had in store. We were strong and determined that nothing would impede progress, and success was starting to seem possible even though failure never crossed our minds.

What we hadn't bargained for, however, was what the weather had in store for us.

Chapter 11
Seeking Solitude by the Rivers

June 29th to July 17th
Mile 1300 to 1643

The state lines of New Jersey and New York teased us several times. The trail dipped over into one, then fell back to the other, undecided, so we never knew if we'd left New Jersey or not. Finally, at mile 1360, we began hiking the eighty-eight miles of state number nine: New York.

It was June 29th, day ninety-one of my hike. Although I was happy that the Appalachian rains had generally held off up to that point, a new problem presented itself that was far worse. New York State was sweltering. Temperatures were hovering around or above 100°F and the humidity never fell below 100%. It sapped my energy; I was soaked in sweat all day and most of the night, and prayed for a respite. I wrapped a bandana around my neck, dipping it into water as I passed a creek or stream, and constantly wiped my face. Within minutes it had dried. Suddenly, food was taking second place to a new resource; everyone was chasing water.

We drank constantly, keeping an eye on upcoming water sources, of which New York had numerous. Occasionally we'd pass a hosepipe by the side of a farm or building and took it in turns to hose each other down. The relief was exhilarating and our soaked clothes kept us cool for an hour or so.

Following one hiker, I laughed as instead of taking the bridge over a river, he swerved right and approached the bank, dropped his pack and flinging off his shoes, and continued without breaking stride straight into the water.

I strove for starts around 6 a.m. to pull in some decent

mileage before the furnace fired up. Even the nights were hot; I often pulled my quilt to one side and there it stayed.

Goggles and Thirsty were also suffering, but faring slightly better than I, they were usually ahead by a couple of miles. That said, when Thirsty dropped back behind, I knew he was approaching, as his footfall reverberated through the ground like a runaway bear. Most times, when I was aware he was just a few feet behind, I merely stepped off trail for a second and let him steam past as though his brakes had failed.

"Thanks Fozzie!" And off he sped.

The trail tumbled along, rarely flat but without any major hills. It twisted, turned, emerged into sunlight and then plunged back into the woods. Board walks suspended us over swamps and marsh where the mosquitos droned annoyingly. The trail was easy but the heat was taking its toll on all of us. Embittered, I breathed deep, drank and resisted the urge to scratch my insect bites.

Keep going, Fozzie — you must keep going.

We stopped for food at a store in Unionville. The sheltered porch and flickering lights advertising 'deli' and 'breakfast' were too tempting to resist. I devoured a roll stuffed with bacon and two eggs before deciding I was still hungry, then ordered another — all washed down with two pints of chocolate milk, now our preferred choice of protein. I promptly ordered another roll to go.

New York is one of the most densely populated states on the AT but hikers never really notice. Although quiet road crossings were common, and stores, cafés and other amenities cropped up regularly, we were still in the most part oblivious to it as the trail shied away, hidden in the woods.

Bush Goggles was suffering badly from sexual frustration. So obsessed with the fairer sex had he become that when describing anything great, or even just good, it was referred to as 'titties'.

"How was your food?" I asked him outside Heaven Hill Farm, where we had stopped one afternoon.

"Oh yeah," he replied, "Titties."

***

Arden Valley Road, where Juggles had agreed to collect us, was approaching but not before a section known as 'Agonies Grind'. We made short work of the higher areas. The Eastern Pinnacles,

Monbasha High Point and Buchanan Mountain all passed as the AT clung to broad, rocky ridges, bordered with forest. The small community of Greenwood Lake was visible below us.

Agonies Grind wasn't marked in our guide so it caught us by surprise. Reminiscent of the Roller Coaster just before Harpers Ferry, it was a section of sharp climbs and descents that, while not particularly taxing, finished us off in a constant, searing heat. We emerged from the woods battered, bruised, and dripping a trail of sweat behind us.

Juggles, true to his word, arrived and took us back to the house he shared with his father James in Midland Park, New Jersey, where we eventually took three days out. Rest was required, I needed new shoes as Pennsylvania had finished my last pair prematurely, and we all had chores to take care of.

Juggles had taken advantage of a few days' work. The TV show *America's Got Talent* had contacted his agent, as they were in need of a juggler to perform, with others, to Will I Am's latest single. He needed a week to prepare under the choreographer and was constantly darting about to and from the city.

Lazagne had emailed stating his intention to come up and join us. He was back on trail but his two weeks out had put him a way behind. When he expressed a wish to walk with us, the guys had no problems with it so I invited him up. His intention was to return to the section he missed after reaching Katahdin and polish off that last little bit. Daffy was also back on trail but content to carry on from where he left off.

We spent a day in the big city. The Tick Tock Diner, on the corner of 34th Street and 8th Avenue, served us breakfast in typical, frantic, New York style. The streets were busy, traffic was noisy; I felt claustrophobic and couldn't breathe. Thank God for Central Park at least, an oasis in the big smoke, where we spent most of the afternoon.

"Wait, listen to this," Juggles said on the way back to the car in the evening. He approached a complete stranger coming towards us and motioned him to stop.

"What do you think of the Appalachian Trail?" he asked the bemused guy.

"I think I like it," he replied.

"How long did it take you?" Juggles questioned, trying not to giggle.

"Two hours."

With this, Juggles turned to me with a look of complete anguish on his face as he tried to suppress a laugh. He pushed one last question.

"What was your favourite part?"

"The top!"

***

Lazagne had arrived the following day and dropping us all back at the Arden Valley Road, Juggles explained he had around a week committed to the TV show but would be back on trail and, hopefully, would catch us up. Our new four-man team was rested and looking forward to the final 800-mile section.

West Mountain Shelter lay thirteen miles up the trail. We stopped there as its position commanded fine views of the New York suburbs and, being Independence Day, with the promise of fireworks, our perch offered the best outlook of the pyrotechnics.

The four of us camped in the woods and took our stoves to settle in front of the shelter. As our dinners cooked, we picked on snacks, and chatted to some locals who had also hiked up to watch the display. What we hadn't anticipated was the added spectacle of a lightning storm. As the fireworks exploded below us, a huge bank of cloud blew in from the west. Passing to the side of our overlook, the black mass bubbled, grew, and lightning bursts illuminated the cloud's interior. Forks of lightning cracked down, ominous rumbles reverberated around us and more firework displays joined the performance. It was better than any movie, even *The Great Escape.*

***

The lowest point on the AT was situated in a zoo, of all places. The Trailside Museum and Zoo to be precise. At just 124 feet above sea level, the trail passed directly through the zoo and didn't charge hikers an entrance fee. A nice gesture, but I wouldn't have paid it anyway. I hate zoos — in fact I loathe them. As it turned out, the zoo was shut and the gates locked. Unbeknown to us, there was a side trail for hikers to use when this was the case. Instead, we shimmied over the gate.

I know zoos educate us to the reasoning that their animals are kept because they were found injured, or orphaned and unable to survive by themselves, so they need to be looked after. I accept this in the cases where it may be true, but my dislike for these prisons stems from the other animals incarcerated there purely for show.

This was brought painfully home as I walked through the Trailside Zoo. I passed at an enclosure and abruptly stopped, saddened by what I saw. A lone fox, in a pen no bigger than most people's lounges, sat motionless and stared at me. I stopped as the guys went on, calling out that I'd catch them up.

I dropped my pack and sat down, watching my new friend. He didn't move, just returned my gaze; and despite the lack of communication, it wasn't needed. I quickly realised how unhappy this creature was. He lowered his head slightly as if ashamed, kept eye contact for long periods but then gazed off aimlessly, lost. Then I swore he was trying to tell me something, although I don't know how. An overwhelming sense of sadness hit me, as if this innocent fox was pleading with me to set him free. At one point he whimpered — a pathetic, lost cry of surrender. Resigned that he would never get out, be free to run through the woods, sleep in the grass, drink from a creek and start a family.

It wasn't right that I was free, and he was imprisoned. Surely it should be the other way around? At times my standard life felt like imprisonment and I longed for the outdoors. Here, the roles had been switched. I was wild and he was locked up, desperate to return.

He looked again, pleading with me almost to the point that I could hear him.

Open the gate. Please, open the gate and let me escape.

I looked around; no one was about and the zoo was still locked. It was quiet. I wished Thirsty was with me. He had a knack of seeing when something wasn't fair and acted on impulse. I knew he would have helped me.

Please. Please, let me free.

Compassion replaced logic, and overwhelmed by what I was seeing, emotions conquered resolve and I started to cry. Looking just inside the outer fence I saw an iron bar lying on the ground. I glanced at his pen; there was just one, feeble padlock on the gate. I reached for the latch.

Grab the bar, Fozzie. Break the padlock and set him free.

I got up and reached for the gate.

"Hey, morning! You know there's a side trail around the zoo

when we're closed? You're a thru-hiker right? Are you OK?" she asked, seeing my damp eyes.

I grabbed my pack and ran, eventually stopping at the Bear Mountain Bridge, which passed over the Hudson River. I stopped, caught my breath and composure and walked quickly towards the sanctuary of the trees. If anywhere could heal the hurt, it was the woods.

To this day I still see that fox. I still remember his forlorn expression, I still sense his pleading, I still hear him and I still feel as though I let him down. I would gladly have spent a few days locked up in exchange for his freedom.

And to this day, I still believe — animals shouldn't be locked in cages.

Rising away from the Hudson, trees moved in and huddled all around me as I crunched over gravel roads that intersected the trail. I climbed over Canopus Hill and descended. Lost in my thoughts I missed the turn off for Canopus Lake, eventually pulling up by the Shenandoah Camping Area for the night after thirty-one miles, to camp with the guys.

The heat and humidity continued to tire us the following day. Since Duncannon there had been no let-up. Dust from the trail clouded up around our legs and stuck to the sweat, resulting in a sticky brown residue.

Lazagne had already gelled well with the group. I knew he would; he was easy going, pulled in the miles and got on with the mission in hand without complaining, although he had commented on his sore knees. Goggles and Thirsty were suffering badly from sore sac syndrome, which had now spread between their buttocks. My legs were tired for some reason, and I was also sore in the same places. We had enough creams, powders and sprays to start a small pharmacy and each of us stopped regularly during the day to apply something, somewhere. Water seemed to help. If nothing else it did clean the area and the cold relief was welcome, as well as pleasantly numbing.

However, I couldn't figure out what was wrong with my legs. The point at which the lactic acid became too much, and my legs started to hurt after exertion, seemed to be kicking in earlier. Ascents seemed harder. I couldn't move as quickly and became frustrated. When setting off first thing it was usually my calves that ached, particularly going uphill but my quadriceps were also complaining. Thinking it may be some electrolyte problem, I increased my intake of a powder that replaced lost minerals, salts and electrolytes and hoped for the best.

We were all tired and our bodies were showing signs of wear. We had passed 1,450 miles, with around 734 left. As fit as we were, experience had taught me that the body starts complaining around that mark on any trail. The break in New York had been a good idea — we had refuelled, rested and returned full of enthusiasm. We got up each day, hoisted our packs and carried on walking north. It was now habit, ingrained and accepted. No one spoke of quitting. Katahdin was our focus and Katahdin would be reached.

We kept to around 1000 feet through most of New York State but the trail was starting to ripple. Short, steep hills meant summits arrived just as we started to breathe hard, and we caught up on oxygen going down, just in time for it to start over again.

Old, moss-covered stone walls in the woods marked long-forgotten boundaries. Sometimes I caught glimpses of a solitary building, or what was left of it, the last corner standing defiant amidst a pile of rubble.

I ascended down the 700 feet of Ten Mile Hill to the Ten Mile River, crossed over the Ned Anderson Memorial Bridge as sunlight bounced off the river, blinding me. Passing into Connecticut, the tenth state, I still had four more to negotiate: Massachusetts, Vermont, New Hampshire and Maine. I climbed again to Indian Rocks. Gaps in the trees teased with glimpses of the countryside below.

***

Lazagne and I finished off a long downhill to reach the CT-341 at Schaghticoke Road. Thirsty and Goggles were ahead of us and discovering the best places to renew fat levels in the town of Kent, just under a mile east. Tired and hot, neither of us could fathom which way east was. Having downloaded the data book onto our phones, we both peered helplessly at the screen, trying to see the directions as sunlight blinded us. Eventually we just went with the direction that seemed right and met up with the guys shortly after. Thirsty's uncle, John Lundeen, had agreed to put us up for the night. He collected us and drove us to his house in Darien where we were able to clean up and feast. We even managed to stumble on *America's Got Talent* that evening whilst watching TV and cheered as Juggles plied his trade effortlessly in the background, even managing a cheeky grin for the camera as he sped past on a unicycle. Again, glad of the rest, we left the following morning and were back on trail quickly.

A soft, sandy path hugged the Housatonic River as it kept us company for most of the day. Its wide, shallow and clear waters weaved around submerged boulders. Thinly spaced trees lined the banks. Thirsty and Lazagne floated down river whilst Goggles, unsurprisingly, napped on a warm rock, as did I.

The rivers on the AT were wonderful, particularly from Connecticut north. As the woods were often so dense, we had no idea what was coming up, except for checks made in the data book. Gradually, as I approached, the sound of water filtered over and met me, and the sunlight intensified, creating beams that spliced through lingering mists and silhouetted the trees.

Then I broke out from the forest into the light. After the dark woods it was a revelation to be free. Often I'd pick a route over the rocks until I reached the middle and just stood there. Facing downstream I could do little more than remain motionless, amazed, watching that huge ribbon of water gradually shrink and narrow, lines of perspective decreasing as I lost sight completely.

Although there were plenty of rivers intersecting the AT, I always became excited when I stumbled across one. Sometimes they seemed out of place, strange and unexpected. A long, silver slither parting the trees, a warm and bright oasis that demanded I stop and rest.

In fact I knew when I'd indulged in a little too much river therapy because the guys were always a way ahead. These warm, light strips where the trees parted and the rivers flowed became an addiction. The Housatonic either crossed my path or glided alongside me several times in Connecticut, and one morning was no exception.

It was cooler than usual, goose bumps speckled my arms and I spent several minutes contemplating whether to put on a jacket. A solitary silver birch stood sentry. Then, slowly, the trail descended, its soft sandy surface easing my feet into the day and the woods parted like a theatrical curtain. Mist spectres glided effortlessly across the water, a solitary crow called and I hopped out to a lonely rock. It was quiet. A gentle breeze tickled the tree tops and they replied with a genial rustle. I tilted my head skyward and, grateful for the early morning sun, just sat there.

The Housatonic slid past and, save the occasional gurgle, was silent. My rock was warm and I spent an hour revelling in the solitude, letting the wilds of Connecticut soothe me. I adored the rivers.

I caught the guys in the afternoon and we managed a quick lift into Salisbury to top up the fat levels and buy some food. Riga Roast Coffee solved my immediate caffeine crisis before we holed up in the Country Bistro, eagerly eying the menu. The waitress suggested we move nearer the back door, as 'there was more space on the table'. Returning, she took our orders, placed an industrial-strength fan pointing straight at us, and flicked it onto hurricane mode. Most of the napkins blew off the table and I guessed our aroma wasn't improving.

I was becoming hooked, for some unknown reason, on ginger cookies. The two supermarkets in Salisbury failed to deliver and I left despondent, hands in pockets, kicking the dirt. When I reached the end of a quiet road before disappearing back into the woods, a car pulled alongside me and stopped. The woman beckoned me over.

"Hiking the AT?" she said.

"Yes, I am."

"Well here, take these. I have two and figured you might like one of them."

With that I accepted the pack she held out and, before I could even thank her, she had driven off as if she knew something that I didn't. I looked down to be met by the sight of a pack of ginger cookies nestling in my hand. Go figure.

Stocked with good food we left town and made inroads into the ascent up Bear Mountain. I had concentrated on buying food with not only fat, but healthy sources of it — such as a small bottle of olive oil slipped into the outside of my pack. A tub of fresh pesto was finished quickly, dipping a fresh tear of Kaiser Bread into the green paste. I supplemented my stocks with cheese, olives, various nuts and even carefully wrapped up an avocado in a pair of socks to protect it.

I increased my intake of electrolyte powder and also started to drink a protein shake in the morning. Good, nutritious food wasn't the lightest or easiest to carry but it always revived me.

Passing the Riga and Brassle Brook Shelters, we climbed from 720 feet to 2316 feet strongly and smoothly to summit Bear Mountain. A hiker called Easy Mile was resting at the top, and we exchanged a few pleasantries. I was to bump into her several times that afternoon. We descended to Sages Ravine, crossed the Connecticut–Massachusetts state line and then our path forced us up harshly to the summit of Mt Everett. The afternoon levelled somewhat and we relaxed.

I was happy, content with my world. The 102 days now behind me were already imparting lifelong memories, filtering out the least important and leaving me with vibrant recollections. I was fit. Several weeks of nature's nurturing had calmed my mind and I felt healthy. My breathing seemed easier, problems that played with my consciousness had either been resolved or had vanished, and my body slowly responded to the nutrients I had eaten.

All these factors made me smile but, occasionally, I also felt sad. Sad because I was on the home stretch. Instead of walking away from the beginning, I now felt as if I were walking towards the finish. There were perhaps six weeks left to reach Katahdin, at which point the inevitable feeling of helplessness would come back to haunt me.

Most of the reputable thru-hikes in the northern hemisphere require finishing near the onset of the winter. After months of freedom, escaping the constraints of my normal life and becoming recharged, there was little to look forward to. I would invariably return home to England with nothing more than a bleak winter to battle through. Sounds despondent I know but post-thru-hike depression is common.

It takes time for us to readjust to society. After plentiful time in the wilds the shock of leaving is hard for many to comprehend. I tend to cope reasonably well; I'm not one for wallowing in self-pity, although it may take me a week or two to merge back.

Houses seem confining, the air dry, there are too many distractions and unwanted noise, and I hate dealing with the boring, mundane activities that civilisation demands. It feels like an alien environment and many times I entertain the idea of a walk with no set direction, a walk with no end. An adventure to escape to, forever.

A walk with no end is just that. To spend the rest of my life drifting through the world, with what I need strapped to my back. Perhaps I'd have a dog for company, but one thing is for sure — my route would not be planned. The walk with no end doesn't stick to one, marked trail; it meanders on many, undoubtedly through Europe, probably starting in England. I always dreamt of starting with no ideas other than to walk on an approximate southeasterly bearing.

I didn't want a schedule mapped out of where I was heading. I wanted to be free to go wherever I wished. There would be no daily mileage targets and no overall distant goal. After catching a ferry over the English Channel I'd listen to my senses, be open to suggestion and flow along able to accept opportunities as they appeared.

The only plan I'd entertain would be the approximate direction. I could see myself progressing through northern France in the direction of Switzerland. As the Alps rose up I'd probably veer east and explore the foothills, occasionally rising up higher to the summits. Liechtenstein and Austria seem obvious choices but my options, always open, meant that if the Mediterranean called, I could work over the Alps and hike down through the Dolomites, reaching Italy's Po Valley.

The Adriatic Sea would beckon and, passing Venice, perhaps I'd pay a visit to Trieste before crossing into Slovenia. From there Croatia has always been on the wish list along with the lesser-visited countries of Hungary, Serbia, Romania and Bulgaria before the vast Black Sea came to view. Or perhaps I'd travel further north, taking advantage of the summer through such delights as Slovakia, Hungary, Poland and Belarus.

Live their cultures, taste their cuisine, marvel at the history, and lose myself in the forests and mountains. Perhaps spend a day in town once in a while, drink coffee and read the newspaper then move on, feed the nomad.

And all the while I'd be free, indulging the dromomaniac, satiating its appetite, bowing to its whims. Left? Right? Straight? I wouldn't care, pick the path that seemed right, follow my instincts.

Sweet serendipity. One day …

***

Bush Goggles was like a whippet in an espresso bar, constantly needing to pull in miles. He had agreed to meet his mum at the finish and travel back home with her. His relationship with her was obviously great, and he beamed as he spoke of his plans. However, his plan was affecting me, and I didn't like it.

To that point, Goggles, Thirsty, Lazagne and I spent most of the day either hiking with each other, or in the same approximate vicinity. Sometimes we'd walk alone but we always pulled in a similar mileage, and at some point in the afternoon we would break and discuss the options of where and when to camp.

Goggles had set himself a tough target to reach Katahdin, and although he was more than capable of sticking to it, the constant demands to meet his quota were impacting on me.

If anything, I wanted to slow down. I was still on course for a sub-five-month finish and I didn't need to rush, nor pull in huge miles to achieve it. I was also painfully aware that I didn't want the Appalachian Trail to finish.

Thirsty and Lazagne seemed fine with the pace and distance but I was tiring of it. I was more than capable of pulling in the miles that Goggles had set himself; and as we all enjoyed his company, and didn't want to split the group, we met his targets. I didn't want to see him go but I knew that at some point I would talk to everyone and raise my concerns. At that point Lazagne and Thirsty would either keep with Goggles, keep with me, or we'd disband and figure it all out for ourselves.

The town of Dalton shimmered in a heat haze. We made our way down Depot Street after filling up with stove alcohol at the L.P Adams store. The Mill Town Tavern, profitably placed right on the AT, seemed a good choice to grab a beer. I entered and my choice seemed confirmed as Thirsty greeted me with an ale in hand.

Dalton had places to stay but, for some reason, they were all expensive. We agreed to grab a shower at the Sports Hall, which kindly offered its washrooms free to thru-hikers. Laundry was also dealt with in the shower and, after just a couple of hours, we left to start our sixth day on trail without a zero and make dents into the ascent of Mt Greylock, seventeen miles and 2000 feet away. The shores of Gore Pond offered a great camp spot for the night and amongst some crazy mosquitos, I drifted off to the cries of Loons calling and frogs splashing.

Six a.m. was unreasonably dark. Dense evergreens blocked out whatever light managed to escape from cloudy skies and a dog's cry down in the valley was the only sound. I alternated between packing up camp, sipping on coffee and grabbing a handful of granola to fuel the system.

The guys left as I was finishing off. Working my way down outcrops of marble known as the Cobbles, I paused to take in the view of the Hoosic River and the town of Cheshire below, with Mt Greylock rising up behind.

Cheshire was quiet. The AT joined Church Street before turning right onto School Street. Unable to find the store and grinning at the prospect of being in town at breakfast time, I was soon disappointed to find everywhere shut at 7.30 in the morning. I spotted Lazagne and Goggles coming down a side street and they directed me towards the only open store in town. A bottle of chocolate milk followed by a protein bar worked wonders on my muscles, and I tucked another bottle of protein away in my pack for later that day.

We rested on Mt Greylock, the highest point in Massachusetts, admiring the ninety-three-foot-high Massachusetts Veterans War Memorial Tower, before a cry caught my attention.

"Hey!"

I turned around out of instinct but realised the call probably hadn't been directed at me anyway.

"Hey! Fozzie!"

I turned again to see Pink Bits, sorry, Lady Forward coming towards me. I even got a hug on arrival.

"Pink Bi … sorry, Lady Forward. How are you?"

"Great!"

She was happy, going strongly and focused on finishing.

"Here," I offered. "This is for you. I've been lugging this thing with me since I last saw you. It's your turn, at least until you pass me."

I handed her the gauntlet and she took it.

"You'll have it on Katahdin, you know," she jested.

"We'll see about that."

Another familiar face appeared later. The Congdon Shelter was quiet and seemed empty as I passed.

"Fozzie!"

I turned to see Chez 11 grinning and poking his head out from the interior.

"Chez 11! How the hell are you, mate?"

"Not too bad. Feet have been in bad shape since Duncannon though. You?"

"Yeah, I'm all good."

A few blisters spotted his feet and he agreed that his new shoes were partly to blame, as he was still wearing them in.

"I'll deal with it," he added. "Too close to quit now.

***

Shortly before the Seth Warner Shelter I left Massachusetts and entered Vermont. Along with the two remaining states of New Hampshire and Maine, this area of northeast America was famed for its autumnal colours. Unfortunately we were early, and being the middle of July, the dynamic greens around me showed few signs of surrender. With our progress to date, we would have finished and left Maine before the majestic shades of yellow, red and orange celebrated the end of the summer.

Even so, Vermont was stunning. Wood and forest still occupied vast swathes of the land, which the AT faithfully followed. But we were blessed with wide-open spaces where sunlight streamed down. The air was clean, the skies deep blue and farm buildings we passed retained a sense of age, their colourful wooden exteriors blending with the area.

The terrain was becoming tougher. It seemed that since Pennsylvania, the further we ventured north, the more demanding the hiking became. Elevations dipped to as little as 400 feet, reaching as high as 4000. Any mountaineer or hiker will tell you that a 4000-foot elevation is relatively minor but it was still the constant ups and downs in between where our energy was expended. Mountains rarely entail a straightforward ascent straight up; there are usually sections going down as well.

With the elevation and occasional winds the temperature had dropped; and although still hot, it was slowly becoming more bearable. Clouds cast shadows and cooled our surroundings further still.

The AT was becoming wilder and more remote. The last three states were prone to harsh winters and less populated; regularly we stopped at vantage points and marvelled at the arena surrounding us. A vast sea of green stretched away in all directions, occasionally broken by rocky mountain summits. Lonely, elongated lakes dotted the valleys and shimmered. The huge expanses of open water caught the sunlight and winds whipped across the surface creating alluring patterns.

We tried to camp high, still escaping the mosquitos, where the breeze chased them away. We were humbled by stunning sunsets of reds and oranges bouncing off the waters and casting infinite shadows. Canada was near and Maine, our last state, jutted sneakily northwards into the next country as if claiming a small portion for itself.

Lazagne, Goggles, Thirsty and I reached Stratton Mountain where the lookout tower and caretaker's cabin kept tabs on the weather. We sat snacking under the tower as one of the caretakers strolled over.

"Bad storm coming!" She said, smiling as if it were meant to be great news. "Get into camp early if you can and hunker down! 'Bout eight o'clock I think."

We looked at each other as Lazagne peered into his phone to corroborate the news but ended up just shrugging his shoulders.

"She knows something we don't," he said.

Veering on the side of caution, and remembering the fickle mountain weather patterns, we agreed to camp at Prospect Rock. I left first, keeping a watchful eye out for the William B. Douglas Shelter, which was situated just under a mile before the turn off for the Prospect Rock camp area.

Daydreaming and concentrating on speed to be sure of getting to camp before the storm rolled in, I missed the sign for the shelter, and for Prospect Rock itself. Luckily Spruce Peak Shelter was close at hand. As I pulled in, nodding to Chez 11 who was setting up in the shelter, the wind started to increase. I looked up through the trees and saw the ominous black clouds stream over.

I strung up my hammock first, just in case I got caught out and retired to the table outside the shelter where the others had congregated, as usual, for some socialising.

Catching up with Chez 11 after our brief encounter earlier that day, he introduced me to three, new faces; Danish, Metric and Don Quixote.

Food stock levels varied between the three of us. I was well stocked after a resupply in Bennington. Danish's head disappeared into his food bag, looking disappointed when he emerged. We supplemented his rations and he reciprocated with a few titbits to liven up our dinners.

Dinner time on trail was an interesting time to study the eating habits of others. Because of our raging hungers, most hikers ate quickly, shovelling ramen, pasta or rice dishes down as quickly as possible. Others savoured their food and dined slowly, taking the time to appreciate the contents of their pot.

Conversations were animated; news on how we were all doing, where everyone else was, the weather, mosquitos, and other relevant topics were discussed.

We each cleaned our pots as we finished. I'm sometimes asked how I do my washing up on thru-hikes. How much washing up liquid did I carry? Did I bother with a cloth, and perhaps a small towel to dry my utensils? I don't think I've ever met a thru-hiker who bothered with any of them. The preferred method of cleaning up utilised just water and a finger.

My pot was a perfect depth to accept my middle finger, which just reached the bottom. A small trickle of water was poured in, and then I swept my finger around the sides of the pot, scraping away any detritus clinging to the sides, sucking my finger after each sweep. Then, I'd swish the water around, discard it, and repeat the finger process again. Finally, a quick tickle on the bottom of the pan, and a final rinse was job done.

The interesting point was watching others do the same, as it was the method most used. As we were usually so hungry, with smaller than ideal rations, every scrap of food was eaten. Pots were cleaned to within an inch of being sterile. Fingers precisely wiped pans, sucked carefully after each pass and savoured as though it were a last meal. Concentration was focused, precise checks and observations picking up any stray morsels. Mugs were tipped skyward as we searched for the last dribble that may, or may not, drop out to an expectant tongue; and again a small splosh of water swilled around with care to retrieve that last dribble of coffee. Cutlery was sucked and inspected for any clingers, which were removed with a fingernail or wiped along a suitable piece of clothing, then sucked again, tongues scanning the surface for any irregularities.

Food was gold and, along with water, a valued commodity. We never had enough of it. Portions were never big enough and variety never up to par. However, such was our hunger that it was never wasted and, despite the limitations, always enjoyed and savoured. Such a change to everyday life where obscene amounts of food are sometimes wasted. We never left a scrap and relished our food.

A few fat raindrops splattered our little haven in the woods. We ran for our shelters. The woods hissed and roared as the deluge gained strength and a fierce wind ripped through that little corner of Vermont. I ran for my hammock, suspended my rucksack under the tarp and sat underneath, observing the torrent as, gradually, the light faded. Occasional gusts lifted my tarp, pulling at the anchor points. Eventually, too tired to sit any longer, I slid into my sleeping bag and watched, enthralled, as the woods lit up with lightning bursts, silhouetting the trees above me.

I fell asleep thinking of mountains. The Whites were coming.

Chapter 12
The Whites

July 18th to July 30th
Mile 1643 to 1841

The storm had stopped during the early hours but nature was still clearing up. The trail, overgrown in sections, was littered with deadfall; plants were dripping wet, dampening my clothes as I brushed past. The woods were silent save an occasional plop of water plummeting from the trees above and hitting small pools nestled amongst tree roots. Swathes of mist glided effortlessly through the canopy, chilling my exposed skin as I entered the murk. I stepped up my pace and put on a warm jacket, occasionally holding my trekking poles under my arm to rub my hands together, but the friction did little to alleviate their numbness. Cobwebs constantly covered my face as I frantically brushed them away.

The guys were somewhere behind. I had made an early start from the Spruce Peak Shelter but, eager for them to catch up, I took regular breaks and enjoyed a leisurely pace.

I paused at the VT-11 and VT-30 to contemplate hitching into Manchester Center for breakfast, just over five miles west, but continued progress won the day over bacon and eggs. I sped up the climb culminating at the summit of Bromley Mountain, descended down to Mad Tom Notch and then rose once more to bag Styles Peak and Peru Peak. As I was resting on a footbridge a few minutes later, Thirsty, Goggles and Lazagne finally rolled in.

The pursuit of the hyper light still seemed to be affecting Lazagne. Having extolled the benefits of the hammock to me, which subsequently influenced my purchase shortly after, he had now ditched the system. A solitary tarp weighing barely a couple of hundred grams now acted as his shelter with a small section of plastic forming a barrier between him and the ground. A sliver of foam provided ground insulation, with a lightweight quilt to sleep under. A new rain jacket barely registered on the scales at ninety grams and he had also, remarkably, ditched his stove, fuel, and associated equipment, surviving on cold food and drink.

His new radical approach was inadvertently having an impact on me and the others, and was fuel for constant, light-hearted jibes in his direction. As he constantly made amendments to his equipment, his tweaks had left him short of gear that others would deem necessary. His knife had been a victim of cutbacks, as well as his camp shoes. Camp shoes were just that — usually a pair of light, comfortable and vented offerings to wear in the evening for a little comfort, and for our feet to air and escape the confines of our smelly, damp hiking shoes.

Lazagne's gear refinements had resulted in the occasional plea to borrow an item. A knife was the most common request but his lack of footwear took the situation a little too far. One evening at camp he strolled over and asked to borrow my Crocs. A knife? No problem, but appeals for personal items such as clothing, and indeed, shoes, were taking things a little far. I mean, I even struggled to put my footwear on — camp shoes or hiking shoes — because of the stench and rapidly increasing communities of microbes calling both of them home.

"Fozzie, can I borrow your Crocs real quick?" he asked, sheepishly.

"Where's yours?" I questioned.

"I sent them home, didn't need them anymore."

"Well, obviously you do need them. Don't you think that your pursuit of the mega-light is pushing the boundaries a little too far, Phillip?"

He stuffed his hands in his pockets and shuffled his feet guiltily.

"Yeah. Ditching the shoes may have been hasty."

"You can borrow my shoes but just the once because I don't think it's fair. So, you can keep that 'borrow' in the bag for a later time, or feel free to use them now. Either way, it's only the once, sorry."

On the plus side, the Anglo-American chess championship was back and competitive as ever. Picking up from where we had left off weeks prior, the score had now reached three to one in his favour.

The English had mounted a comeback and after game five that evening at Little Rock Pond I had pulled one back to bring the score to three-two.

Checkmate!

***

Wild swimming was the new activity and inadvertently meant we needed to spend less time in town. We were able to wash ourselves and our clothes, which meant motel rooms and laundrette stops weren't needed so much.

A classic example was the Mill River. As we rounded a corner the impressive, if somewhat wobbly, Clarendon Gorge suspension bridge hung precariously over a rocky drop to the river cascading through the narrow rock walls below. A small path picked its way down to the popular swimming hole and we cooled off and discreetly bathed for an hour. Regular washing seemed to be resolving our sore sac issues as well, and in the main there seemed to be some improvements.

The water in Vermont, and further north as we were to discover, was beautiful. The lakes in particular provided calm waters and cool temperatures. Often, rocks poked out a short distance from shore and we swam to them, then hauled ourselves out to dry off and bask in the sun. The activity also cooled off tired muscles.

Most of us were suffering physically so relief was welcome. I was carrying five injuries: an old battle wound to my right calf throbbed constantly, my right ankle hurt on the back and left-hand side, my left knee ached, and my left elbow was swollen for some unknown reason.

Lazagne's knees were still causing him grief, but Thirsty seemed to be either faring well — or he was also suffering but not complaining about it. Goggles seemed fine in the muscle department but had been grumbling about a bad stomach and feeling lethargic. 1700 miles in and with around 484 left, our adventure was taking its toll.

Mentally, however, we had never been stronger. That first month, where most hikers drop out, was now one of many memories we nurtured. Although our surroundings changed by the minute, our routine and mental resolve remained solid.

Each of us approached the day in our own individual styles but we had formed a unique pattern to get us through it. We rose with the sun, which was now well past the summer solstice so each morning it peeked over the horizon a little later. Lazagne was usually the first to rise. Being quick to pack up, he was usually ten minutes up the trail before the rest of us broke camp. I brewed coffee, snatched a little to eat and Thirsty and Goggles usually left just before me.

We still hiked together, occasionally splitting up as the day progressed but joined each other if someone was resting. We shared the views, conquered mountains, forded rivers — and, each day, got just a little closer to Katahdin.

In the evenings our respective routines came into their own once more. I always slung up my hammock first. Then, I'd stretch out my leg muscles with a series of exercises which took perhaps ten minutes. Although often ignored, I had made efforts to stick with this routine on the advice of my physiotherapist back home.

Then I'd hang my sleeping bag over the hammock so the down expanded whilst some water boiled for a hot drink. Slipping into my camp shoes and donning a warm jacket as my body cooled, I'd take some time to update my journal for the day.

Then food, the highlight of every evening and a much-treasured activity. Each of us would usually commandeer the table if we had camped near a shelter; but, more often than not, we now stayed away from them. Congregating at a suitable spot, perhaps by some trees to act as a backrest, we watched our dinners cook and reviewed the day.

It was not just a time to eat, but to catch up. We chatted together, although sometimes one of us, seeking a little solitude, would remain absent and the rest would respect their privacy. Thirsty and I often shared this trait and would remain either in or near our hammocks. He also liked to make camp near the lake shorelines, enjoying the relative calm and therapy of gently lapping water. Close to the lakes there was a lack of trees so hammock spots were rare. Thirsty regularly bagged the prime spots and spent a few minutes standing sentry like a guard dog; get too close to his patch and he'd look disapprovingly in our direction, narrow his eyes in warning and occasionally he'd even growl.

Goggles was easy. He'd employ a quick scout round of the

available spots, scratch his head and make himself comfortable in whatever area he'd chosen. He could have pitched on a slope, with umpteen tree roots and a small puddle but still he'd merely grin and utter his catch line: 'Oh yeah, titties.'

Lazagne was happy pretty much anywhere. He'd scout around for a few minutes and, after a little head-scratching, make it home for the night.

Once fed and rested, we'd often retire to the camp fire after sunset to stay warm, catching brief glimpses of each other in the meagre light as the flames rose and fell. Often we were quiet. The fluctuating patterns of the blaze became addictive as we stared into their world. Cracking and spitting, glowing embers escaped and rose up before slowly fading.

And slowly, one by one, we bade each other a good night, crept into our shelters, spent a few minutes still as our sleeping bags warmed to our body heat, and slept soundly.

***

As we spilled out onto the VT-103, we were pleased to see a sign for the Whistle Stop Restaurant, just a half-mile down the road. We sat outside on the grassy area while the owners popped out regularly to top up our coffee levels before bringing an afternoon breakfast over — a delicious feast worthy of any thru-hiker's appetite.

A steep climb up a rocky outcrop followed before the trail dipped down to the Clarendon Shelter and rose once more to Beacon Hill. A ten-mile, 2500-foot climb beckoned to the Cooper Lodge Shelter; but, having become tired, we pulled in early near Robinson Brook to camp.

I slept poorly as the bottom of my hammock was still cold. During the early hours I got up and slung my old quilt underneath for insulation, which worked perfectly, the sleeping bag keeping me warm once back inside.

When I did eventually rise, I was surprised to see Pink Bits's, sorry, Lady Forward's tent lurking in the trees a short way off. I hadn't noticed it during the night. Realising she must have arrived late the previous evening, I snuck over.

"Morning, Pink Bits," I said softly.

"I don't answer to that name anymore," came the groggy reply.

"I'm off shortly," I continued. "Just wanted to bring the

gauntlet over for you. Have a great day."

***

While relaxing at camp after a strong afternoon with good miles, Lazagne shuffled over looking a little sheepish.

"You OK?" I ventured.

"Fozzie, I have a bit of a problem," he explained. "I think I might have a tick."

"Well it's not so bad," I said. "They're pretty easy to identify and remove."

"It's not so much the tick, it's the location of it."

I paused from eating my Mexican savoury rice and looked at him.

"Where exactly is it?" I ventured, still chewing.

He paused and scratched his head.

"Between, well, it's between my nuts and my arse."

Laughing was probably not the most sympathetic of responses but I couldn't help it.

"Oh shit."

"Yeah, shit," he confirmed.

He looked at me silently and expectantly until I finally caught his angle.

"Oh, hold on! Wait a second! No! Absolutely not! I consider you a fine friend and there are many things I'd do for you, including pulling you from a river if you were in trouble, right up to looking after you if you fell. However, there is no way I'm surveying the hidden crevices of your anatomy for either a positive verification, or any form of removal. Sorry mate."

"OK, that's cool."

"You could try taking a photo of it for identification?" I added.

As I returned to my dinner, occasional flashes from the direction of Lazagne's camp silhouetted the outline of his legs as he took several exposures with his phone stuffed down his shorts.

"It's OK, Fozzie!" came the cry a few minutes later. "It's just a bit of dirt!"

Vermont had started to roll. Hills of a constant gradient were rare on any part of the AT, which more often involved short, sharp ascents and descents in between bigger peaks. However, Vermont was noticeably tougher. It was slowing us down

although our mileage remained pleasing, between twenty to thirty miles most days — but it was taking longer to pull in the same distances.

This got me thinking how I could better manage my day and I started a list of time-saving methods, more often out of humour to keep me amused as opposed to actually putting them into practice.

Taking the time to roll a cigarette whilst peeing had the potential to save a couple of valuable minutes. With both hands not necessarily required for pee breaks, it seemed obvious to put them to some other use and I did try this method, but discounted it because of the lack of aim and subsequent splash back.

Another potential skill — although not linked with time saving — was the ability to pee in the middle of the night without getting out of my hammock. This proved difficult in a tent but Thirsty and I had already mastered the art of hammock peeing and, often, at some point in the early hours, the sound of splashing on the ground could be heard as one of us relieved ourselves.

I had managed to master the enviable art of either removing or donning my jacket without breaking my stride or completely removing my backpack. This, again, wasn't so much of a time saver, more a personal challenge that I'd seen others employ.

I had perfected the art of weatherproofing when it started to rain. My poncho lived in an outside pack pocket and a quick grope to one side retrieved it whilst I threw it over me and my pack. The umbrella quickly followed as it also lived in the same pocket. I could do all of this without stopping.

Finally, snacking, applying sunscreen, drinking and checking the data book without breaking stride had all been mastered back in the Smokies.

Perhaps I was paying too much attention to time-saving experiments? It was usual to think whilst hiking, and regularly becoming lost in thought; but it had affected my concentration on occasion. Hearing a loud rustle up in the trees, I naturally looked to try and see what was causing it — before walking straight into a tree trunk. Although cursing the mental distraction and a very sore face, shortly after I admit to passing a very attractive female hiker coming from the opposite direction. Turning around to take in the rear view, as is natural for both sexes on trail (she did the same), I promptly walked straight into another tree. Saving any further loss of face, literally, I laughed it off and tried to look more professional.

We skirted the town of Killington, passed Kent Pond and took a side road into town. Food was calling and I also needed batteries, so I entered the Base Camp Outfitters. Whether the woman that served me had seen me lurking around various sections studying equipment and had deemed me prime for a potential sale, or she had excess stock I don't know, but her sales pitch did little to lure me to the object in question.

"Have you seen this, it's brilliant!" she opened with, handing me a silver-coloured piece of cloth about the size of a large handkerchief.

"What is it?" I enquired.

"It's made by NASA," she proclaimed, as if this fact alone would secure a sale. "The technology is amazing. Just soak it in cold water and it stays cool."

I usually turned off when I discovered that anything was made by NASA — or. as the Americans pronounced it, *Narsore*. Responsible as they may have been for making inroads into the space race, and the subsequent technology associated with it, I noticed that most people in the States take everything they produce, or endorse, as sufficient reason to buy it without question. Well, it's produced by *Narsore* — it must be great!

"How much is it?" I asked the assistant.

"It's forty dollars," she answered, her expression similar to a double glazing salesman trying his luck with a high price.

"Forty dollars is a hell of a lot to ask for a piece of cloth," I said. "I use this," holding up my bandana. "Cost me two dollars fifty and does exactly the same job."

I paid for the batteries and left her staring into several redundant boxes containing NASA Cool Cloths, no doubt wondering whether she had been a little hasty.

I found the others at the Killington Deli. Several empty bottles of chocolate milk and sandwich wrappers dotted the table and the guys looked suitably full.

"How was the food?" I asked.

"Titties," Goggles replied and then changed the subject. "Have you seen the elevation graph?"

I peered at my phone to study the data book, which provided a schematic of ascents and descents. By way of comparison, back in Pennsylvania, this line coasted along with barely a ripple. Now it looked more like a cardiograph screen hooked up to a patient with a serious heart condition.

"Crikey!" I exclaimed.

"That's nothing," chipped in Thirsty. "Check out New Hampshire."

I scrolled forward a few pages.

"Flippin' 'eck!"

New Hampshire, home to one of the toughest sections of the AT through the White Mountains, or *Whites* as they are known, looked positively horrific. Mt Washington itself peaked at 6288 feet, and there were numerous other stiff climbs. The elevation graph bounced up and down, steep ascents and descents appeared everywhere and a new term, *notch*, made its debut. Notches, as we were to find out, were pretty common in New Hampshire and Maine. The name pretty much gives them away, but imagine a V-shaped indentation in the terrain, steep on both sides with a river at the bottom. We English would refer to them as gorges. The Whites were a mere fifty miles away, and Vermont, it appeared, was doing its upmost to get us into gear for them.

Our confidence was high and we knew there was nothing that could stop us, but still, I always doubted my own ability. Despite having around six thousand miles of hiking experience, I still looked at difficult terrain, particularly climbs, and didn't know if I could make it. I always relied on my trail mantra of *never, ever, ever, give up* to see me through. Nothing was ever that difficult, was it?

Every evening and several times during the day I vigilantly made checks in the data book. I often preferred to hike in ignorance; whatever the trail had in store for me wasn't going to change, whether I knew about it or not. However, planning each day was necessary. It was no use planning to pull in a thirty when I didn't know that there were 8000 feet of climbs and descents to take into account.

Most hikers will groan when they know any climbing is imminent, me included. Knowing that an hour is all it takes to knock off three miles, perhaps four or even more, and then suddenly faced with a speed drop to less than one mile an hour was a motivation killer.

Despite my grumbles and lack of confidence, when in full flow I loved hills. Covering ground over flat terrain is undemanding, and dare I say sometimes it can be monotonous. There's little energy expended, minimum effort required, and concentration is limited to avoiding detritus on the trail.

Crossing mountain ranges where steep climbs were common always appeared daunting but I relished the challenge.

Climbing was all about keeping near to the limit I had set myself. I knew, roughly, how long a 1000-foot ascent took, and could subsequently adjust my pace, and effort, to see me up to the top without exhausting myself. There were other factors such as the distance those 1000 feet were spread over, what time of day it was, how I was feeling; even the weather played a part. But, after quick mental observations of how those influences could affect me, I then figured out how I needed to react to get up there.

When the hill hit, I went in at the pace I thought best. Sometimes I felt confident and pushed hard, playing around with pain limits and holding it just below them. At other times I completely misjudged them, or was just having a bad day physically, and all the planning went out of the window. But there are few greater pleasures than being at the peak of physical fitness, staring down a mountain and then reaching the top. You just feel superhuman, and nothing in the world is unachievable.

To take it to the next level, after a thru-hike is completed, and all the miles, weeks, physical exertion and metal stamina are behind us, we emerge as stronger individuals. Returning home, we suddenly realise what we have actually achieved and it makes a positive impact on everyday life. To walk 2000 miles and more through the heat, the wet, and the cold tests anyone's resolve — but it imparts strength. Suddenly, anything is achievable. We learnt the power of perseverance, to push through regardless of the odds, to always keep going. Obstacles in everyday life were not viewed negatively, but positively.

I've just walked 2000 miles! I can do anything I want to do!

***

Vermont ended at the Ledyard Bridge spanning the Connecticut River, and heralded our arrival into not only the penultimate state, New Hampshire, but to the town of Hanover as well. We had 161 miles to negotiate through New Hampshire and a further 282 through Maine, the last state — a total of some 443 miles. It was July 22nd, day 114 of my thru-hike.

Hanover was a beautiful town. Dartmouth College sat in an island of grass, occupying a proud position near the centre, its colonial buildings dating back to 1769. With wonderful architecture and old stone buildings, neatly trimmed gardens, parks and clean streets, it was a pleasure to thread a route through town.

We were eager for a motel so we could clean up. Thirsty, Goggles, Lazagne and I loitered outside Dunkin' Donuts as I got stuck into one of their glazed chocolate varieties. The Sunset Motor Inn, situated a couple of miles out of town, seemed to be the only viable option in an expensive area. The logbook stated they were happy to offer rides from town, which a phone call soon confirmed. It was the first time in my thru-hiking adventures that I had ever walked into a town looking for a motel, only to get a ride out again. Normally, I'd be standing by a road trying to get in, not the other way round.

Using a bed rotational system, normally disputed when at a motel, Thirsty and Goggles claimed the two beds whilst Lazagne and I slept on our mats on the floor. A shuttle bus made regular stops outside the motel and, the following morning, I caught an early one into Hanover for breakfast and some gear replacements. My head torch had died, and I needed a new pack towel to replace the one I had lost, not to mention new shorts as well.

The Hopkins Center for the Arts at Dartmouth College was celebrating its 50th anniversary with an unusual but wonderful project called *Hands on Pianos*. The college had dotted brightly painted pianos around Hanover and the surrounding area. The object was simple and invitations open; if you were a half-decent piano player, or indeed couldn't play at all, the idea was simply to sit down and have a go.

Strange as it was to see pianos perched on street corners, they drew regular crowds as participants shared their favourite tunes. I listened to everything from Mozart to Mick Jagger.

We reluctantly prised ourselves away from Hanover and its eclectic music choices at mid-day, managing twelve miles before setting up camp on Holts Ledge. After converging on a rock slab with impressive views down to the lowlands, we sat around watching the sun sink lower whilst slapping mosquitos, leaving bloody streaks on our exposed flesh. I missed the pianos and fell asleep humming songs by the Rolling Stones.

The data book's interpretation of New Hampshire turned out to be accurate, as we would have expected. Plummeting from Holts Ledge at 1937 feet, we bottomed out at the Lyme Dorchester road some 800 feet further down, only to climb again. Passing Lamberts Ridge we carried on to Smarts Mountain at 3237 feet. We climbed the fire tower to get a visual on the terrain surrounding us and bemoaned what seemed like a wasted climb; the trail promptly fell 1787 feet back down to South Jacobs Brook.

Our maps appeared to suggest that the White Mountain section started shortly before the Beaver Brook shelter, at mile 1793. Mt Cube, about twenty miles before, offered a sweet perch for camp and to take in the outlook. The further we ventured north, the wilder America was becoming. Far-reaching views surrounded us as we sat on the flat summit, the rock warm from the sunshine, eating our dinners. A green ocean of trees rose up to the peaks surrounding us as distant, blue hills faded off to the horizon. Quintessential summer clouds appeared motionless, hanging in a contrasting sky, their reflections mirrored far below us in the lakes.

It seemed an inspiring enough location to discuss our plans for the Whites. There was no doubt that our mileage was due to suffer so damage limitation was the name of the game. Everyone was happy with progress and the estimated finish date wasn't of concern. Approximate plans put us on for a finish before the end of August, making a sub-five-month thru-hike. This wasn't breaking any records, nor was it a bad time either — more a typical thru-hike average for the AT.

However, everyone agreed that the Whites looked difficult. A never-ending series of peaks had to be climbed — but what we didn't realise was that it wasn't the climbs that were going to prove difficult, but rather the descents. Also, having psyched ourselves up for the ninety-odd miles through the Whites, we had become dangerously complacent. Such was the reputation of this section of the AT, we were focusing too much on its difficulty when we should have been looking beyond it. The Whites, as difficult as they looked, were just an entrée for everything afterwards.

Up until Pinkham Notch, near the town of Gorham at mile 1865, the trail just went silly. I had a headache from looking at the elevation profile, which switched from ascents to descents at alarming intervals. Thirsty's eyes peered over his guidebook. His eyebrows rose and fell in quick succession, almost like the mountains themselves.

Notches appeared regularly, and the climbs were long and steep, as were the descents. The surface of the actual trail was getting tougher also. Rock slabs rudely protruded over the trail, and tree roots, searching desperately for soft soil, wove crazy patterns everywhere.

Agreed that our daily distances were due to plunge, damage limitation involved nothing simpler than earlier starts and perhaps later finishes as well. One thing was certain: we were about to get our arses kicked. Not just by the Whites, but most of the rest of the AT itself.

Mt Mousilauke was the first peak to fire an opening shot across our bows with a 3746-foot climb. With Thirsty just a couple of yards in front of me, but his feet still level with my head, I realised it was going to be steep, and not easy. We had to fuel up just a few minutes in as my energy suddenly plummeted. The guys took the opportunity to do the same. I chewed on a packet of dried mango slices and, slowly, a sugar rush navigated a route down to my grateful legs.

The trees thinned shortly before the top and rain began to fall as we picked our way along a clear trail cutting over a stony summit. A howling wind whipped us from the west and, scurrying along, we began to curve downwards to the relative shelter of the trees.

Once out of the wind we took a quick break. Goggles and Thirsty dropped their shorts to carry out some treatment for their sore areas. It struck me at that point that I had two arseholes either side of me.

Switchbacks are not favoured by many thru-hikers, but their absence on the descent from Mousilauke wasn't making the going any easier. Sections of slick, wet rock slabs asked a lot of our fading shoe tread. Pinned to alarming angles, we teetered, eyeing up any promising lines. Trusting the grip on our shoes with arms flapping for balance, we cautiously inched our way down, sticking to the sides of the trail where trees offered hand holds, their roots edging onto the rock for sketchy foot placements. Even a series of steps hewn into the rock were difficult. As Beaver Brook joined us for company, we eventually landed at Kinsman Notch after a descent of 2932 feet in just four miles. Our first day venturing into the Whites had nevertheless reeled in an impressive twenty-three miles.

Sobos were a reliable source of information and Mike, fresh out of the Whites, stopped as we gleaned some advice from him.

"You've got this far," he began. "You'll get through but just keep an eye on the weather, it changes quickly."

The town of Lincoln was just six miles east on route 112. We were all suffering — not just with sore sac syndrome, but with burning rashes where the straps from our packs had been rubbing in the humid atmosphere. Our shoulders, hips and backs were raw and demanded attention. A quick ride dropped us at the Econo Lodge and we each took turns for a shower.

Thirsty emerged cringing a few minutes later.

"That was one of the most painful experiences of my life," he announced, tentatively sitting on the edge of the bed and trying to decide which ointment would be the least painful.

Cries of pain floated out from the bathroom shortly after Goggles went in. Lazagne followed in silence but his facial expressions as he came out did little to placate my concerns.

As I cautiously entered the shower, looking at my beaten and raw flesh, I didn't know which way to turn, literally. My shoulders burned as the water hit them from behind; turning to lower the temperature, my hips fared little better.

I dabbed the towel hesitantly. Unable to face the prospect of actually rubbing in the antiseptic cream, instead I gently smeared a generous squirt over everything that looked like it needed treatment and left it. We spent most of the evening lying horizontal in front of the TV as, gradually, our bodies succumbed to the treatment and the pain slowly faded.

However, it hadn't faded enough for us to contemplate carrying on the next day. Lazagne had made the best progress and left with Chez 11, also in town, to knock off the section over Mt Wolf, South Kinsman Mountain and North Kinsman Mountain. Thirsty, Goggles and I rested in between eating, overdosing on ointment applications and striving to perfect some form of painless walking style.

The rest, several showers and cream applications appeared to work well and, the following day, we got a taxi back to Kinsman Notch. Once again, the rain started just shy of South Kinsman Mountain's summit, complete with lightning and thunder claps although, thankfully, not in the immediate vicinity.

A familiar pattern was already emerging. The AT constantly rose and fell through the Whites, and the name of the game was to bag a high peak or two, usually around the 3000 to 6000-foot mark. Once summited, it was then a steep descent back down to a notch — at which point, the whole process started over again. It made sense to use the areas around the notches as overnight camps. They were situated in sheltered positions and down from the higher altitudes where rain and lower temperatures were common. As sheltered as they were, they didn't benefit from much sunlight.

We didn't consider this a problem; in fact it made complete sense to camp at the notches. However, my problem with the section through the Whites centred on the rules and regulations. The area was popular with hikers — not just AT thru-hikers but day hikers also — and foot traffic presented problems with erosion.

The Appalachian Mountain Club (AMC) maintained a 122-mile section from Kinsman Notch in New Hampshire to Grafton Notch in Maine. They offered hikers overnight stays in eight mountain huts and several shelters. The huts, as wonderful as they were, were basic; most didn't have showers or heating, and the fees to stay there started around $80 each. A couple of positions were usually available on a work-for-stay basis for thru-hikers in exchange for sleeping on the floor, and leftover food.

The Randolph Mountain Club (RMC) maintained the section from Edmands Col to the Madison Hut and maintained four normal shelters in the Northern Presidentials Range, also charging for overnight stays there.

Charging high fees, and charging for shelters period, instead of encouraging us to stay there, did nothing more than to tempt us out to camp off the trail. Stealth campsites, as they were known, were common and information made available on the web by previous thru-hikers was easily obtainable.

Areas within a quarter of a mile from AMC and RMC facilities, and everything above tree-line were part of the Forest Protection Area (FPA). Camping was prohibited in these areas, and within 200 feet of water and trails anywhere. Trail boundaries were often marked with small, rock scree walls, off trail was out of bounds to protect plant life.

Suddenly, after weeks of living free with few restrictions, it wasn't just the amazing environment in the Whites under threat from erosion — it was our freedom.

Thru-hikers take on the challenge of a long-distance trail, and escape to the wilds, for various individual reasons. A yearning for a sense of living free is high on that list. To suddenly be told that camping in most areas was illegal, and to then feel forced to pay over the odds for accommodation, to keep to marked trails and to adhere to restrictions did little more than encourage us to rebel. It felt as though the Mountain Clubs had used erosion prevention to impose an accommodation monopoly with ridiculous prices.

I understand that areas of high traffic in wilderness areas need to be protected. I respect plant life, know to camp away from water sources and follow all the recommendations we were made aware of. However, we seem to forget that carving the Appalachian Trail in the first place — and the building of the AMC and RMC huts, the shelters, and the clearing of the ground surrounding them — is, by definition, erosion from the word go. For all this to happen and to then be told not to camp was hypocritical, especially as the vast majority of thru-hikers were always respectful, and practiced a leave no trace policy.

The net result was that Goggles, Thirsty, Lazagne and I stealth camped for most of the Whites. We were extremely careful: we didn't camp near water, resisted the urge to light a fire, took everything away with us and did our upmost to make no impact. The hammocks were ideal for this, keeping us off the ground and opening up sites on sloping terrain that a tent wouldn't be able to utilise. Although Goggles still had his tent, he often managed to squeeze into a flat space with us.

I never met a thru-hiker who had stayed at one of the shelters or the huts, and the usual reason they offered was that the cost was prohibitive. So stealth camping was how most of them got through.

***

Franconia Notch had proved a good place to stay. Getting ready for our second day in the Whites, I jumped out of my hammock and looked skywards. The sun was up but not yet high, the steep walls of the notch reaching up and covering us in shadows. I pulled on a jacket, started to jump around for warmth and made a coffee. We had a steep climb up to Franconia Ridge, taking in Little Haystack Mountain and Mt Lincoln before culminating at Mt Lafayette, 3831 feet above us. Franconia Ridge was a highlight of the AT, mainly because it was above tree-line for two miles and offered amazing views of the alpine scenery around us. Getting above tree-line was a rare treat in New Hampshire, as well as Maine, and the views offered insights into the wilderness we were travelling through.

"Here, I believe this is yours." I turned to see Pink Bits, sorry,

Lady Forward, with an outstretched arm offering me the gauntlet.

"Just finishing my lunch," I replied. "I'll be off before you so you best keep hold of it."

Stuffing my snacks back into my food bag I discovered a rock at the bottom. Goggles started grinning, suggesting he was the culprit.

"How long as it been in there?" I asked.

"What in where?" he replied. "Don't know anything about a rock."

"I never said it was a rock?"

Thirsty also grinned, feigning surprise. I merely smiled and planned revenge.

Our route, for two miles at least, was clearly visible ahead along Franconia Ridge. Hikers speckled its length, clinging to the rocky top. It was so different to what we had become used to, spending days in the woods with few glimpses of what lay around us. Suddenly to be out in the open with views all around was incredible. We were all smiling.

After summiting Mt Garfield, we descended 1000 feet to get away from the exposed peak and tucked into the woods, just off trail, for the night. We had managed just ten miles.

South Twin Mountain faced us the following day but, once summited, it was 3625 feet downhill to Crawford Notch, fourteen miles away. South Twin was steep but we warmed quickly. With muscles loose, we made short work of the descent, pulling in at a small car park next to the US-302 at Crawford Notch.

Crawford Notch was essentially the start of the ascent of Mt Washington, 5000 feet above us and sitting pretty at 6288 feet. The summit was thirteen miles distant and renowned for its highly unpredictable and often violent weather patterns, even in the middle of summer. Despite having hiked just over twenty miles to Crawford Notch, it was a long and steep climb up to Washington. We needed to get up, over, and descend the other side out of any potential bad weather. The trail descended from Washington to the Peabody River, twenty-two miles away — so, keen to get up and over the mountain, we left late afternoon to climb the 2000-foot, two-mile section to Webster Cliffs. This, we hoped, would place us perfectly for the next section over Washington.

The 1000 feet per mile rule, signifying anything steep, was on our minds as we left Crawford and climbed. Progress, as expected, was slow. Tree roots wrapped over the trail to provide natural steps as we climbed, weaving around huge rocks encroaching on the trail edge. Ten minutes in we realised we had no water for camp. Goggles and Thirsty were good enough to track back down to the bottom and collect some water — not just for themselves, but for Lazagne and I too as we sat and waited.

When we reached Webster Cliffs, a large area of flat rock opened up before us with far-reaching views away to the valley below. Some of our gear was damp from the recent rain, so we pulled out our sleeping bags and hung them from the trees, setting up camp in a small clearing behind. The sky over the hilltops at the other side of the valley was streaked with oranges and reds, gradually rising up to blues and higher still to a darkening border as night fell.

The rocks were warm. We sat, cooking our dinners and discussing the big day ahead of us. The Whites were hard and we weren't though them yet. Stunning as they were, the immediate focus was to get through New Hampshire and into Maine, some sixty-one miles distant. After that we figured we could breathe easier on kinder terrain, and push some higher miles in our last state.

How wrong we were.

Chapter 13
Cambers, Sinkers, Bouncers, Sliders, Rockers, Rottens and Floaters

July 31st to August 8th
Mile 1841 to 1953

I was up at 3.30 a.m, unable to sleep. I didn't know if the anticipation of summiting Mt Washington and hiking the Presidential Range was responsible, but for over two hours I sat on Webster Cliffs. The Milky Way blazed its own trail over me and, slowly, the horizon started to glow red. With enough light to have breakfast and pack, I was away before the guys. The forest thinned the higher I ventured. I found regular opportunities to rest on rocky perches with views ahead and behind. As I watched the guys closing on me a little further down, I shouted regular taunts that they were either going too slow, were too far behind, or that their hiking was rubbish. They stopped, looked up at me a couple of hundred feet above, laughed, threw a few insults and started to speed up. At this point I flew off, increased my speed to gain further ground and subsequently re-appeared at another vantage point for further bantering.

With Goggles leading the hunt, they eventually caught me as we rolled over Mt Jackson. The terrain unfolded before us, occasionally broken by solitary, rocky peaks floating on a sea of green. The trail was invisible beneath millions of trees, but our route was clear. Numerous pinnacles, each a little higher than its predecessor, stepped up to the clear outline of Mt Washington itself, standing proud over everything it surveyed. Perched on its majestic throne, we, its subjects, bowed in acknowledgement, humbled.

The Presidential Range, within the White Mountains, contained thirteen mountains named after American presidents and other prominent figures from the eighteenth and nineteenth centuries — Mt Washington, Mt Eisenhower, and Mt Franklin to name just three. The area was a tempting lure for many hikers and mountaineers.

I had read so many accounts of this section that I was convinced we were going to be in for a very wet and windy ride. Washington is a melting pot of weather patterns. Fierce winds regularly rip over the summit and it once laid claim to the fastest wind speed recorded anywhere in the world, of 231 miles per hour. This record, set on April 12th 1934, remained solid until 1996, when a tropical cyclone called Olivia registered 253 miles per hour at Barrow Island, Australia. Mt Washington had lost its claim to fame but still holds the record for wind speed outside a tropical cyclone.

Washington's reputation as the most dangerous small mountain in the world is well founded. Even calm days with clear blue skies can, in a short space of time, descend rapidly into fierce winds, with temperatures plummeting to below freezing. Inexperienced and experienced hikers alike regularly get blown off course. Resisting the urge to battle the gales, they succumb to them and end up disorientated and lost, miles from anywhere. Often on day hikes with no equipment, they die from exposure and hypothermia. It is not a mountain to be taken lightly.

Unofficial fatality lists for the area date back to the 1800s. Figures vary, but around 147 people have reputedly lost their lives there.

It immediately reminded me of a quote by Edward Whymper, an English mountaineer, illustrator and author who was born in 1840.

There have been joys too great to be described in words, and there have been griefs upon which I have not dared to dwell; and with these in mind I say: Climb if you will, but remember that courage and strength are nought without prudence, and that a momentary negligence may destroy the happiness of a lifetime. Do nothing in haste; look well to each step; and from the beginning think what may be the end.

Always wary that the weather could change, I looked up amazed at how lucky I was. We couldn't have wished for a better day. In fact, a day hiker I met coming south stopped to chat to me.

"How's the view up there?" I opened with.

"Wonderful," he replied, grinning. "I've walked up to Washington many times, and the Presidentials. I can honestly say this is the best weather I've seen up here. Enjoy!"

When we reached the Mizpah Spring Hut and nearby campsite, the caretaker called Bearsweat called us over and brewed hot drinks for us. He had also hiked the AT and shared his experience, confirming we were lucky with the weather.

"The descent from Mt Madison down to Pinkham Notch is long and steep but you're well on course to get down there today. Have a great hike!"

Our next target was the Lakes of the Clouds Hut, five miles further up and itself a mere one and a half miles before the summit of Mt Washington. The trail climbed steeply from the Mizpah Hut over awkward sections of tree roots before emerging above tree-line. With the summit buildings of Mt Washington now clearly visible, we passed the Lakes of the Clouds Hut and the prospect of a hot meal in the summit café was enough to haul us up the final 1200 feet.

Scrambling over the final section of rocks we arrived in a different world. Tourists spilled out of the train, after ascending 3588 feet on the three-mile cog railway built in 1868. Many seemed out of their element, surveying the view in T-shirts and shorts before retreating to the warmth of the café. Warm from the climb, we felt no need to put on another layer, instead queuing for a few minutes for the obligatory summit photo.

We weren't keen on staying, partly due to the crowds and the need to get down to Pinkham Notch. Hot food, however, was on blatant display; and, following our unwritten rule of never passing sustenance by, we retreated inside for a quick bowl of chilli before leaving for the decent.

One of several trail customs on the AT entails baring one's bottom, or mooning, in the direction of the tourist train. So popular was this custom that apparently the authorities had taken a dim view of the practice. Police were known to ride the train and arrest perpetrators on occasion. I was under strict instructions from Pockets, a friend with whom I had hiked a fair chunk of the PCT.

"Don't forget to moon the train," he ordered. "If the police are on board, run!"

Intrigued by the possibility of being arrested, Goggles and I, the first to descend, stopped as the train chugged and strained up the final few hundred feet to the summit. The passengers peered out curiously at two strange-looking, bearded beasts. Goggles turned to me.

"Ready?" he said, smirking.

"Yup."

Not wanting to push our luck further than necessary, a quick drop of the shorts with raised arms was sufficient and we glanced back to applause and shouts. With no police in pursuit, we nevertheless upped the pace a little and sped off north.

At first the descent was relatively easy, over open ground with good visibility. We reached Edmands Col and then the Madison Spring Hut, refuelling once more with snacks. Rising steeply to Mt Madison, the final climb was over and we began the 3100-foot descent to the Peabody River three and a half miles down. Picking our way over rough rock slabs slowed my pace and Goggles, Lazagne and Thirsty pulled away. I fell below the tree-line and negotiated the trail steeply, watching my step, weaving over and around rocks with tree roots reaching out and gripping the surface like giant hands.

Finally I bottomed out at the Peabody River where the guys had set up camp with a new thru-hiker, Grok. We hadn't managed to reach Pinkham Notch, but having pulled in an impressive twenty miles over difficult terrain, no one was complaining.

I was sore, though. A minor stumble had blooded my thigh and my knees were tight from such a long and steep descent. At the end of each day it felt as though I had gone several rounds in a boxing ring. Having won each bout thus far, I seemed to be facing far heavier, tougher opponents every time I ventured out for another round.

"It roughed us up but we won the fight," Goggles commented, wisely, as we chatted with raised voices over the roar of the Peabody River. Grok, also sporting some grazes, complained that he needed several beers for medicinal purposes.

***

After a short, and welcome, four miles from an early morning start we emerged at Pinkham Notch. The visitor centre offered a decent but expensive breakfast, which we declined in favour of getting a ride into Goreham, eleven miles west. Apart from bacon and eggs, we all needed to resupply with food, get cleaned up and wash our clothes. My shoes, also, were on their last legs and pair number four was beckoning.

We had heard of a trail angel called Miriam in Goreham who welcomed hikers at her small house three miles from town. Our ride dropped us in the centre of town at the Moonbeam Café. Timing couldn't have been more perfect; as we emerged with full stomachs she pulled up and took us back.

"I have to go to work," she said. "But feel free to use the washer, make yourself at home and I'll see you later."

I took the opportunity to call Pockets, who had hiked the AT some years prior, and asked him for advice to get through the last state, Maine, just a few miles ahead.

"No problems really," he explained. "Just watch the biting flies."

"Biting flies?" I ventured.

"Yup, come out latish summer, nasty little bastards."

With breakfast already a fading memory, and our clothes drying outside, we walked back to town for more food and also for me to try and get a new pair of shoes. There was just one outfitter in Goreham, and that would have better been described as a hardware store. My first pair at the start, a brand called Inov-8, had lasted an impressive 1000 miles. Pennsylvania fought a running battle with their replacement, a pair of Brooks, which gave up after just 250 miles and some New Balance had fared well until Goreham, but they too were finished.

Lazagne came to the rescue with a suggestion that, at first, I dismissed. He had ordered a pair of Brooks Cascadia 7's, which had been delivered to the post office in Goreham. They were too small for him but curiosity got the better of me when he offered them to me for the original purchase price. The only problem was the size, which was two full US sizes up from what I normally wore.

Unwittingly, it solved the problem of my wider feet up front. Although clearly too big and with a gap at the ankle I could slide a thumb into, I walked up the road for half a mile and returned. Apart from sliding around at the back, as I might have expected from being too large, they remained firmly secure; and with my feet pushed towards the back, the toes also moved back and away from the narrowest part of the shoe. It was a revelation. Not only were my feet away from the edges up front, they were unbelievably comfortable. I have hiked in Cascadias ever since with no problems. I didn't see them as shoes; they were so comfortable I referred to them as my slippers.

We left Goreham on Thursday, August 2nd. 1865 miles into our adventure, and with 319 miles left to Katahdin. Confidence was high. We had finished the Whites, one of the toughest sections. We climbed the 2000 feet from Pinkham Notch up to Wildcat Mountain, having left most of our gear at Miriam's, taking just lunch and clothing. The trail intersected the US-2 twenty-one miles further up, but taking into account the twists and turns, it spilled out just a few road miles back into Goreham so we could walk back. The chance of hiking with little weight over rough terrain made the decision for us. More wet, slick, green rock hindered our climb. Huge rock sections at alarming angles were becoming more common. It was a big leap of faith to plant a shoe down, taking all my weight, and then hoping it held as the other foot searched for grip. Coming downhill, the horrible feeling that at any second my feet would be whipped out from under me constantly teased. We crawled, slid, shimmied, and grasped anything at the side of the trail that would accept a hand. If the trees and their roots hadn't been there to help, I don't know how we would have got down, or up.

Instead of the AT becoming easier, if anything, it felt much harder. The notches were killing us; always steep on both sides, the only saving grace was that some of them crossed roads at their base and offered the chance of trail magic, or a quick ride to town. We were reduced to a plodding pace, our legs not so much stepping ahead, more lifting up. Breathing hard with legs screaming we eventually reached the open summit of Wildcat.

"I thought this was supposed to be getting easier?" I said. "The further we venture north, the harder it seems to be getting."

Thirsty, bent over double trying to regain his breath, agreed.

"That's not all," Goggles chipped in. "The Mahoosuc Notch is only twenty-four miles away. We'll probably be there tomorrow."

The Mahoosuc Notch took notches up another notch. We had heard stories about this mile-long section of trail, and indeed its reputation preceded itself. Fallen boulders, some the size of houses, littered the passage through. It wasn't so much hiking as crawling.

Goggles and Thirsty moved ahead of Lazagne and me. My lower back was sore after a night on Miriam's unforgiving sofa, and Lazagne's pace had also suffered because he had little grip left on his shoes. He was treading cautiously, especially through the rock sections.

It was exhausting. After recovering from Wildcat Mountain we promptly plunged back down 900 feet, bottomed out near the Carter Notch Hut, and then faced a 1500-foot climb back up to Carter Dome.

As we reached the higher sections, the trees gradually thinned and became more stunted. Light flooded the trail and the wind increased until we met rocky summits with astonishing views. It became a familiar pattern: descend to the dark depths of a notch, sunlight diminishing as the trees grew thicker further down, the walls of each notch closing in like a dungeon. Then, we picked our way back up, through a dank, murky underworld where the environment was quiet, sometimes eerie. The climbs always caused me to overheat. Peeling off a jacket, I remained undecided — too hot or too cold, I never got it right.

After North Carter Mountain and Mt Moriah, we gently eased our way down 3200 feet to the road. The gentle decline was a welcome reward for our hard work — so welcome, in fact, that Lazagne and Thirsty started to jog two miles from the road, free from their pack weight. I followed and before long our legs were scrambling to stay with the momentum. With fading light we leaped over obstacles, not seeing them till the last moment.

"Log!" Lazagne screamed from the murk a few feet ahead. "Stream! Rock, shit! ROCK!"

Swerving, running hard, focusing on the trail, jumping and cutting corners we reached the road crying with laughter from the adrenaline rush, drenched in sweat and giggling uncontrollably.

Goggles, resting and confused as to why we were totally out breath, hoisted his pack and we road-walked back to Miriam's. After hiking twenty-one miles and following every curve of the trail, it was strange to be back, just a short distance from Goreham.

The run had inflamed my shin splint, which had given me no problem for weeks. Obviously my free-spirited jog had caused it to retaliate and I made a mental note to keep my speed down. I debated resting it the following morning but any delay meant the guys would be ahead and I might not catch them.

We were two weeks away from the final 160 miles of the AT. Occasionally I'd flick a few pages ahead in the data book, as did the others; during that final section, the gradients eased, the hills diminished, and the going appeared flat. Of course, there was the small matter of summiting and descending from Katahdin. The mountain entailed a climb of over 4000 feet spread over five miles, the first half of which was renowned for its hard going, and then we had to get back down again.

The weather had also turned and we longed for the heat wave that had plagued us through New York State. Temperatures had dropped, especially at night, but we still wore T-shirts and shorts throughout the day. Angry clouds swept over us and, each minute, threatened to open.

The Mahoosuc Range is a notorious section of trail starting at Mt Hayes and is renowned for many steep climbs on difficult terrain. It hit me for six.

I picked my way over rock slabs, following a weak line of cairns to the top of Mt Hayes after a storm. I was alone. Various injuries screaming at me to slow down had won over my resolve. I dropped my pack and sat on the summit, enjoying the warm rock. A strong sun somehow discovered chinks in the clouds, casting searchlights all around me and flooding the valleys with light, broken up by racing cloud shadows. Steam rose from the rocky summit as it dried and I surveyed my world. Mt Hayes dropped away, its speckled, grey slopes surrendering to the tree-line and merging into green. I could see no trace of man's intervention. No roads or buildings spoilt my panorama; the wilds were just as they had been for thousands of years.

Rivers, like silver ribbons, threaded routes through infinity, sparkling as the sun bounced off them. They emptied into vast lakes, mirrors nestling in the lowlands. Then the land rose majestically once more, cloaked in evergreens before succumbing to the rocky peaks. A weak wind offered the only noise, the trees gently reciprocating, bowing over in surrender and gently rustling. I could have stayed there forever.

In retrospect, Mt Hayes somehow seemed to talk to me. I stayed up there for two hours, just thinking and questioning. This is something I often did at home when I needed space. Escaping to the outdoors often not only forced me to accept problems, but gave me the space and time to resolve them.

I was exhausted — there was no escaping that problem. My shin throbbed, the injured calf complained constantly, my ankles ached; and as I looked at my bloodied legs the solution became obvious. I had to slow down. I was lethargic, sluggish, not just in body but also in mind. My pace was slow and so was my decision making. Everything seemed like hard work, something was wrong.

I needed to make a decision. Bush Goggles was pushing hard, both the miles and the pace. He had agreed to meet his mum at Katahdin where she would drive him home. The target he had set himself had rubbed off on us. We didn't want to lose him; we were a team, and a damn good one, but I was at risk of bailing out if I continued to push myself like this. Confident of reaching Katahdin, and well ahead of schedule, if anything, I wanted to slow down and take more time, not speed up.

My body needed rest. When I hauled myself down from Mt Hayes I was too tired to go on. After covering just four miles for the entire day, I pitched the hammock and made a decision. I would talk to the guys — even let Goggles go, if that's what he needed to do, as much as I didn't want to see him leave. Whether Lazagne and Thirsty would go with him or we would stay as a three-member team I didn't know.

By the morning I had deteriorated. Making decisions was exhausting and hiking was slow. Something was wrong; physical tiredness was a problem I could usually sort out, but with judgements to be made and navigation choices to follow, my mind just didn't seem up to par. At times I just couldn't be bothered with any of it and entertained thoughts of quitting the trail for good.

I caught them mid-morning. We shook hands on passing into Maine and somehow I managed to make it to camp on the west peak of Goose Eye Mountain. Stiff, tight, low vegetation hindered camping and there were no trees to sling our hammocks. As the sun set we sat on the flat, rocky summit and watched the sunset, staying there for hours as the night sky came out to play. Away from the city lights, the stars were intense and the Milky Way arced, soaring above us. Mesmerised, we said little. I woke several times during the night to take it all in again.

Realising the others would be ahead of me straight away, I voiced my concerns over breakfast.

"I'm tired, guys," I ventured. "I'm nowhere near a hundred percent and I need to slow down, if not rest for a day. Something isn't right. Goggles, I know you have to meet your mum but I can't keep with your distances. I'd love to finish with you but I don't think I can."

No one spoke as I turned to Thirsty and Lazagne.

"I don't know what will happen with the group, and we all know there is no commitment to walk together. I *have* to slow down. Chances are I'll rest at the next opportunity and, then, I plan on fifteen-mile days until Katahdin."

We discussed the situation sensibly. Although we came to no decision, we all knew that Goggles would be out front, I would be bringing up the rear, and Lazagne and Thirsty would take time somewhere in the middle to figure out their next move.

Suddenly, everything seemed to be going wrong.

Four miles later, somehow, I had managed to stick with them and a good job it turned out to be. Suddenly, we stared down at the jumbled, rocky calamity otherwise known as the Mahoosuc Notch. Awol had described the notch in his guidebook as '*The most difficult, or fun mile of the AT*'. I guess it depended on your perspective.

Tiredness and group dynamics were pushed to one side as each of us realised that prudence, and a team approach, were advisable to get through. We surveyed the terrain ahead of us. Planning went out of the window. It became clear that the only approach was to descend and take each obstacle as it appeared.

The walls of the notch narrowed towards the base where countless massive boulders had become lodged, blocking the route. Faded white blazes indicated the optimal route but we lost them many times. Balancing on rock ledges, we peered down into dark crevices, seeing the faint gush of water below us as streams also battled a way through. Sometimes we picked a way through the base, crawling, sliding and squeezing. Occasionally we were forced higher up the notch, inching along narrow ledges, all the time scanning ahead for the right line.

Two hours later we emerged, having averaged a dismal half a mile an hour. We smiled, looked at each other's dirt streaked clothes and laughed.

I lost them in the afternoon. After the adrenalin of the notch, my fatigue kicked in once more. I dropped my pack on the shore of Speck Pond, sat down and eased off my filthy socks and shoes, pulled off my T-shirt and waded out into the water. My muscles slowly eased, grateful for the therapy. For an hour I alternated between swimming and sitting on a rock a few yards from shore. The sun warmed me as gentle waves lapped over my feet.

I dried myself off and checked my injuries for any swelling but found nothing. Ten minutes into the next climb, I was stopped by a couple of day hikers who questioned why I had started so late for a south bounder.

"I'm heading north to Katahdin?" I questioned. "I'm north bounding?"

"Well, currently you're headed back towards the Mahoosuc Notch," one replied. "Are you OK? You look done in."

"I'm fine, thanks," I said, offering a weak smile. I turned around and headed back the way I had just come.

It was obvious that I wasn't fine. Somehow I managed to climb 600 feet, passing the turn off for Old Speck Trail. Two more day hikers, Eric and Samantha, enthralled when they discovered I had walked from Georgia, forced me to stop and chat. I couldn't focus on the conversation and felt light-headed, but did my best to appear friendly.

"You sound like, British or something?" Eric said.

Oh crap, not now please.

"I'm from the UK, yes; I'm English."

"You *walked* here all the way from Georgia? That's amazing!" Samantha chipped in.

They wished me good luck and some minutes later I arrived back at Speck Pond. I had walked the wrong way again, all the way back down the hill I had just climbed.

That's it, Fozzie. Get the fuck off trail and rest. Sort this out, you need to take time out.

Again, I plodded back up to the Old Speck trail, sat down and checked the data book. There was a 2500-foot descent to Grafton Notch just over three miles away where the ME-26, a quiet road, offered the chance to get a ride out.

Staggering down, somehow I managed to catch up with Eric and Samantha. I must have looked terrible because, again, they asked me if I felt OK.

"I don't feel great, no," I answered. "I don't know what's wrong with me but I need to get off trail and rest for a couple of days."

Before I knew it, my pack was in the back of their car and they had dropped me at the Pine Ellis Lodge in Andover. David, the owner, checked me in for two nights and provided a brief tour of the hostel.

Pine Ellis was quiet save for a few hikers. Most of them were in bed despite it being mid-day. Being as quiet as possible, I inadvertently woke Rachael, a section hiker sharing my room.

"Sorry," I said. "Didn't mean to wake you."

"That's OK," she mumbled, rubbing her eyes. "Surprised you're not ill."

"Really, why?"

"You haven't heard? Most of the hikers within a ten-mile radius are sick," she explained.

"No, I hadn't heard?"

I walked to the Andover General Store, which also served food from its deli. Two hikers I had not met, Willie and Indiana, along with Bad Dinner and Metric, peered up from their fries and shuffled over to let me in. Everyone looked pale, unimpressed as they poked their food.

"How's the food?" I opened with.

"It's good," Bad Dinner replied, somewhat contrary to his trail name. "Are you not sick?"

"I feel incredibly tired, something is definitely not right but I'm holding on to my bodily fluids. Do you have any idea what's going on?"

"Norovirus," he explained. "Apparently the CDC was in the area recently trying to locate the source but didn't find anything. Everyone is sick. I'd say at least eighty percent of hikers are down with it."

I'd never heard of norovirus but it is very common. With a twenty-four to forty-eight-hour incubation period, the symptoms include vomiting, diarrhoea and tiredness. There is no cure. The usual advice is merely to rest, drink plenty of water and let it run its course. I hadn't been sick, and my bowels seemed fine although I was tired. Either I was in the early stages or I had something completely different.

Lazagne arrived at Pine Ellis the following morning.

"I thought you were ahead?" I asked.

"I was. I got off at Dunn Notch. I'm sick, feel like shit. Thirsty too. He was too weak to even get up."

"Where's Goggles?"

"I think he's at the next notch, South Arm Road."

Dunn Notch was ten miles ahead of where I had bailed out, and South Arm Road was a further ten more.

Despite sleeping for ten hours straight overnight, I was still tired and dozed off again for another four hours. I walked slowly downstairs, sat outside on the porch, drank a Coke and watched a car pull up outside. Goggles got out. Before he could even shoulder his pack, another car arrived and Thirsty emerged, looking very much the worse for wear.

Goggles appeared fine and confirmed he felt OK. Thirsty was far worse, saying he couldn't even muster the energy to get out of his hammock to be sick, so he just poked his head out to vomit.

Rest was on the cards. In between drinking plenty of water, the chess championship picked up from where it had left off. England was making a determined comeback; beating Lazagne twice, I pulled the score to four against five. One more win for me would secure a draw.

Thirsty slept but Goggles only rested briefly, ate some food and set off with David for a ride back to the trailhead. Knowing that we probably wouldn't see each other again — at least not on that trip — we shared a hug before he left. I'd hiked with plenty of companions but was going to miss Goggles for sure. With Thirsty, Lazagne and I all sick, and with his schedule to meet, we all understood that he had to leave.

Andover was quiet, the streets narrow, and we occasionally passed timber-clad houses dotted around the town. Although we were desperate for some vitamins and nutrients, the general store, amazingly, had no fresh fruit. I walked over to the Little Red Hen Diner. The door creaked open to reveal Pink Bits — sorry, Lady Forward — Chez 11 and a new face called Warlie.

"Are you ill?" Lady Forward asked.

"I'm not a hundred percent. Tired but holding on to the fluids. You?"

"We've all been ill, everyone's been ill."

"I think we're out the other side mate," Chez 11 chipped in, his Scouse accent pronounced.

The Little Red Hen, a wonderful little country diner, saved the day with fresh orange juice and a salad. I rested and continued to drink water with rehydration powder. Slowly, my lethargy faded; and, although still not completely up to par, I made plans to leave the following day.

Rising early, I left Lazagne and Thirsty at Pine Ellis. Both had ten miles on me anyway so they weren't in any rush. David drove me back to Grafton Notch.

Johannes, a German thru-hiker, was gearing up to leave as David dropped me off. He had started ten days before me back in Georgia and was struggling through the Mahoosucs. Either he was ill or I was recovering; climbing 2167 feet from the notch up to Baldpate West Peak I left him quickly. There were ten miles to Dunn Notch, where Lazagne and Thirsty had bailed out and I knew they were planning a ride there with David, probably getting there before I did. We knew our plans and agreed that we'd either meet later, or certainly the following day. The beauty of the AT, and other trails, was that firm plans weren't needed. We hiked on a strip of trail perhaps a couple of feet wide. You would always pass others and could never really lose anyone.

I felt almost back to normal. My legs coped without complaints but, more importantly, my head was clear. Decisions came easily and with little effort.

Taking a quick break, I looked around. Broadleaf trees were in the minority in Maine, replaced with evergreen pine and firs. They grew right up to the trailside, their thick growth transforming my surroundings into a dense, eerie darkness. Although the way was clear, stray off trail and it was easy to see how anyone could get lost and never be seen again. Many hikers have gone missing in Maine when they never showed at expected points, despite searches. Not only was it sad but this last state on the AT definitely had a sense of mystery about it.

One thing was for sure — Maine was wild, very wild. Surveying that barren corner of America from many vantage points, there was usually little to remind a hiker that they lived in the twenty-first century. It was rare to see a building or road. Even planes passing overhead seemed scarce.

But wilderness was precisely the reason many people came. The lack of intrusion, and wanting to keep that beautiful countryside unspoilt, drew many outdoor enthusiasts. In fact, the state slogan said it all: *Maine – The Way Life Should Be.*

The winters were harsh. Low temperatures and high snowfall made much of the area out of bounds except for a dedicated few, experienced at winter hiking and other such activities.

Climbing higher, the trees gradually became more stunted. Unable to cope well with the harsher climate at altitude, their height diminished to just a few feet. This feature of subarctic and subalpine trees is known as krumholtz, from the German *krumm,* meaning crooked or bent, and *holz,* meaning wood. The exposed upper sections of the trees were often devoid of foliage. Growth concentrated around the base where it was more sheltered. At lower elevations, the growth became more normal, away from the upper climes.

The predominant rock in Maine, granite, often covered the mountain tops. Vast sections also stretched down from the summits. Bathed in sun, they were wonderfully warm and great places to sit. Even lower down, the surface alternated between soft, dark soil and this grey, sometimes bluish rock. My shoes stuck to the gritty texture. It was like walking on sandpaper. After a while getting used to its whims, it proved a trustworthy platform to hike on. I could always count on it to hold me securely while ascending steep sections. Striding purposefully uphill, leaping from boulder to boulder, Maine granite held me securely.

However, away from the exposed sections, where the sun made few inroads, this rock was often damp and covered in a slimy texture that demanded caution. Many descents were spread over vast sections of rock, appearing like a flight of steps, each one several feet high. With the weight of my pack bearing down, slips were common; I continued to utilise the edges of the trail where trees steadied me and their roots offered foot holds.

My hiking style had to adapt to these sections. It was common to clamber, slide on my bottom, teeter precariously and generally look completely inexperienced.

The soil, a rich, chocolaty dense brown colour, was wonderful to walk on. The soft texture gave just a little underfoot to cushion each footfall. Even then, at the beginning of August, sections were still wet. Vast amounts of snow melt over the course of the summer, coupled with the rainfall, meant much of the ground never dried out. Puddles speckled the way and boggy sections were common.

To prevent erosion and make the trail negotiable, the authorities had installed many sections of boardwalks. The majority of these were welcome, preventing soaked and muddy feet. The upper sections of these walkways were constructed using two parallel lengths of wood, with shorter planks fixed widthways, similar to what you might expect on a pier.

The dodgy versions consisted of two planks of wood side by side, sometimes logs sawn in half so the underside was semi-circular but the top flat. At the ends, a block or two of wood lay on the ground at right angles for the planks to anchor onto — foundations if you like. To negotiate these boardwalk versions required an awkward stance with legs slightly apart, with one foot on each plank.

Boardwalks became a pet hate for me, so much so that I studied the various types. I divided them into various categories, in order of difficulty starting with the easiest.

There were right or left cambers, sinkers, bouncers, sliders, rockers, rottens and floaters. Most exhibited just one trait but some shared two or even more.

Cambers were the easiest, mainly because they gave themselves away visually. On approach, it was easy to spot the angle, the surface sloping either to the left or right. A slight posture adjustment was enough to counteract most of the cambers.

Sinkers were hard to detect because it wasn't until I had set foot on one that its character revealed itself. They thrived on ground that was either saturated or muddy. Once my weight bore down, one section or more would sink alarmingly into the ground, catching me unawares.

Bouncers were closely related to sinkers. Instead of remaining in the downward position, they mustered enough energy to counter my weight and bounce back up — just at the point when one foot lifted for the next step and the pressure released somewhat.

Sliders were, frankly, lethal. Wood has many positive properties but grip can never claim to be one of them, especially when wet. With the damp conditions and regular traffic, most boardwalk surfaces were slippery. It was the one aspect that was common with all of them. Feet merely skidded when any pressure was applied. Some lured me in with a couple of sections of dry wood; I became complacent and sped up, only to enter *the slider zone*. Once the leading foot was planted it suddenly slid forward, resulting either in a very ungraceful parting of the legs, or the splits, which had me clutching my groin in pain. Sometimes one leg flung up wildly skyward, shortly followed by the other, as in the classic cartoon sketches where someone steps on a banana. During this split second of airborne travel came the realisation that no part of my body was in contact with the ground and I was, in fact, horizontal. My pack, thankfully, cushioned many a hard fall.

Rockers gave an entirely new perspective on fulcrums. Loose ground on the end sections left the base points without any anchor points. I often stepped on the first section only for it to sink and the opposing end to lift up, just like a seesaw. Or, reaching the far end, suddenly the section behind me did the same.

Rottens were easy to spot, but difficult to judge. The older sections, those in need of some maintenance or replacement, gave themselves away with deep surface ridges, chips, breakaways and holes. Tentative steps were crucial to establish just how bad they might be if any progress was to be achieved. Trust in placing all my weight had to come into play at some point. The usual warning was a loud splitting sound when the wood finally decided that life in Maine was not as ideal as it might have hoped for. One foot, sometimes both for double points, fell a few inches to the ground where mud invariably engulfed my new Cascadias and an unpleasant feeling of moisture greeted my socks.

At the far end of the difficulty scale, floaters were extreme. Actually, they were fairly easy to spot because one end was over water. The trick was judging whether they were securely anchored below the surface, or were prime floaters. Applying foot pressure over the suspected area was usually enough to ascertain whether they had a firm base; they either didn't move, sunk a little or, in a worst-case scenario, plunged down into the murky depths. Once more, although testing was obligatory, complacency regularly overruled. With an overwhelming feeling of impending wetness, the universe seemed to pause as my platform sank in anticipation of meeting anything solid. Some merely sank a few inches but the worst culprits, the crème de la crème of floaters, sank into oblivion and called their cousins, the sliders and rockers, into action. Either a quick retreat or a forward jump saved the day; but if I was caught out in the middle sections, the only escape was to jump sideways into the water.

Over time, I became quite adept at judging the boardwalks but one particular specimen, despite appearances, hid a far deeper, evil character. It looked innocent on my approach. A right camber was obvious but not severe, and the ground seemed boggy which made me suspicious of anything in the sinker, bouncer or rocker categories. The surface seemed dry so a slider didn't really cross my mind but the opposing end was hovering over water.

The initial left foot placement held and I felt confident. My right foot swept past, but instead of making firm contact, merely glanced across the camber and was promptly whipped from under me. It collided with my left foot which decided to join its partner in flight. Both feet hurtled out to the left, momentarily leaving me in midair before I fell off the other side.

After dusting myself off and glancing quickly behind for any possible witnesses, I stepped on board once more and progressed to the apparent safety of the middle haven. The centre sank alarmingly and proceeded to bounce, reverberating, as I clung there like a tightrope walker pausing to regain composure.

With half the stage complete, I inched bravely towards the obvious floater but it remained solid. Already bruised and muddy, I figured things couldn't get any worse; and, despite the solid anchor point, little did I know that a small sliver of wood was holding on for dear life on the edge of a submerged rock.

Feeling proud and all-conquering, I reached the end and raised my arms in triumph. Despite an ungainly start, I congratulated myself on a successful finale — until, that is, the aforementioned sliver finally slipped off and my world sank by two feet. I fell backwards, missing the wood behind me which angled off to the right, and clipping the edge I rolled over in mid-flight for an unceremonious finish, head first into a foot of mud.

It wasn't the ideal end to the day but I saw the funny side. A sense of humour through Maine was a welcome attribute but I didn't realise how much I would come to rely on it.

Chapter 14
Why didn't Anyone Tell Me about Maine?

August 9th to August 27th
Mile 1953 to 2184

Old Blue wasn't some ageing old hillbilly — the somewhat friendly sounding name had also been claimed by a mountain. My approach from the south descended gently from Moody Mountain to a wide col and then curved up to the 3600-foot summit. I scampered quickly down to the col, making the most of my momentum to get stuck in to the uphill. My shoes clung to smooth granite, fuelling confidence to plough upwards with firm steps, hopping and jumping through the traverse. Occasionally I had to call my arms into play to hoist myself up natural steps and ledges.

I dropped my pack at the top for a quick rest. I preferred the summits for breaks because I could pick up again straight into a downhill. Krumholtz surrounded me as I rested my back against a weather-beaten post, topped with a sign for Old Blue itself. The limited growth of the trees meant I was taller, allowing for a decent 360-degree view. A clear line of erosion was visible back down in the col where thousands of hikers had etched a faint passage over the rock.

It was incredibly quiet. I heard nothing except the occasional bird call. Quintessential late summer clouds appeared motionless, barely mustering a glide against the blue canvas behind. The sun was hazy, its light bouncing and ricocheting around, making me squint. A storm raged far to the south, angry clouds crowning a distant mountain.

I briefly calculated where I thought Lazagne and Thirsty might be. They had ten miles on me, but taking into account my earlier start by perhaps an hour, I figured they were no more than two hours ahead. Knowing how both of them approached the trail, and their mileage, I estimated they would probably end up at the Sabbath Day Pond Lean-to, meaning I had a twenty-mile day.

I found them sunbathing on a beach at Moxie Pond, half a mile before the lean-to.

"How are we all doing?" I asked.

"OK," Thirsty replied. "Not a hundred percent but a shit load better than yesterday."

I thought Old Blue had been peaceful but the lake was pure nirvana. A thin strip of beach lined the shore before meeting the forest edge. Sand gently sloped away to meet the flat, calm waters that stretched away to the far end where two hills either side shelved diagonally down to frame the view. Despite a lack of wind and our proximity to the water, the mosquitos seemed to have taken a welcome vacation for once. We sat on the warm sand, took an occasional dip and relaxed.

"Heard from Goggles?" I asked.

"No but he'll be at least ten ahead," said Lazagne. "He'll need twenty-five to thirties to meet his mum. I don't think we'll see him."

"Presumably, then, you two aren't hot on his heels and have decided to take it easy?"

"Yup," Thirsty answered.

This was great news. Although I missed Goggles, there was no way I was going to catch him. My plan to drop the mileage down, and take the last 230 miles at an easier pace, seemed to have rubbed off on Lazagne and Thirsty. We hadn't spoken about our conversation to let Goggles go, and I felt no need to bring it up again; but having lost one member, our team appeared to be solid once more.

Lazagne, making further inroads into his pursuit of the pack that weighed nothing, had now ditched his tarp, trekking poles and one of his quilts. His philosophy for the final section was to sleep in the shelters. This made sense but he was counting on the shelters having space which, although wasn't impossible, might catch him out.

It rained overnight. Packing away at camp, water drops fell and splashed on my back, making me shiver in the colder, early morning hours. I passed a new face, Catwoman, at the Sabbath Day Pond Lean-to. I was warming up as I walked so I didn't stop, but we both nodded an acknowledgement to each other.

We dodged rain showers for most of the day and hiked cautiously over wet ground and slick rock. When we met the ME-4, the town of Rangeley lay nine miles west. We were lucky to get a quick ride down to the supermarket for a food resupply and back again.

Maine liked to refer to its shelters as 'lean-tos' and our destination for the day was the Piazza Rock Lean-to. Thirsty didn't stop; but with rain clouds threatening, Lazagne and I grabbed a spot inside. We were pleased to see Chez 11 and Groc who were setting up their beds along with Catwoman.

The privy had a sign on the outside which read *Your Move*. Curious, I ventured inside to see not one but two seats for doing one's business. In between the two was a cribbage board. Quite why anyone would want to have a crap next to someone else, or even indulge in a game of cribbage at the same time, defeated me. Apart from the strange setup, it did at least have a roof to stop me getting wet. Believe me, taking a toilet stop in the rain presented all sorts of logistical problems.

The rain didn't let up all night. As Lazagne and I watched a few sobos head off, the warmth of our beds did little to persuade us to get up and hike. The forecast was dire: rain all day and the temperature wasn't encouraging either. There was only one solution, a trail zero.

Trail zeros are just that — instead of taking a day out in town, you do it on the trail. I had only ever entertained one, back on the PCT in the Sierra Nevada, where the scenery alone was enough to make me want to experience it for a whole day. At Piazza Rock, the weather had made the decision for us. Our gear was still damp from the day before so it made sense to dry it out, start a fire to keep us warm, and of course have a game of chess.

We played two games. I won the first to bring the scores level at five apiece. Sensing the possibility that I could pull away from America, I focused intently on the game that culminated in a masterly pincer movement utilising my Queen and Knight to finish off Lazagne. I punched the air, grabbed his phone and held it aloft with pride as those immortal words floated around the lean-to:

Checkmate!

The only downside of my victory was that I had forgotten my

shoes were drying by the fire.

"These yours, Fozzie?" Groc asked, holding up my right shoe and quickly tossing it between his two hands, the heat too much for him to hold. He blew on the sole as a faint wisp of smoke curled upwards.

"Shit!" I cried. "Shit! Are they OK?"

A small section of the side sole had bubbled slightly but, thankfully, they seemed intact.

We tended the fire all day but Groc took the mission to heart and cared for it like a treasured possession. Constantly glancing over towards the flames, he adjusted the fuel to provide more air, occasionally blew on the embers and placed piles of wet wood on the stone surround to dry out. In between rain bursts, we all raced over to breathe life back into our heating system, sitting at the fire edge and chatting. We tended it well into the evening. Its flickering light danced around the inside of the lean-to and picked out trees before fading into the darkness of the Maine wilderness beyond.

Everyone's mood seemed happy, but I also sensed a little sombreness. I, too, was feeling somewhat sad. The thought of finishing was becoming a real prospect. Mixed feelings played havoc with my moods at the end of thru-hikes. Ecstatic that I would soon be successful, thoughts turned away from the usual day-to-day planning and life after the trail entered the fray.

It wasn't unusual for my feelings to run riot on the final stretch, and it was confusing to know how to deal with them. The high of completion is unmatched by any other feeling of accomplishment I've ever experienced. I become emotional, thoughts turn to family and friends, those people that I love, and the burden of returning to civilisation weighs heavy. My dromomania becomes dormant, satiated by time in the woods; but I knew that even after a couple of weeks back home, my attention would turn to the next adventure. My wandering thoughts would call and there was little sympathy to be found in the upcoming cold and dark winter months back in England.

I sensed it in others as well. Camp fire conversations inevitably turned to home, and my hiking friends began to touch the surface of life after the trail. I think the elation of success, coupled with the inevitable prospect of finishing what many would eventually regard as the best few months of their lives, created confusion. Most thru-hikers become extremely emotional near the end.

It wasn't unusual to see people cry, some openly, some more reserved. I was often tearful; and even though I was aware of why, it still caught me off-guard. In full hiking flow one minute and then bam! Suddenly, I was sobbing.

Often, I paused and battled the urge but many times I shed a few tears openly, albeit when I was on my own. A failed relationship just prior to leaving for the trail weighed heavy. I dwelt on what could have been. Contrary to how this sounds, all these mixed emotions were actually calming and I often tempered them even further by planning the next trip. I think it pleased my wandering side.

I woke at 3 a.m. with an overwhelming feeling that something wasn't quite right. After rubbing my eyes and taking a moment to get centred, I realised that, firstly, I felt terrible; and secondly, I needed to get to the toilet as quickly as possible.

A game of cribbage was the last thing on my mind as I pulled on my camp shoes and raced with clenched buttocks to the faint silhouette of the privy, stumbling on the uneven ground. With not a second to spare, I lifted the lid, sat down and relaxed my muscles with an overwhelming feeling of relief.

As my bowels emptied it became quickly apparent that the consistency wasn't optimal. In fact, the splashing sound from the inner depths of the privy pit confirmed that my stomach was not in a good way.

I stumbled weakly back to the shelter, feeling slightly nauseous, and crawled back under my quilt. By 10 a.m. I felt I had spent more time in the privy than in the shelter, making a further five emergency visits. Groc and Lazagne had left for the climb up to Saddleback Mountain.

I was confused, thinking my lay up in Andover had been due to norovirus and that it had left my system. Perhaps I had just caught a mild case of the illness. I figured I had a stronger immune system than others, and had escaped the diarrhoea and vomiting that others hadn't.

I was also tired again, felt mildly nauseous but hadn't been sick. One thing was for sure — I wasn't going anywhere for a second day and settled down to another trail zero.

"Fozzie!"

I looked up to see an old friend. The sight cheered me.

"Juggles! Where the fuck have you been!"

"Where the fuck have *you* been?! Where is everyone? Lazagne? Thirsty? Bush Goggles? Why are you here?" He paused, tentatively, on his approach. "Are you sick?"

"That's a lot of questions, Mr World Champion. Er, answers in order. They're walking, obviously — Lazagne left this morning, Thirsty two nights back. Goggles has pulled away to get to Katahdin and meet his mum on time. I'm here because I got that bloody norovirus thing which answers your last question; yes I am sick."

He stopped, eyed me cautiously and, throwing caution to the wind, gave me a hug.

"Don't get too close," I said. "Have you had the bug yet? Everyone's had it, mate, or it seems that way."

"No, I've been lucky," he said.

It was mid-day so Juggles had no reason to stop. I said to get the message up trail that I'd be back hiking the following day.

With no more visitors either in the afternoon or the evening, I had the place to myself. I continued to drink water and also some rehydration sachets, along with the occasional mouthful of sugar and a little salt. As my toilet breaks stopped, my nausea faded and my energy levels began to increase. With my hunger returning quickly, I cooked dinner and picked on almonds through the evening.

Despite my almond supplies, a squirrel was taking a dislike to my presence in camp. He screamed loudly at me for most of the afternoon, occasionally jumping up and down on a tree branch as if unable to get his own way.

"He's a local," the shelter caretaker explained when he came over to check on my progress. "Thinks he owns the area, doesn't like visitors and just stomps about airing his feelings."

By 9 p.m. I felt as though I was on the mend. I made the decision to leave early the next morning to catch up with the guys, hoping that Juggles would replace our absent team member, making us four once more.

With no privy visits during the night, I made a strong coffee, wolfed down a bowl of porridge, and was away by 6.30 a.m. I felt strong, amazed at the speed of my recovery. Saddleback towered 2000 feet above me; but, surrounded by trees, I couldn't see it. After a mile I passed Ethel Pond where a low-slung mist hung motionless over the water. The only sound was the occasional plop of a fish.

I thrived on the expectation of views. Since Georgia I hadn't been disappointed and Maine had saved the best until last. I expected magnificence on every mountain and every summit delivered, still managing to throw in a surprise.

Saddleback was no exception and, in retrospect, became one of my favourites. Looking down, endless hills rolled away to the horizon. Bands of cloud stretched across the sky, their ivory tops blending to darker bellies. Rain seemed imminent but never came. A rocky path swept down, curving away around the north side of Saddleback and disappeared into the trees. The trail was still unbelievably quiet. I took an hour at the top to snack, surveying my world.

My illness defeated, I was back. The wind raged and I stood firm, leaning into it, arms and legs outstretched and screamed "I'm back! I'M FREE!" I punched the air and celebrated.

"YES!"

We English are generally a little reserved. At most, if we're having a great day, we don't usually voice our thoughts — certainly not shout them — but linger in the feeling, perhaps the only signal a satisfied smile. The Americans, more unabashed, often feel free to express themselves verbally. On sunny days, or during lively conversations around a camp fire, perhaps breaking for lunch in a jovial mood, they often aired their joy by simply saying "Good times!"

It seemed strange when I first heard it, thinking it somehow wrong that verbal confirmation of happiness should be shared. Realisation of enjoying a moment might seem obvious but we often let it pass by without indulging a little in that feeling. Admitting happiness at a precise moment, and taking a moment to wallow in it, records it for posterity — verbalising it even more so and often resulted in fond recollections after those moments, often months or years later.

***

I was eager to catch up with the guys and concentrated on pulling in a decent day. After bagging Lone Mountain, Mt Abraham, Spaulding Mountain and Sugarloaf Mountain, I eventually reached days end, after twenty-two miles, at the south branch of the Carrabassett River.

The woods parted like a curtain to reveal this gently moving, boulder-strewn ribbon of water. A few tent sites on the opposing bank indicated the perfect spot to spend the night and attack both South and North Crocker Mountains the following day. The ME-27 intersected the AT some eight miles further where the town of Stratton lay five miles west. Lazagne mentioned he was planning to stay there overnight and gear up for the next section.

Small clearings in the wood, just a few feet from the Carrabassett, proved an ideal spot to string up the hammock. A couple of day hikers were my only company. I retreated to the river and took a quick swim, washing a few items of clothing in the process.

I had heard that bears were often spotted at the campsite so nodded off cautiously, keeping one ear cocked for movement. Sure enough, around 2.30 a.m., a paw fall snapped a few twigs as I listened to what could only have been a bear move slowly closer.

"Hey, bear! Sod off!"

Immediately a loud crashing sound reverberated around the woods as the culprit sped off. The annoying aspect of marauding bears is that I could never be content when they left. Experience showed that, more often than not, they usually returned. Sleep never came naturally after the initial visit. By 3.30 a.m. I was resigned to the fact that I wouldn't fall back to sleep, even though a return visit didn't seem likely. I got out of my hammock.

I took my stove to the river and splashed some water on my face, then filled my pot and lit the fuel to brew a coffee. I looked up at the river. Its lines of perspective narrowed as the moon reflected and glinted in the water, throwing around just enough light to see.

My head torch picked out the path on the steep climb up to South Crocker Mountain, dipping momentarily and climbing further to the north peak. Stopping briefly to fill up my water bottle from the spring, I reached the road shortly before 7 a.m. and stuck out my thumb.

Brian pulled up, on his way to work. "Where you heading? Stratton for breakfast?"

"You read my mind," I replied.

He dropped me outside. When I swung open the door of the Stratton Diner, Lazagne, Thirsty and Juggles looked up smiling.

"You OK, Fozzie?" Lazagne asked.

"Fighting fit and back into the fray! How's the breakfast?"

"Awesome," Thirsty mumbled with a mouth full of eggs.

The Stratton Motel and Hostel was just over the road. The owner kindly allowed me to use the laundry facilities. Whilst waiting for my clothes to dry, a sheet of paper pinned to the wall caught my attention.

It concerned Paul 'Parkside' Bernhardt, who had set out on his AT thru-hike well before me on February 17th. Registering as the eleventh thru-hiker to start, he was at the front of pack. Making camp near Pierce Pond on June 15th, thirty-three miles up trail from the Stratton, he went to the pond to take a swim, not thinking it necessary to tell anyone of his intentions.

Shortly after, those at the shelter heard cries from the pond and raced down to see Paul go under the water. He never surfaced again. Despite brave attempts by Achilles and Carpenter, they couldn't find him. His body was discovered later that evening by rescue workers.

The likely cause of death is unknown but thought to have been cramp. Parkside had covered twenty miles that day — not an unusually high amount at that stage of the trail but still a hard day's hike, taking the terrain into account. Low potassium levels may have played a part as well as the notoriously cold water.

Achilles, Dropout, Germanator, Swivel, Spiral and Catwoman took time out from the trail to attend Paul's funeral in Queens, New York. Two weeks later, on June 29th, they carried Paul's ashes to the summit of Mt Katahdin.

With such an uncommon trail name, I assumed the Catwoman I had met the previous day was the same hiker who was with Paul and had returned two months later to hike some more. I never saw her again to ask.

It's a sad and sobering thought to know that some hikers never come back. Worse, always at the back of my mind was the fear that I, one day, could be one of them.

Maine seemed to be the state where most hikers go missing, and many were never found. With such hazardous terrain, one slip or fall could mean a hiker ended up in inaccessible areas at the base of cliffs or gorges. It's a sobering thought, and one that many try not to dwell on. Besides, if we all took notice of the warnings associated with some outdoor activities, we probably wouldn't get involved in them.

The clothes drier beeped, shaking me from deep thought. Rain had started to fall once more and we paused, contemplating staying at the hostel but eventually caught a ride back to the trailhead and hiked the five miles up to Horns Pond Lean-to.

The caretaker turned up late evening and took time with us, expressing his sadness surrounding the events at Pierce Pond. He also confirmed that Avery Peak, three and a half miles further on, was the last major peak of the AT except for Katahdin itself. It was downhill to East Flagstaff Lake. The final, flatter section we had studied in our data books was close.

We had just 183 miles left to call ourselves AT thru-hikers.

***

Light rain fell as we broke camp in the morning. We glanced up to see the cloud level tickling the mountain tops. Climbing strongly and warming quickly, we reached South Horn first, with views of the west peak of Bigelow Mountain ahead. Above tree-line our direction was clear. Despite heavier rain and a ferocious wind we eventually summited Avery Peak and hunkered down behind some rocks to take in the view and eat some snacks.

We were smiling. Nothing could stop us now, not even Katahdin. That icon was the last in a long stretch of mountains starting 2000 miles and 138 days behind us.

Dropping from Avery, we met the East Flagstaff Road and suddenly remembered our mileage total had exceeded 2000. For the second time in my life I had passed this point. We marked the moment by taking a soft rock and writing '2000' on the road.

We called it a day after just thirteen miles, and had good reason to stop. East Flagstaff Lake glinted through the trees to our left as a beach shelved gently into the waters. With more rain due it seemed a good excuse to stop, but I think, secretly, we knew that the end was close. The fewer miles we hiked each day, the more time we had to stretch out our remaining time on trail.

Lazagne, being without a shelter, carried on to the West Carry Pond Lean-to whilst Juggles, Thirsty and I set up camp on the beach, alternating between swimming and resting before the rain came.

The pattering on my tarp didn't abate all night. The following day, soot-black clouds offered little to suggest any let-up so there we stayed, indulging in our decision to slow down and make the most of our last days.

The temperature dropped that night. I woke cold and pulled on a jacket. Despite the chill, I knew the reason for the sudden cold was that the clouds had cleared and that the morning, hopefully, should dawn bright.

I wasn't disappointed. I woke to calling loons, a gentle breeze lifting the tarp, and a perfect morning.

***

River crossings were common in Maine, as were wet feet. The Kennebec River, thankfully, was the only exception. With its fast-flowing water and wide berth, the Kennebec had a ferry service in operation.

Dave Corrigan of the Kennebec River AT Ferry Service was on the opposite bank. As soon as he saw us waving, he was in his canoe quicker than an otter taking a dip. There was no fee and Dave gave us a quick briefing on what to expect. There wasn't room for all of us so I went first with Thirsty, figuring if anyone could paddle with power it would be him, whilst Juggles and Lazagne waited for the return voyage.

Dave had been ferrying hikers and other outdoor enthusiasts for the previous six years and told me that already he had carried around 1500 hikers over the waters that year. It was just starting to get busy as the nobos were in full flow and closing in on their goal. We thanked him and left.

Despite the kinder terrain away from the mountains, there was one final test of our resolve in addition to river crossings as we reached the last town on the AT. The ME-15 heralded the start of a section of trail known as the Hundred-Mile Wilderness. It ended at Abol Bridge, itself just fifteen miles from the finish. Northbound hikers often caught a ride to Monson, four miles east, to resupply before the section.

The Hundred-Mile Wilderness was just that: no towns, no road crossings, nothing except the occasional desolate logging track. We had figured on five twenty-mile days to get through. We could have done it in four, perhaps even three; but with the end of our adventure closing, we wanted to make the most of it.

We secured a quick ride into Monson. Shaw's Lodging provided a bed for two nights, taking a final zero to get cleaned up and resupplied for the final assault.

I was walking back from lunch at the Lakeshore Pub. I turned around to see Snot Rocket, Anchor and Chef getting out of a car. I hadn't seen them for weeks and welcome hugs were freely dispensed. It reminded me that even though I had lost contact with those I had met, they occasionally turned up when I least expected it.

The Lakeshore Pub, being the only place to serve draught

beer, tempted me back in the evening where I sat with Lazagne, Thirsty and Juggles.

"Goggles made it! He reached Katahdin today!" Juggles screamed, passing me his phone. There he was, Goggles, astride the summit sign proudly holding a flag with 'Wisconsin' emblazoned across it.

"He's on his way back home now," I said. "What are you going to do when you get back, Juggles?"

"A different kind of survival," he answered wisely as Thirsty and Lazagne smiled and nodded in silent approval.

We left Monson the following morning, still in no hurry, keen to eke out every last minute.

A campsite caught our eye late afternoon, but getting there meant fording Little Wilson Stream. Lazagne crossed last; when the rest of us had made it over safely, we turned to check on his progress.

Reaching half way, he decided a better approach would be to throw his pack to the bank, leaving him unencumbered for the last few feet. Unfortunately, before we could grab it, the pack slid slowly down to the water's edge and slipped gently into the stream before floating in the direction of Little Wilson Falls. 'Little' was not the first adjective that sprung to mind for the cascading torrent disappearing alarmingly over an abyss to our left.

"Fuck!" Lazagne screamed as he increased his wading speed. He reached a small rock and leapt for another to cut off his pack's own little adventure. He promptly fell sideways into the water but re-surfaced just in time to grab his pack before it disappeared over the edge.

I negotiated Little Wilson carefully the following morning and was away before the others had broken camp. Maine continued to amaze me with its dense forest, regular river crossings and quiet hiking. True to form, we continued to hike together but often drifted off on our own, occupied with thoughts of finishing and what we would do after trail life.

All 3650 feet of White Cap Mountain rose up before me. I appeared to have missed that while checking the last 'flat' section of trail in my logbook. I filled up with water from a stream near the Carl A. Newhall Lean-to, where Meat, whom I had just met, joined me to do the same.

"Meat, I still look at mountains after all this time and doubt my own ability to get up them," I offered as we sat on a rock drinking.

"I know exactly what you mean, I do the same," he agreed. "Always doubt if I can make it up."

"See you up the top then?" I said.

"Hell yeah!"

White Cap wasn't just famed for being the last major peak apart from Katahdin on the AT. A side trail along the north summit, through a short section of trees, offered the first view of what most AT thru-hikers had spent several months dreaming about.

I crested White Cap, turned north through the woods and, after a minute, emerged from the other side. The land swept down, rippled along the lowlands dotted with a few lakes, then rose majestically. My eyes slowly eased upward to settle on a sight I sometimes thought I'd never see. I cried as emotions caught me out.

There, seventy-three trail miles north, Mount Katahdin soared skywards to command absolute dominance over all it surveyed. The upper plateau, known as the Tableland, was clearly visible. Forest ascended its lower flanks, finally surrendering to the harsher conditions further up. A few wispy clouds tickled the summit; I hoped the fine weather held, for I, hopefully, would be standing on the summit in days.

With White Cap behind me, the trail settled down to the level section I had hoped for. A smooth trail wove through the forest. My feet were gently cushioned by soft soil and a sprinkling of pine needles. It was easy hiking all the way to a waterside camp at Nahmakanta Lake, where the guys arrived later.

Discussing logistics that evening, it was agreed that a 3.45 a.m. alarm call followed by a start time of 4.30 a.m. would be prudent. We wanted to see Katahdin at first light around 5.30 a.m. and our logbooks advised that Nesuntabunt Mountain was a great vantage point.

I struggle with early morning calls on trail. It's invariably chilly and the complete darkness doesn't lend itself to getting out of a sleeping bag. Usually I waited until someone else stirred before moving myself.

The next morning, we took a short side trail on Nesuntabunt to reach a cliff where the trees cleared. Sitting down near the edge, our finishing point was clearly visible. An orange glow brushed the eastern skies, softened by blankets of mist caught in the valleys.

Katahdin's silhouette beckoned.

***

On the afternoon of the 25th of August, I emerged from the Hundred-Mile Wilderness onto Golden Road, frantically grabbing my sunglasses as the sun caught me off-guard. A small café and store were pretty much the only buildings there. With a hunger that was borderline dangerous, and an unhealthy yearning for fat, I ordered two large burgers, two packets of crisps, ice cream, three coffees, a chocolate milk and an orange juice. My choices wouldn't have made the front cover of any healthy diet magazine. Lying outside on the ground after the indulgence, my stomach certainly regretted it. I wobbled over to the Abol Pines campsite where Lazagne, Thirsty, Juggles and I warmed with a camp fire and watched the Penobscot River glide sweetly past.

We woke to find Juggles missing. He had mentioned that he needed to get a ride to Millinocket, nineteen miles east, to collect some juggling batons that he had mailed to the post office. His plan was to juggle with fire on the summit. We sent him a text explaining our intentions of taking advantage of a decent weather window on the Monday, two days away, so he could join us for the finish.

He also had a suspected broken toe but didn't intend to visit the doctor for fear of a confirmed prognosis. Talking to Meat about walking with broken bones that morning, he relayed some unfortunate news about Danish. I had met him a couple of days before and we had shared a brief conversation. He explained that it was his second attempt on the AT; the previous year, his visa had run out before he could finish the trail.

"What happened?" I asked Meat.

"Got one foot caught in a tree root or something. Momentum carried him forward and now he's got a broken tibia and fibula," he replied, cringing somewhat.

"Oh shit! So, he's off for the second year?"

"Knowing Danish," Meat said, "He'll be back next year again."

It was a welcome short day to the Birches Lean-to and campsite. At least fifteen thru-hikers had congregated for the final approach and our last day's hike to Katahdin in the morning. Our base camp was bustling. Juggles had shown and, along with my regular companions Thirsty and Lazagne, we also had Pedestrian, Houdini, Great Dane, Banjo, Meat, Skunkape, Roadhouse, Chesty, Stingray, Poncho, and Jonathan the caretaker for company.

We built a roaring fire in the evening and Houdini invited everyone over for a smudging ceremony. Common amongst the Native Americans, smudging or purifying the air by burning herbs creates a positive atmosphere. Sage is a common choice for this; but Houdini, unable to find any, had settled for the noble alternative of a cedar bundle.

We sat in a circle around the fire. Having lit the cedar, Houdini blew it out and wafted the smoke over each of us with the aid of a feather. He explained that every person was then invited to speak about their experience, adding that each of us should hold the feather in turn. The rest of the group should be silent as the person with the feather spoke. When finished, they handed it to the next person.

It was a wonderful ceremony, of particular poignancy because everyone respected the feather and the person that held it as they spoke. There were no interruptions. I thought what a pleasant change it made for each of us to offer our story without disruptions.

Stories of a serious nature were openly told, as well as humorous tales and everything in between. We laughed, joked, pondered, reflected and left for our beds feeling positive.

My thoughts centred on the rumour that Katahdin was the first landmass in America to receive light from the rising sun. Anyone standing on the summit would be the first in America to witness sunrise, but in fact this is not true. According to the time of year and the equinoxes, Cadillac Hill, Mars Hill, and West Quoddy Head share the claim.

However, Katahdin was right up there. I peered in annoyance at my alarm which broke my slumber at 2 a.m. I packed, and hung around for a few minutes waiting for Lazagne, who had agreed to join me. No one stirred. At 2.26 a.m., I left and began my final day of the Appalachian Trail.

I was still hauling the gantlet. Pink Bits, sorry — Lady Forward — had beaten me to the post a few days before.

I glimpsed clear skies studded with stars through breaks in the trees. It was warm and the climb soon had me shedding clothing and walking in just shorts and a T-shirt. The hiss of Katahdin Stream Falls filtered through the trees as I passed, and then faded. My head torch easily picked out trees with white blazes. A stream glistened and frogs hopped out of my way as I picked my way up the trail. Not even the drone of a mosquito spoilt a definitive silence and occasionally I stopped, turned off my light and looked skyward to swaying pines framing a magical night sky.

I caught Skunkape, who had started a few minutes before me, fumbling with his failing head torch. I offered to share my light. As the going steepened, I took the lead, crawling and scrambling over rock slabs, occasionally turning around to shine my light for him.

After just over three miles, at 4538 feet, the ascent suddenly eased onto the Tableland. Meagre light spread from a glowing horizon and picked out our passage through a rocky environment. An occasional lonely white blaze was caught in the dawn fire. I turned back to see two head torches behind, sweeping around the landscape like lost astronauts on a distant planet.

And suddenly, there it was ahead of me. Backlit with orange, as if rightly commanding a solitary presence on stage, the silhouetted, iconic summit sign that I had seen so many times in photos straddled the summit.

At 5.15 a.m., just under three hours after leaving, I placed my palm on its cold and damp surface, and slowly ran my hands over the carved letters.

KATAHDIN
Baxter Peak – Elevation – 5267 FT
NORTHERN TERMINUS OF THE
APPALACHIAN TRAIL
A mountain footpath extending over
2000 miles to Springer Mtn. Georgia

A fierce wind ripped over the Tableland. I pulled on my jacket and sheltered behind a rock with Skunkape, soon joined by Banjo and Meat whose lights we had seen behind us. We faced east and watched, mesmerised but impatient for our sunrise. At 5.51 a.m. a hazy, ruby circle tentatively poked over distant hills, battling for supremacy with lingering cloud. The Knife Edge Ridge to our right gradually illuminated, dropping and arcing away to the north. The light met our faces, inching down our chests as Katahdin gradually brightened.

We stayed there for three hours, observing the light change, watching the shadows appear and the temperature rise. Finally, after weeks of carrying my imaginary gauntlet, I launched it over the side of Katahdin and watched it plunge down before smashing into the rocks to disintegrate into a thousand pieces.

I heard footsteps behind.

"YEAH! FUCK YEAH!"

I peered over rocks behind me to see Thirsty beyond excitement, punching the air and yelling. Lazagne arrived shortly after. Juggles, somewhat emotional, greeted me with a wobbly bottom lip and watery eyes. Others gradually filtered in. From a quiet, reflective and silent atmosphere, the mood turned to celebration.

Juggles had indeed carried up his juggling batons. He held a lighter under each one, and the flames caught, licking skyward. He balanced on top of the sign, plying his trade for several minutes with no drops and to rapturous applause.

After a group photo I shook some hands and left, descending back over the Tableland and occasionally turning back. The group slowly faded. Unable to control a barrage of emotions but trying to resist the urge to cry, I suddenly let everything go and burst into tears.

Months of planning and hiking, time spent thinking about my life, reflecting on my past and pondering my future, and the uncertainty about my next step all surfaced — but they weren't sad tears, they were joyful. I had made it. I was a Double Crowner, an Appalachian Trail thru-hiker, and a member of a rare breed of individual successful in completing the most iconic hiking trail on Earth.

Before dipping away from the Tableland I turned for one last, lingering look at Katahdin. Visually it was exceptionally beautiful, but also a decisive and poignant landmark offering confirmation that I had been successful. It stirred massive emotions, so powerful I couldn't ignore them even if I wanted to.

It had made people cry, sing, and dance. They basked in their own glory and that of those around them. It held them in the moment and, suddenly, realisation dawned that they had achieved possibly the biggest challenge they would ever face, that they are capable of far more than they ever thought possible. Katahdin offered encouragement to pursue dreams and a life away from the ordinary. It wasn't so much a realisation that the adventure was over, but that new ones were just beginning.

My dromomania was silent, still and satiated; but it stirred as I descended, eager for sustenance. Hungry for the next adventure, the nomad already demanded feeding.

Chapter 15
Epilogue - The Separating

Peter 'PJ' Semo

Resting my injury was a hard and frustrating decision to make. For a few short weeks I had been given a wilderness present and then, abruptly, it was taken away before I could properly unwrap it. But rest was what I had to do — an obvious choice to make when the only other option was to quit. Returning to continue my hike after a month's break, I reached Katahdin on October the 5th. I'm immensely proud of what I achieved.

I don't often bring my adventure up in conversation but I do find it holds a common bond, being an easy story to make small talk with. Most of the time people's eyes light up when they realise what I have achieved. It helps people understand where I have come from in life and what type of person I am. It imbues a certain wonder and curiosity, and that's all I could hope for — to inspire others to experience nature and possibly go and hike the AT for themselves.

Post-hike I went to Dalton, Massachusetts, to work at a hostel and then I decided to return to my original home near Latrobe in Pennsylvania. Readjusting to society was very difficult, and post-hike depression, which I had heard about, was disturbing. It was a sense of tremendous loss like a family member had died. A part of me had disappeared and the memories became foggier and foggier. The winter was tough. I wasn't sure where I wanted my life to go and, frankly, at times, I couldn't really care either.

My mood improved during the spring of 2013. I started to work at an adventure park, making some fantastic friends. In the summer I was promoted to rides supervisor and now I'm very happy.

The trail imparted a certain understanding of life and helped me on the journey, like finding a meaningful book in the library with answers to a specific topic. Having hiked I now understand life more. With increased confidence in myself, I know where I want to go; and more importantly, I have the confidence to get there. My big goal is to hike the Pacific Crest Trail and the Continental Divide Trail to earn my Triple Crown.

Socialising and communicating are easier now and I'm able to discover areas that excite people. I can inspire them to do something that is really meaningful in their lives. Everyone is full of possibilities, capable of wonderful things and I hope they view me in the same way.

I value my friends much more and my family is really important. Not a day goes by in which I don't think about my dad. I miss him dearly. But he would be proud of the journey I undertook and the mental effort I put into sorting everything out, both the tangible and intangible. Whilst I have regrets about the events between us, I have made peace with myself. I'm blessed to have my family back in my life and I love coming home from work where I can talk to my brother and mum, or my sister when she visits. I'm grateful I have learnt the importance of friendships.

I feel loved and I couldn't be happier. The trail has been a philosopher's stone for my life and I wouldn't be where I am today without it.

Phillip 'Lazagne' Colelli

The train was a wise choice of transport to return home on. I had nine hours to ponder my adventure but never really figured much out. My dad was waiting to collect me and I was overjoyed to see him. Realising how important family was to me, we had grown even closer.

I had little idea of what my next move should be but I knew I had to work. Returning to my old job was the easiest option; despite my original yearning to escape from grilling burgers, at least I had money coming in, breathing space to calculate my next move. That was a big mistake.

I was still peaking from the AT, on a high from what I had achieved and no one else's negative energy could affect me. However, after a couple of months I realised that I was back where I had been before I began my hike, and I didn't like it. I missed the trail, the amazing people I had met and the simple existence I had thrived on.

I started to plan more adventures. If getting away made me happy, then I thought planning another trip would take my mind off work. I researched North Carolina's Mountains to Sea Trail and cycling across America. The anticipation of this planning woke me up to the mistake I had made of returning to a job I hated.

"Shannon, I'm done, I'm leaving now," I said to the general manager after my last shift, right before the Friday night dinner rush.

"You realise you won't be rehire-able if you don't work your two weeks' notice, right?" she replied.

"I don't care."

In retrospect, subconsciously, I think I left them in the lurch so I wouldn't be rehire-able. I didn't want to go back.

Working with my dad in construction gave me more time to think. He knew I was viewing it as a stopgap until I figured out my next move. Then Sam called. He was contemplating a move to Denver, Colorado, to rent a house there and asked me if I would be interested. I said no, on the basis that I wasn't 100% sure — but called him a week later and said I had changed my mind.

Packing most of what I owned into my tired old car made me realise what the trail had taught me about materialism. It had 200,000 miles on the clock and was only worth about $500 but I loved it. I had no desire to own anything other than the crappiest car in existence. It also acted as a people-filter. I had little time for anyone who judged me on the basis of my car, and you would be surprised how few people that left.

I had high hopes for Denver but it was tough at first. A few dead-end jobs came and went until one day I saw an advert for a vacancy at a marijuana-growing facility, shortly after the plant became legal in Colorado. I had no experience but figured it would be a complete change of scene. The interview went well, I got the position and I've now been there for a few months. The people are great and the managers treat me with respect, which was always more important to me than money.

A co-worker called Adam mentioned that his lease was running out, and as mine was also coming to an end we looked for somewhere together. This proved difficult as he had a dog —

albeit a service dog — and landlords were reluctant to take it on. After a few weeks of wasting our time I suggested the mad idea that we go and live in the woods. I had the gear, there was no rent to pay, it was quiet with no neighbours and it just seemed like a brilliant (if somewhat crazy) idea. Adam jumped at the chance, so for the summer that's exactly what we did.

It was something I had always wanted to do. We packed up and found a nice spot in Pike National Forest, although we abide by the forestry regulations and move camp every two weeks. I still get a shower every day, decent meals and I'm warm at night.

I suppose I have been unsettled since I completed the trail but that is possibly something that the trail has done to me. I realise that I have to work to earn money for the everyday expenses that we all have, but I'm unsettled because for a few, short months, I had complete freedom. Indeed, I now realise that long-distance hiking, or whatever adventure I choose, is the best method for being as truly free as I can ever hope to be.

I live my life day by day and I have no idea what may come along next. Tomorrow I could be living on the other side of the country, but to taste true freedom — or as close as I could wish for — at some point I'll pick up my pack and head off for another long-distance hike to rekindle how I really love to live.

Sam 'Daffy' Ridge

I swore I'd never do it again. Don't get me wrong, it was fun, but directly after finishing, believe me, the last thing on my mind was doing it again. As much as I loved my journey, there's only so much rain, so much hunger, tiredness and time in your own head that a man can take. I felt beaten up. It hurt physically and mentally I was exhausted as well, but elated that I finished.

The negativity wore off quickly. After a week or so I started planning the next one, which is going to be the Pacific Crest Trail in 2015. Day hikes just don't do it for me anymore. Why escape for a day when you can immerse yourself for months? It's different out there if you commit the time. Generous periods in the outdoors are rewarded by leaving them with an entirely different perspective and appreciation.

I did the AT to get away from people, otherwise known as the world. I hated both at the time; but, over the course of those summer months in 2012, my opinions of both changed dramatically. I'm now sure that I couldn't have done it without the people.

I made new friends, some of whom I now share a place with. I met my girlfriend on the trail too. I moved to Colorado to be nearer the outdoors and because the weed's legal here now.

I smoked marijuana almost every day on the trail and concluded that it wasn't as limiting or bad as the masses perceived. I now work legally at a weed growers for a living. I just received manager of the quarter and I'm in charge of more than fifty people.

I'm still on my trail, or *the* trail, in many ways. I still read poems that I wrote on the AT and look at the pictures. I do feel like I was stronger, more at peace, or more Zen on the trail.

John 'Thirsty' Beshara

I returned to Juggles' place in New York and stayed with him, Fozzie and Lazagne. Of all the things we could have done, we decided to return to the woods and spent a few days by Lake Placid. It was by mutual agreement, mainly to experience just one, small, isolated place amongst the trees without moving on. Perhaps we just didn't want to leave.

Before my flight home, I was milling around near the ticket counter as the flight crew walked in. The pilot noticed my pack and we starting talking about hiking. It turned out he was a section hiker who had done much of the southern half of the AT. We talked about the Smokies for a minute before he went off to prepare for the flight. It was a short trip back to Minneapolis; I don't think they were even offering a snack. So you can understand my surprise when the stewardess came over to my seat.

"You're the hiker, right?"

I considered the question for a moment, wondering if there had been a complaint about the odour coming from seat 34A, before eventually responding.

"Yes," I replied, tentatively.

"What would you like? The pilot wants to buy you a beer."

It was one final, uplifting gesture of trail magic before I returned to locations where that concept wouldn't have any meaning.

I stayed in Minneapolis for about a month. The beard and hair were big hits with my friends, but eventually I shaved and trimmed in favour of a less conspicuous look.

I didn't have much trouble re-integrating. People are different when you're in the city. You have to get used to the idea that you can't just walk up to someone and expect them to be friendly as they were in the mountains. Most were very interested to hear about the trail, but their interest would wane the longer I rambled on. They wanted to hear about the animals, the weather and the food. I ended up with a couple of anecdotes about bears and snow that served me well whenever someone asked about the trail.

I left Minneapolis in October with a one-way ticket to Saigon. My plan since graduation had been to go abroad and teach English. I gained a contact through my sister who was teaching in Vietnam and I got in touch with him. He sold the lifestyle well, so I packed my stuff and took off. After completing the trail I was confident in my abilities to make it on my own in a place very different from anything I had known — to be able to adapt to new people and surroundings, to sleep anywhere, and eat just about anything. The first week or so in Vietnam was difficult. I kept getting lost, I couldn't understand anything that was said to me, and it was sweltering hot. But it got easier, if not less hot, as time went by.

My experience in Vietnam lasted for a little over a year. Taking advantage of the opportunity, I also travelled around much of Asia. The highlights were Koh Rong Island off the coast of Cambodia, where I met my beautiful Argentinian girlfriend; and a one-month motorbike tour down the coastline of Vietnam. I'm currently in Barcelona, Spain, and I'll be heading to Buenos Aires soon.

Spending time outdoors is still a big part of my life. I haven't done anything longer than a few days since the AT, but I still get out fairly often. I just finished four days in the Catalonian Pyrenees, and the GR-11 trail is now on my long-distance list. The PCT will likely be my next attempt, though. I hope to be on the border of Mexico in May 2016. When I get there I'll be adopting the trail name 'Moses', which Fozzie unofficially gave me on the AT due to my apparent likeness to the biblical character.

Hiking the AT didn't breed any wanderlust in me that wasn't already present. It did give me the foundation of skills and confidence that allowed me to pursue the life of adventure that I've always dreamt of.

Advice on the AT? None really. Just pack your shit and go!

Dallas 'Bush Goggles' Nustvold

I finished my thru-hike on August 20th. I missed the guys and it was a hard decision to leave them but sometimes life is about making tough decisions. I was incredibly proud to have made it, and sitting on top of Katahdin I felt very optimistic about my future. All those weeks of hiking provided plenty of time to think about what was ahead of me.

Optimistic, that is, until I returned home. I fell back into the old routine and returned to my old job. I moved in with my parents to give me some time to find a place of my own. Whilst interesting at times, I never really liked my job. Then I stumbled into a post-hike depression. All I wanted to do was lie around, relax and eat. Even though I stopped hiking, my appetite remained. By Christmas I had gained forty pounds. It's worrying how easily we can change from being a thru-hiker at the peak of our game to lying around doing nothing.

I knew there and then that if I didn't make some radical changes to my life I would be unhappy so I hit the gym. It felt good and the fat just burned off. With my body back in shape, my mind quickly followed. I focused, realised I missed the hiker lifestyle and decided to take on the Ice Age trail in Wisconsin.

I left on March 15th 2013. Winter hadn't subsided and it was too early for hiking season. The trail was deserted. It was a different kind of hike — obviously it was colder, but I also missed my hiking family, especially in the evenings.

I faced a lot of challenges. It was bitterly cold but I still had a blast. I finished 700 miles of the 1050 before the weather finally defeated me and my deadline to return back to work arrived. I even managed to hike fifty-four miles in one day.

I spent the following summer training to run a marathon, which I completed. I finished another one in the fall. In just over a year I hiked 3000 miles and ran two marathons.

Not a day passes in which I don't think about the AT. I daydream about those morning climbs, fresh spring water and beautiful sunsets. I think I will be a slave to my wandering ways forever. Something deep and strong inside just urges me to go and explore. I know that another thru-hike, somewhere, will happen at some point.

I have learned to slow down and live in the moment. I allow my anxieties to take hold sometimes and I start rushing for some reason. I'm not in a race to my death, so I have to remind myself to relax, just like I did on the AT.

I just wish every day could be like that Appalachian Trail hike in the summer of 2012.

Chris 'Juggles' Chiappini

I guess perseverance pays off eventually. If you want something badly enough, I think you need to put in the effort and never admit defeat. This was true for the trail; and, having hiked it, I carried away that philosophy to my everyday life. We are capable of truly wondrous things, but it's not until a challenge is undertaken and completed — whether it be the AT or anything else — that we fully comprehend them.

I returned home to New York to pick up my life where I had left it. In March 2013 Lazagne came to stay and we hiked the New Jersey section of the AT. That August I took a trip to Colorado to climb some 14,000-foot peaks.

In September 2013, the chance of my dream job came out of the blue. A juggler I knew was leaving his position and they needed someone to replace him. He put my name forward as the ideal replacement and even said he wouldn't train anyone else. Eventually, after a nerve-wracking wait, I received a call from their HQ in Vancouver asking me to come for an interview.

More waiting followed before I knew if I had been successful but finally the news came. I couldn't believe I had landed it. After a lot of training, I'm now proud to say I juggle for Cirque du Soleil all over the world.

Although I get a few weeks off between shows, it's not enough time to go back and do another long-distance hike. I take trips out between shows, in whatever country I'm lucky enough to be in. So far I've seen New Zealand and Australia. I'm incredibly happy and very lucky to be doing what I love.

I nurture fond memories from the AT, and made many friends whom I still keep in contact with. Such a beautiful and eye-opening way to spend a few months. I miss the mountains and often reflect on my adventure there. I will do another long-distance hike someday.

I was very taken by Maine — so much so that I would like to return to live there. I have a dream of buying some land, building a log cabin and letting some close friends have separate parcels of land to do the same. It's wild up there, quiet, beautiful, and I can't think of a better place to put down some roots.

Keith 'Fozzie' Foskett

From Georgia, I had traversed north on a slim ribbon of trail over the Appalachian mountain chain for 150 days. Through snow, ice, rain, storms, humidity and unbearable heat I inched a little closer to Katahdin every day.

I witnessed stark, bare trees come alive as my world turn green. Riding a series of rocky waves I smiled, emerging above tree-line to survey America's wild lands from a lofty perch. I had battled fatigue, illness, stress and emotional storms, clung stubbornly to my resolve and refused to give up.

Some mornings I woke and doubted if I could go any further. I stood in valleys, mesmerised by the hulk of mountains towering before me. I willed myself up to summits that I never thought I could conquer. Despite all my fears of failure, I stood strong and arrived at camp knowing that, for another day, I had won.

The continual search to placate my dromomania, to satisfy the nomad, and to appease my travelling addiction continues. But I've written another chapter of a never-ending adventure to be as close to freedom as can ever be truly possible.

From a teenager that initially viewed my wanderlust as a curse, I learned over time that it was, in fact, a valuable and cherished attribute. I accepted my feelings, nurtured them, learned from them and acknowledged how I was supposed to be, instead of trying to pick a more conventional life that I know would have made me unhappy.

I know I'd be just as fulfilled cycling around the world, taking a long road trip or bumming around Europe for the summer. The ultimate goal has, and always will be, to be as free as is ultimately possible in this world.

As I write this, in January 2015, a piece of paper nestles on the corner of my desk. There are a few scribbles haphazardly inked in one corner, a list of actions, plans needing to be implemented in order to fulfil my next adventure. The culmination of years of planning, months spent in the wilderness — training, if you like, for the big one.

That scrap of paper is titled 'The Continental Divide Trail'. The last of the big three American hikes. 3000 miles from the Mexican border to the Canadian border along the length of the continental divide. From the lowest point, Waterton Lake in Glacier National Park at 4200 feet, soaring to 14,270 feet on Grays Peak in Colorado, this is the next instalment of my life adventure.

My dromomaniac ways still beckon. I doubt they will ever be truly satisfied. In the unlikely event that the nomad shrinks into obscurity and declares, *OK, I've had enough, I'm full up*, that will be a sad day.

My wanderings keep me alive, urge me ever forward, constantly searching for the next adventure, a new escape. The call to freedom, the cries of the wilderness, the desire to roam is all I dream of.

Can I recommend you walk the AT? Of course! However, if hiking isn't your cup of tea, perhaps take whatever pastime you prefer and make a plan to do it for a few months.

If you're stubborn enough to make it happen, when you get there, open your eyes. Observe and admire everything as much as possible. Take mental photos, study them for a few seconds, remember them, hold on to them, and tuck them into an imaginary file. Place that file in the back of your mind and label it:

The Best Few Months of my Life.

No, wait.

I don't mean in some weak font, in lower case, and printed when your black ink level is low.

I mean use a striking font, in capital letters, bold, and with a fresh ink cartridge:

THE BEST FEW MONTHS OF MY LIFE.

Printed in Great Britain
by Amazon